THE FUTURE FROM THE PAST
EXPOS: A CATALYST FOR CHANGE

WORLD EXPO MUSEUM

从过去向未来
引领时代进步的世博会

世博会博物馆 / 编

上海人民美术出版社

Editorial Board

Editor-in-Chief:
LIU Wentao

Deputy Editor-in-Chief:
ZHOU Yongping, ZOU Jun

Executive Editor:
HONG Lina, WANG Shu

Content Editor:
HONG Lina, WANG Shu,
SUI Zhiying, LAN Wenxuan

Literature Support:
WANG Pei, ZHANG Jie,
LUO Yunqing

编委会名单

主编：刘文涛

副主编：周永平　邹俊

执行主编：洪丽娜　王姝

内容编辑：洪丽娜　王姝　隋知颖　蓝文轩

文献支持：王珮　张婕　骆云卿

Preface of Congratulations

Dimitri S. Kerkentzes
Secretary General of
the Bureau International des Expositions (BIE)
February 2025

On behalf of the Bureau International des Expositions (BIE), I extend my heartfelt congratulations to the World Expo Museum (WEM) for the publication of this remarkable book, which explores the evolving vision of the future through the history of Expos.

As the only official museum and documentation center authorized by the BIE, the WEM has carefully built an extensive collection of Expo-related documentation in collaboration with the BIE and other partners. Drawing upon these archives, this volume takes "the future" as its thematic lens, offering a comprehensive account of over 170 years of Expo history. Through engaging visual storytelling, the following pages reconstruct significant moments in which Expos have played an important role in advancing human civilization. From tangible innovations to transformative ideas, Expos serve as milestones in our shared history, helping us understand the past while inspiring future generations.

Expos shed light on both the realities and aspirations of their time. The visions of the future explored within these pages are rooted in history—emerging from World and Specialised Expos held between 1851 and the modern day. From their very inception, Expos have showcased the cutting-edge technologies and pioneering ideas of their time, with the common goal of shaping a better world. The history of Expos represents a chronicle of human ingenuity and cooperation—a testament of how societies have imagined, shaped, and ultimately realised the future.

Each Expo documented in this book expresses a unique vision, imbued with its own character and interpretation of "the future". These narratives remind us of the innovative ways in which past generations have leveraged technology to address the challenges of their time. Reflecting on these past insights provides valuable context and inspiration for tackling the pressing challenges of today. By publishing this volume, the World Expo Museum reinforces its role as a bridge connecting the past to the future, encouraging us to embrace new ideas and advance humanity's collective progress.

尖端技术和先锋思想，其共同目标是建设一个更加美好的世界。自诞生起，世博会始终在展现当时当下最先进的技术与理念，而这些技术与理念都旨在构建人类共同的美好未来。世博会的历史也是人类共同应对挑战的历史，也是『未来』不断被构想、被塑造、被实现的见证。

本书所记录的每一届世博会都表达了独特的愿景，充满了自己的特色和对『未来』的诠释。我们惊叹于前人如何以技术革新回应时代命题。通过对历史的思考，更为我们应对当今的紧迫挑战提供了宝贵的背景和灵感。通过该书的出版，世博会博物馆体现了其连接过去与未来的桥梁作用，鼓励我们拥抱新思想，从而推动人类的集体进步。

迪米特里·科肯切斯
国际展览局秘书长
2025年2月

贺序

该书通过对历史探索呈现了世博会不断发展的未来愿景，值此新书付梓之际，我谨代表国际展览局向世博会博物馆致以诚挚祝贺。

世博会博物馆是国际展览局唯一官方博物馆和官方文献中心，经过与国际展览局、世博国际社区的多年共建，已形成较为完善的世博文献收藏体系。在此丰厚文献基础上编纂的这本书，以「未来」为切口，系统梳理了170余年的世博记忆，以生动的画面再现世博历史上促进人类文明进步的珍贵瞬间，将世博会的宏大叙事转化为启迪未来的智慧之书。

世博会启迪了当前时期的现实和愿望，书中探讨的未来愿景源自于1851年至今举办的综合类世博会和专业类世博会。世博会展示了当时的

005

Foreword

LIU Wentao
Director of World Expo Museum
February 2025

As Expo 2025 Osaka approaches, the world will once again gather to celebrate human ingenuity and progress. In this moment of renewed global ambition to "Design a Future Society for Our Lives", we pause to reflect upon more than a century of human aspiration, innovation, and exploration of the future—using the Expos as our guiding landmark.

This volume serves as both a commemorative chronicle and reference compendium of the future. Organized chronologically, it presents a carefully curated collection of photographs, prints, blueprints, and hand-drawn sketches from 72 World and Specialised Expos. From the awe-inspiring sight of spectators gazing up at a giant astronomical telescope at Expo 1851 London to the unveiling of the first lunar rock samples at Expo 1970 Osaka, these images together form a visual timeline—charting the evolution of our visions for the future.

Beyond documenting history, this book invites us to examine how once-distant dreams have shaped the world we inhibit today. The Midway Plaisance of Expo 1893 Chicago laid the foundation for the modern amusement park; the moving walkway introduced at the Expo 1900 Paris has become a staple of airports worldwide; and the wireless telephone unveiled at Expo 1915 San Francisco has evolved into the indispensable smart phone. More than a century ago, visitors to the Expos gazed beyond the present in search of the future—unknowingly glimpsing the world we now inhabit.

Most importantly, this book serves as a guide to action for the future. As early as Expo 1878 Paris, visionaries anticipated the world's growing demand for renewable energy, leading to the invention of the solar-powered engine. Today, sustainability has become one of the most pressing global challenges, and Expo 2025 Osaka is set to advance the United Nations Sustainable Development Goals through international collaboration.

We have gathered these diverse and layered visions of the "future" into a single volume because, together, they form a profound and enduring legacy of human civilization. To read about the future is not to predict its endpoint, but to embrace the boundless possibilities that lie ahead.

Now, let us embark on this journey aboard the Expo express—a time-travelling vessel spanning generations—as we set forth from the past towards our next destination: the future.

道,现在是各大机场的常见设施。"1915年旧金山世博会展出了无线电话,"而如今,几乎没有人可以离开手机生活。一百多年前,人们在世博会上眺望未来,那眺望的远方正是我们现在生活的地方。

更重要的,这还是一本关于未来的行动指南。翻阅本书,或许你会讶异于早在1878年巴黎世博会上就有人预见了未来对可再生能源的需求,发明了太阳能发动机,而如今,可持续发展已成为越来越重要的课题,2025年大阪世博会即将为推动全球可持续发展目标的实现提供国际合作的平台。

我们将这些层层叠叠的『未来』收集成册,因为它们共同构成了人类文明的重要遗产。阅读『未来』不是为了预言终点,而是为了永远追寻无尽的可能性。此刻,让我们搭乘世博会这辆穿梭于时代的快速列车,从过去出发,直达下一站:未来!

世博会博物馆馆长

2025年2月

卷首语

2025年大阪世博会召开在即，全球将再次因世博而汇聚。当各国在大阪『设计未来社会、让生命绽放光彩』的时候，我们却选择在此时回望来路，以世博会为坐标，回顾人类百余年来对『未来』最炽热的想象与最务实的探索。

这是一本关于未来的纪念画册。以时间为序，书中收录了72届综合类与专业类世博会上那些具有未来指向性的照片、版画、图纸和手绘稿。从1851年伦敦世博会人们抬头仰望巨型天文望远镜，到1970年大阪世博会展出的第一批月球岩石标本，这些画面共同组成了未来演进图谱，具有不言自明的叙事力量。

这也是一本关于未来的检索手册。那些曾被称为未来的愿景，有的已成为我们司空见惯的现实生活，有的仍在等待实现的契机。1893年芝加哥世博会上的大道乐园，勾勒出现代游乐场的最初模样；1900年巴黎世博会上的自动人行

What is an Expo?

Expos are a global event dedicated to advancing human knowledge, addressing societal aspirations, and driving progress in science, technology, economy, and society. Organized and facilitated by governments of host countries and bringing together countries and international organisations (Official Participants), these major public events are unrivalled in their ability to gather millions of visitors, create new dynamics and catalyse change in their host cities.

Four types of Expo are organised under the auspices of the Bureau International des Expositions (BIE): World Expos, Specialised Expos, Horticultural Expos, and the Triennale Milano.

About World Expos

Held every five years and typically spanning six months, World Expos are unparalleled in their scale, duration, and visitor numbers. Each World Expo is built around a specific theme, allowing Official Participants to design and construct their own pavilions to express their interpretation of the Expo's theme, address contemporary challenges, and seek collective solutions.

About Specialised Expos

Specialised Expos are organized in the interval between two World Expos, with a maximum duration of three months. Though smaller in scale, Specialised Expos are also global events that are equally designed to respond to a precise global challenge. Official Participants are not required to build their own pavilions, as the host provides the exhibition spaces. The purpose of Specialised Expos is to enable more countries to host and participate in the World Expo.

About Horticultural Expos

Recognised by the BIE and approved by the International Association of Horticultural Producers (AIPH), Horticultural Expos are recognized as Category A1 events. These Expos must be held at least two years apart, and at least ten years between events held in the same country. Running for up to six months, Horticultural Expos focus on advancing innovation in agriculture, horticulture, and landscape design, offering sustainable solutions for healthy living, green economies, and sustainability.

Triennale Milano

The Triennale Milano—formally known as the Milan Triennial Exhibition of Decorative Arts and Modern Architecture—is a recurring International Exhibition held in Milan dedicated to architecture, design and craftsmanship. Held every three years in Milan, with an exhibition period of approximately six months, each edition of the Triennale Milano is organised around a theme that reflects modern-day issues and promotes experimentation and debate in a contemporary and interdisciplinary perspective, linking art, behavioral sciences and scientific research.

专业类世博会

专业类世博会在两届综合类世博会之间举办,会期最多为三个月。专业类世博会也是全球性的盛会,同样致力于全球问题的解决,但它的活动规模较小,参展方无需自建展馆,场地均由主办方提供。设立专业类世博会的目的在于让更多的国家举办和参与世博会。

园艺博览会

国际展览局认可经国际园艺生产者协会批准的A1级别园艺博览会。两届园艺博览会之间至少间隔两年,同一国家至少间隔十年方可再度举办园艺博览会,会期一般为六个月。园艺博览会致力于促进农业、园艺和景观服务等方面的创新发展,为健康生活、绿色经济、可持续发展提供解决方案。

米兰三年展

米兰三年展(即米兰装饰艺术与现代建筑三年展)是在米兰举办的致力于建筑、设计和工艺的国际性展览。每三年举办一次,会期一般为六个月。每届均围绕特定主题展开,而主题通常反映当代问题,并以当代和跨学科的视角促进实验与辩论;将艺术、行为科学和科学研究联系起来。

什么是世博会

世博会是全球性的盛会,致力于提升人类知识水平、关注人类和社会的意愿,强调科学、技术、经济与社会进步。世博会由各个举办国政府组织推动,汇集世界各国和国际组织参展方,通过极具吸引力的展览与活动,吸引数百万甚至数千万游客,并深刻影响主办城市的未来发展。

国际展览局是管理世博会的国际组织,在其监管下,世博会分为四种类型:综合类世博会、专业类世博会、园艺博览会和米兰三三年展。

综合类世博会

综合类世博会每五年举办一次,会期一般为六个月。相较于其他类型,综合类世博会的规模、持续时间和客流量均是无可比拟的。每届世博会都有其特定的主题,允许各参展方自建展馆,表达对世博会主题的理解,面对时代挑战,共同寻求解决之道。

013

Bureau International des Expositions

The Bureau International des Expositions (BIE) is the Intergovernmental Organisation in charge of overseeing and regulating all international exhibitions that last more than three weeks and are of non commercial nature ("Expos"). Today, 4 types of Expos are organised under its auspices: World Expos, Specialised Expos, Horticultural Expos and the Triennale di Milano.

The mission of the BIE is to guarantee the quality and the success of these world events, protect the rights of their organisers and participants and preserve their core values of Education, Innovation and Cooperation.

The BIE do this by:

◎ Choosing the host countries of future Expos

◎ Providing candidate and host countries with expertise in event management, national branding and public diplomacy

◎ Regulating the organization of the event and making sure the host country and all participants respect the Convention of the BIE and the rules of the Expo

From the 31 countries that created the BIE in 1928, the Organisation has grown to 184 Member States, as a result of the success and the appeal of Expos. The BIE Member States take part in all the decisions of the BIE and they strive to continually improve the quality of Expos.

The headquarters of the BIE are located in Paris.

管理、国家品牌建设和公共外交方面的专业知识;

◎ 规范活动组织方式,确保举办国及所有参与者遵守国际展览局公约及该届世博会的制度。

得益于世博会的成功与吸引力,国际展览局的规模不断壮大,其成员国从1928年创立之初的31个发展为184个。成员国参与国际展览局的所有决策,共同致力于提升世博会的品质。

国际展览局的总部位于法国巴黎。

国际展览局

国际展览局是负责监管和规范持续时间超过三周且非商业性质的国际展览（世博会）的政府间组织。目前，其管辖范围内的世博会共有四种类型：综合类世博会、专业类世博会、园艺博览会和米兰三年展。

国际展览局的使命是保障这些世界性活动的卓越品质与圆满成功，保护其组织者和参与者的权益，维护世博会的核心价值——教育、创新与合作。

国际展览局通过以下方式实现这一目标：

◎ 选择未来世博会的举办国；
◎ 为候选国和举办国提供其在活动

World Expo Museum

World Expo Museum (WEM) is jointly built by the Shanghai Municipal Government and the Bureau International des Expositions (BIE). According to the Memorandum of Cooperation on World Expo Museum signed by the two parties in November 2010, the WEM, as the only official museum and official documentation and research centre of the BIE, aims to fulfil the mission of inheriting the legacy, preserving the essence and expanding the effect of the Expo. It is committed to becoming the global culture reference in Expo culture and innovation, and it is dedicated to archiving the exhibition center, promotion center, education center, training center and the documentation research center, and a platform for Expo-related culture exchanges.

Exhibition Centre

With a building area of 46,000 square meters, the WEM thoroughly reflects the Expo's development since 1851. It provides the public with an immersive experience through up-to-date temporary exhibitions and age-specific educational and leisure activities, creating a comfortable cultural space for the general public. In the past two years, annual visitor attendance has approached nearly one million.

Promotion Centre

As an important part of the cooperation between the BIE and the Shanghai Municipal Government, the WEM has participated in the past four Expos in a row and will join the upcoming Expo 2025 Osaka. On this basis, the WEM is now exploring a full-cycle cooperation model with future Expo organizers to further enhance its role as an official museum for the international organization.

Education Centre

The WEM has unified its public services under the 'WE' brand, highlighting the mutually beneficial and symbiotic relationship between the WEM and its visitors. The WEM's social education covers a wide range of areas, including in-house exhibitions, guided tours, lectures and events, as well as mobile exhibitions outside the museum and co-curricular programs developed in collaboration with schools at the compulsory education level.

Training Centre and Documentation Research Center

The WEM is dedicate to building a documentation center for the collection and utilisation of Expo documents, an exchange centre for Expo academic research and a training centre for Expo theories and practices, providing services to academic research institutions and experts and scholars from various countries. The WE Library houses valuable documents related to the Expo, dating from 1851 to the present in 14 languages, making it a specialized documentation and research center for Expo documents in the world.

推介中心

作为国际展览局与上海市政府的重要合作内容,连续参展包括2025年大阪世博会在内的5届世博会。在参展的基础上,逐步探索建立与未来世博会主办方的全周期合作模式,进一步凸显国际组织官方机构属性。

教育中心

世博会博物馆把众多对公众提供的服务统一为『WE』品牌,以此体现博物馆和参观者之间教学相长、共生共荣的关系。从馆内展示、讲解、讲座、活动到馆外流动展览,世博会博物馆开展各类社会教育服务,并与义务教育阶段学校共同创设相关课程。

培训中心和文献研究中心

世博会博物馆致力于打造为各国世博会学术研究机构及专家学者提供服务的世博会文献收藏利用中心、世博会学术研究交流中心、世博会理论实务培训中心。世博图书馆藏有1851年至今、涉及14种语言的世博珍贵文献,是目前全球世博文献资料较为集中的文献研究中心。

世博会博物馆

世博会博物馆由中国上海市政府和国际展览局合作共建。根据2010年11月双方签署的《世博会博物馆合作备忘录》，世博会博物馆作为国际展览局唯一官方博物馆和官方文献研究中心，以传承世博遗产、保留世博精髓、延续世博效应为宗旨，致力于成为全球世博文化与创新方面的知识库，世界博览事业的展示中心，推介中心、教育中心、培训中心和文献研究中心，并为与世博会相关的国际文化交流提供平台。

展示中心

建筑面积4.6万平方米，全景式展现自1851年以来的世博会历史发展，并以常换常新的临展、分龄分众的教育和休闲活动，为公众提供丰富的多感官体验，致力于成为市民舒适愉悦的文化客厅。近两年，年参观客流接近百万。

Introduction

1. There are four types of Expos: World Expos, Specialised Expos, Horticultural Expos and the Triennale Milano. Due to space limitations, this book only includes the contents of World Expos and Specialised Expos held between 1851 and 2030, omitting Horticultural Expos and the Triennale Milano.

2. The name and definition of World Expos have been revised several times. The 1928 Paris Convention initially referred to 'General Exhibitions of the 1st category' and 'General Exhibitions of the 2nd category'. Following a protocol to the Convention in 1972, the two categories were replaced by a single classification 'World Exhibition'. A new amendment adopted in 1988 and applied from 1996 gave World Expos their current official term 'International Registered Exhibition'. For ease of understanding, based on the classification instructions of the Bureau International des Expositions (BIE), all the expos in this category will be uniformly referred to as World Expos in this book.

3. Similarly, the name and definition of Specialised Expos have been revised several times. The 1928 Paris Convention initially referred to 'Special Exhibitions'. A protocol to the Convention was adopted in 1972 redefining them as 'Specialised Exhibitions'. The current classification was adopted by the 1988 amendment which gave them their current official designation as 'International Recognised Exhibitions'. For ease of understanding, this book will uniformly refer to all the expos in this category as Specialised Expos based on the BIE's classification instructions.

4. Each Expo has its official name. For example, the official name of the Expo 1851 London was 'The Great Exhibition of the Works of Industry of all Nations'; the official name of the Expo 1937 Paris was 'International Exposition of Arts and Technology in Modern Life'. Based on the naming instructions of the BIE, the name of the Expos in this book is referred to in an abbreviated form of 'Expo + year + city'.

5. Although the World Expo Museum (WEM) has been mobilising multiple resources to search for and collect Expo documents since its establishment, there are still some sessions for which information is limited, resulting in the lack of suitable pictures to support some of the content in this book. The WEM welcomes international Expo organisations, collecting institutions and individuals to provide valuable historical materials and to continue supporting the Expo-related collaborations.

有过几次修订。1928年制定的《国际展览公约》将其命名为特殊博览会。1972年，国际展览局对公约进行了修订，将其改名为专业类世博会。1988年通过的新修订，规定了这类世博会的官方名称为国际认可类博览会。为便于理解，本书依据国际展览局的分类说明，统一将其称为专业类世博会。

4. 每届世博会均有其官方名称，例如1851年伦敦世博会的官方名称是『万国工业品博览会』，1937年巴黎世博会的官方名称是『现代生活中的艺术与技术国际博览会』。本书依据国际展览局的命名办法，统一使用『年份＋城市＋世博会』的简称方式。

5. 尽管世博会博物馆自筹建之日起，即联动多方资源开展世博文献的查找与征集工作，但仍有部分届次的世博会资料较为稀缺，致使书中部分内容缺乏合适的图片作为文字的佐证与补充。世博会博物馆欢迎国际世博组织、收藏机构及个人提供珍贵史料，持续开展世博相关合作。

写在前面

1. 世博会分为四种类型：综合类世博会、专业类世博会、园艺博览会和米兰三年展。受篇幅限制，本书仅收录1851年至2030年间举办的综合类世博会和专业类世博会的相关内容，未能涉及园艺博览会和米兰三年展。

2. 关于综合类世博会，这一分类的名称和定义有过几次修订。1928年制定的《国际展览公约》将这类世博会分为两种——第一类一般博览会和第二类一般博览会。1972年，国际展览局对公约进行了修订，将这两种类别统称为综合类世博会。1988年通过并于1996年开始实施的新修订，规定了这类世博会的官方名称为国际注册类博览会。为便于理解，本书依据国际展览局的分类说明，统一将其称为综合类世博会。

3. 关于专业类世博会，这一分类的名称和定义也

Contents

002   Preface of Congratulations
006   Foreword
010   What is an Expo
014   Bureau International des Expositions
018   World Expo Museum
022   Introduction
026   Contents

Infographic of Expos

目录

- 005　贺序
- 009　卷首语
- 013　什么是世博会
- 017　国际展览局
- 021　世博会博物馆
- 025　写在前面
- 027　目录
- 　　　世博信息表

WORLD EXPOS

EXPO 1851 LONDON	001	EXPO 1913 GHENT	161
EXPO 1855 PARIS	015	EXPO 1915 SAN FRANCISCO	167
EXPO 1862 LONDON	025	EXPO 1929 BARCELONA	179
EXPO 1867 PARIS	035	EXPO 1933 CHICAGO	189
EXPO 1873 VIENNA	045	EXPO 1935 BRUSSELS	199
EXPO 1876 PHILADELPHIA	053	EXPO 1937 PARIS	211
EXPO 1878 PARIS	065	EXPO 1939 NEW YORK	229
EXPO 1880 MELBOURNE	077	EXPO 1949 PORT-AU-PRINCE	265
EXPO 1888 BARCELONA	087	EXPO 1958 BRUSSELS	321
EXPO 1889 PARIS	095	EXPO 1962 SEATTLE	335
EXPO 1893 CHICAGO	105	EXPO 1967 MONTREAL	353
EXPO 1897 BRUSSELS	115	EXPO 1970 OSAKA	369
EXPO 1900 PARIS	119	EXPO 1992 SEVILLE	457
EXPO 1904 ST. LOUIS	131	EXPO 2000 HANNOVER	487
EXPO 1905 LIEGE	139	EXPO 2005 AICHI	499
EXPO 1906 MILAN	145	EXPO 2010 SHANGHAI	517
EXPO 1910 BRUSSELS	153	EXPO 2015 MILAN	539
		EXPO 2020 DUBAI	557
		EXPO 2025 OSAKA KANSAI	567
		EXPO 2030 RIYADH	579

年份	名称	页码
1915	旧金山世博会	167
1929	巴塞罗那世博会	179
1933	芝加哥世博会	189
1935	布鲁塞尔世博会	199
1937	巴黎世博会	211
1939	纽约世博会	229
1949	太子港世博会	265
1958	布鲁塞尔世博会	321
1962	西雅图世博会	335
1967	蒙特利尔世博会	353
1970	大阪世博会	369
1992	塞维利亚世博会	457
2000	汉诺威世博会	487
2005	爱知世博会	499
2010	上海世博会	517
2015	米兰世博会	539
2020	迪拜世博会	557
2025	大阪世博会	567
2030	利雅得世博会	579

综合类世博会

1851 伦敦世博会 ... 001
1855 巴黎世博会 ... 015
1862 伦敦世博会 ... 025
1867 巴黎世博会 ... 035
1873 维也纳世博会 ... 045
1876 费城世博会 ... 053
1878 巴黎世博会 ... 065
1880 墨尔本世博会 ... 077
1888 巴塞罗那世博会 ... 087
1889 巴黎世博会 ... 095
1893 芝加哥世博会 ... 105
1897 布鲁塞尔世博会 ... 115
1900 巴黎世博会 ... 119
1904 圣路易斯世博会 ... 131
1905 列日世博会 ... 139
1906 米兰世博会 ... 145

1851	1855	1862	1867	1873		1876	1878	1880	1888	
1889	1893	1897	1900	1904	1905	1906	1910	1913	1915	1929
			1933	1935				1937		1939
								1949		
			1958			1962		1967		
		1970								
	1992						2000	2005		
2010		2015				2020	2025		2030	

SPECIALISED EXPOS

EXPO 1936 STOCKHOLM	205		EXPO 1968 SAN ANTONIO	363
EXPO 1938 HELSINKI	223		EXPO 1971 BUDAPEST	381
EXPO 1939 LIEGE	241		EXPO 1974 SPOKANE	387
EXPO 1947 PARIS	247		EXPO 1975 OKINAWA	395
EXPO 1949 STOCKHOLM	253		EXPO 1981 PLOVDIV	403
EXPO 1949 LYON	259		EXPO 1982 KNOXVILLE	409
EXPO 1951 LILLE	273		EXPO 1984 NEW ORLEANS	415
EXPO 1953 ROME	279		EXPO 1985 TSUKUBA	423
EXPO 1953 JERUSALEM	285		EXPO 1985 PLOVDIV	431
EXPO 1954 NAPLES	291		EXPO 1986 VANCOUVER	435
EXPO 1955 TURIN	297		EXPO 1988 BRISBANE	445
EXPO 1955 HELSINGBORG	303		EXPO 1991 PLOVDIV	453
EXPO 1956 BEIT DAGON	309		EXPO 1992 GENOA	467
EXPO 1957 BERLIN	315		EXPO 1993 DAEJEON	471
EXPO 1961 TURIN	329		EXPO 1998 LISBON	479
EXPO 1965 MUNICH	347		EXPO 2008 ZARAGOZA	509
			EXPO 2012 YEOSU	529
			EXPO 2017 ASTANA	549
			EXPO 2027 BELGRADE	573

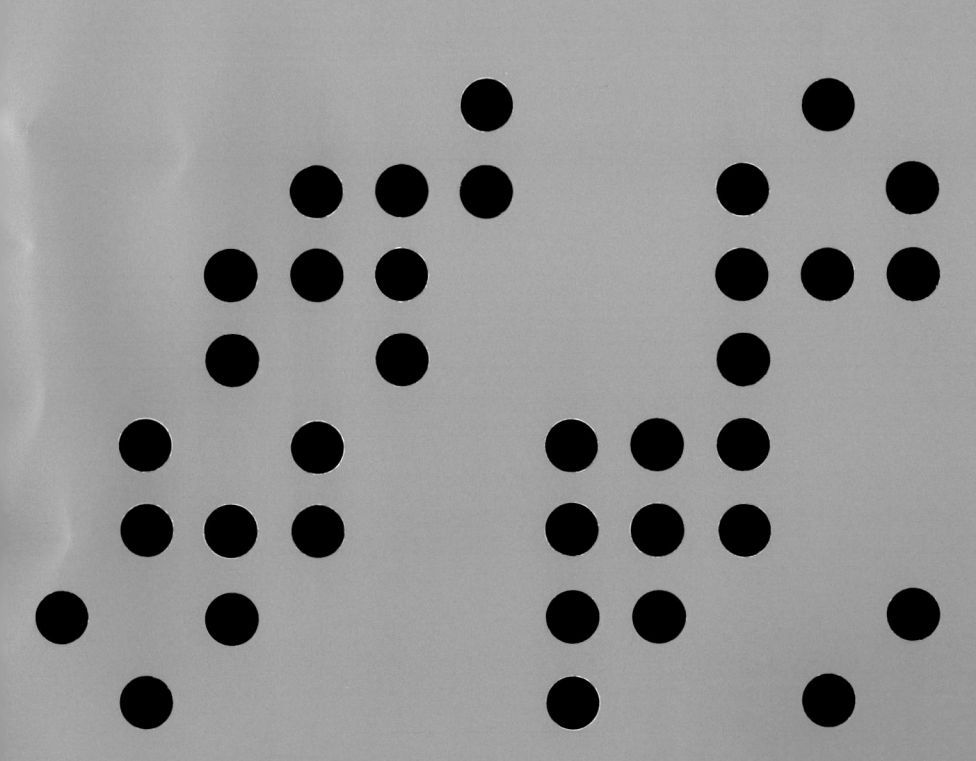

1965 慕尼黑世博会	341
1968 圣安东尼奥世博会	363
1971 布达佩斯世博会	381
1974 斯波坎世博会	387
1975 冲绳世博会	395
1981 普罗夫迪夫世博会	403
1982 诺克斯维尔世博会	409
1984 新奥尔良世博会	415
1985 筑波世博会	423
1985 普罗夫迪夫世博会	431
1986 温哥华世博会	435
1988 布里斯班世博会	445
1991 普罗夫迪夫世博会	453
1992 热那亚世博会	467
1993 大田世博会	471
1998 里斯本世博会	479
2008 萨拉戈萨世博会	509
2012 丽水世博会	529
2017 阿斯塔纳世博会	549
2027 贝尔格莱德世博会	573

专业类世博会

1936 斯德哥尔摩世博会 205
1938 赫尔辛基世博会 223
1939 列日世博会 241
1947 巴黎世博会 247
1949 斯德哥尔摩世博会 253
1949 里昂世博会 259
1951 里尔世博会 273
1953 罗马世博会 279
1953 耶路撒冷世博会 285
1954 那不勒斯世博会 291
1955 都林世博会 297
1955 赫尔辛堡世博会 303
1956 贝特达贡世博会 309
1957 柏林世博会 315
1961 都木世博会 329

72

从过去向未来
引领时代进步的世博会

THE FUTURE FROM THE PAST EXPOS: A CATALYST FOR CHANGE

EXPO 1851 LONDON

伦敦世博会

Theme: **Industry of all Nations**
Location: **London, United Kingdom**
Category: **World Expo**
Dates: **1851.5.1-10.11**
Area (ha): **10.4**
Visitors: **6,039,195**
Participants: **25**

Birth of the World Expo

The first World Expo was held in London, England, in 1851. Masterminded by Prince Albert, the husband and the consort of Queen Victoria, and Sir Henry Cole, the Expo aimed at educating the public about technical progress and showcasing British design and manufacturing. The Expo was born in the midst of the Industrial Revolution, and its success highlighted the notable advances in the area of industry and technology.

The Crystal Palace

The Crystal Palace, 563 meters long and 124 meters wide, and was specially built for the Expo in a few months using modular design and prefabricated components. With more than 300,000 glass panes, the structure offered an immense and naturally-lit area of 92,000m^2 for the exhibition.

"Every Conceivable Invention"

More than 100,000 exhibits were on display in the Crystal Palace. In the words of Queen Victoria, it displayed "every conceivable invention", many of which were icons of the industrial era. Exhibitors from the world were explaining to visitors how new technologies could contribute to improve people's work and life.

"The Peoples of the Earth Rushing to the Crystal Palace"

The initial ticket price kept visitors away, so the Royal Commission opted to introduce "shilling days", with the modest price of one shilling per ticket, encouraging more people to visit the Expo. On the other hand, the expanding railroad network made cross-country travel possible, setting the basis for modern tourism services.

Ever-lasting Impact

The first Expo received many visitors and made a considerable revenue. The Royal Commission used the proceeds to increase the means of industrial education and extend the influence of science and art upon productive industry, with institutions such as the Museum of Manufactures (now the Victoria & Albert Museum) being created as a result of this idea.

主题：万国工业
举办地：英国伦敦
类型：综合类世博会
时间：1851年5月1日至10月11日
占地（公顷）：10.4
参观者（人次）：6,039,195
参展方（个）：25

世博会的诞生

首届世博会于1851年在英国伦敦举办，由英国维多利亚女王的丈夫阿尔伯特亲王与亨利·科尔爵士策划发起，旨在向公众宣传技术进步，展示英国的设计和制造。世博会诞生于工业革命时期，它的成功举办彰显了人类在工业技术领域的巨大进步。

水晶宫

水晶宫是为了举办世博会而专门设计建造的展馆，其长563米，宽124米，采用模块化设计和预制构件组装，仅耗时数月即完成建设。水晶宫使用了超过30万块玻璃，为展览提供了约9.2万平方米的自然采光空间。

『所有能想到的发明』

水晶宫里展出的展品超过10万件。用维多利亚女王的话来说，它展出了『所有能想到的发明』，其中很多都是工业时代标志性产品。来自世界各地的参展商向参观者介绍了新技术是如何改进人们的生产与生活的。

『冲向水晶宫的世界人民』

最初的门票价格限制了客流量，皇家委员会因而设置『先令日』，规定该日门票价格仅为1先令，鼓励更多人参观世博会。此外，不断扩大的铁路网络使跨国旅行成为可能，类似现代的旅游业服务应运而生。

巨久影响

首届世博会吸引众多游客，其收益亦相当可观。皇家委员会用这笔收益丰富工业教育手段，将科学和艺术的影响扩展到工业生产中，制造博物馆（即现在的维多利亚和阿尔伯特博物馆）等机构的创建都是这一理念的产物。

首届世博会的展馆水晶宫,它的诞生具有开创意义,后世诸多公共建筑的设计深受其影响印刷品:1854年,《狄金森的1851年万国博览会全记录:原为阿尔伯特亲王所创作》

Constructed for the first-ever Expo, the Crystal Palace was an architectural milestone, having a profound impact on the design of public building.
Dickinson's Comprehensive Pictures of the Great Exhibition of 1851, from the original painted for Prince Albert. 1854. Print.

Prince Albert and Queen Victoria visiting the machinery division. Exhibits at the early Expos were mainly large machinery, showcasing the leading role of technology in development.
Printed and Published by John Cassell. *The Illustrated Exhibitor, Tribute to the World's Industrial Jubilee.* 1852. World Expo Museum Collection. Print.

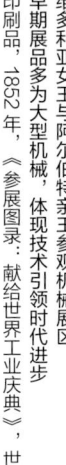

维多利亚女王与阿尔伯特亲王参观机械展区 早期展品多为大型机械,体现技术引领时代进步 印刷品,1852年,《参展图录:献给世界工业庆典》,世博会博物馆馆藏

010 Telescope at the First Expo
The Illustrated London News. 1851. World Expo Museum Collection. Print.

"首届世博会上展出的望远镜印刷品",1851年,《伦敦新闻画报》,世博会博物馆馆藏

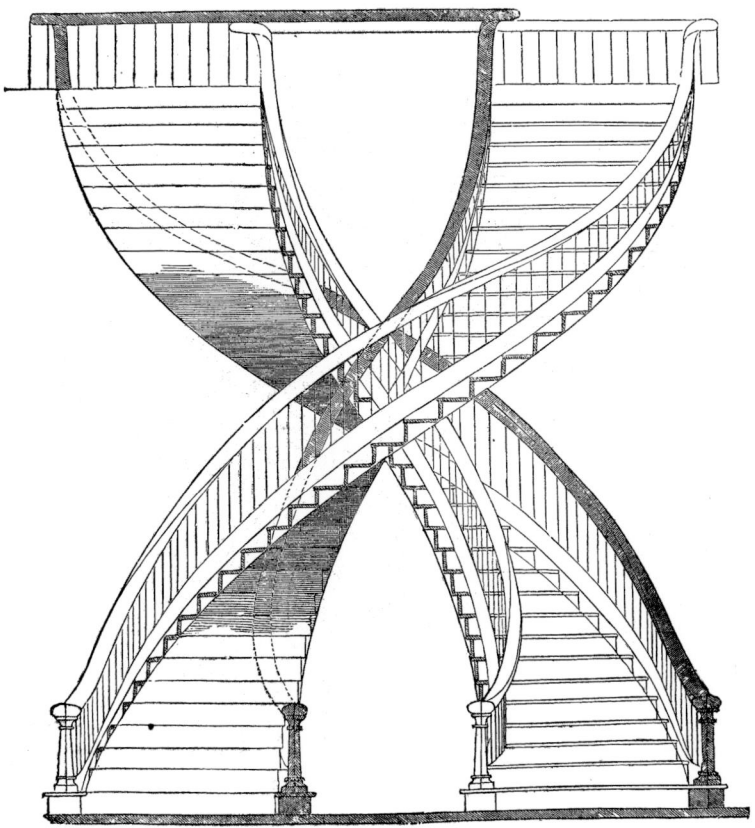

首届世博会上展出的双螺旋楼梯，为解决如何在小空间内疏导参观人流提供了一种方案印刷品，1851年，《伦敦新闻画报》，世博会博物馆馆藏

As an exhibit presented at the first Expo, double spiral staircase provided a crowd flow control solution for a limited space.
The Illustrated London News. 1851. World Expo Museum Collection. Print.

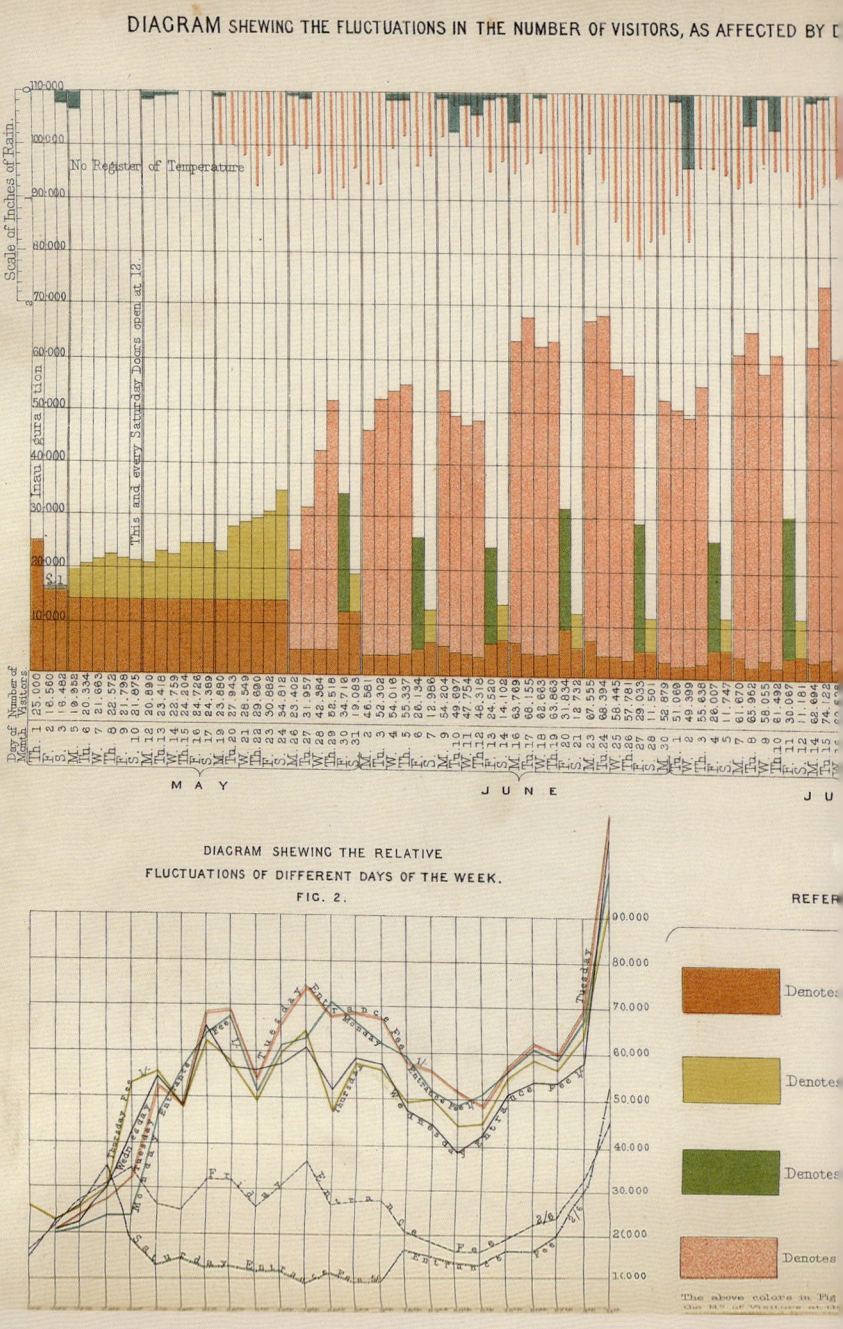

首届世博会组织方记录了票价、雨水、温度对客流量的影响,对未来举办大规模活动具有借鉴价值印刷品",1851年,《1851年伦敦万国工业品博览会委员会报告》,世博会博物馆馆藏

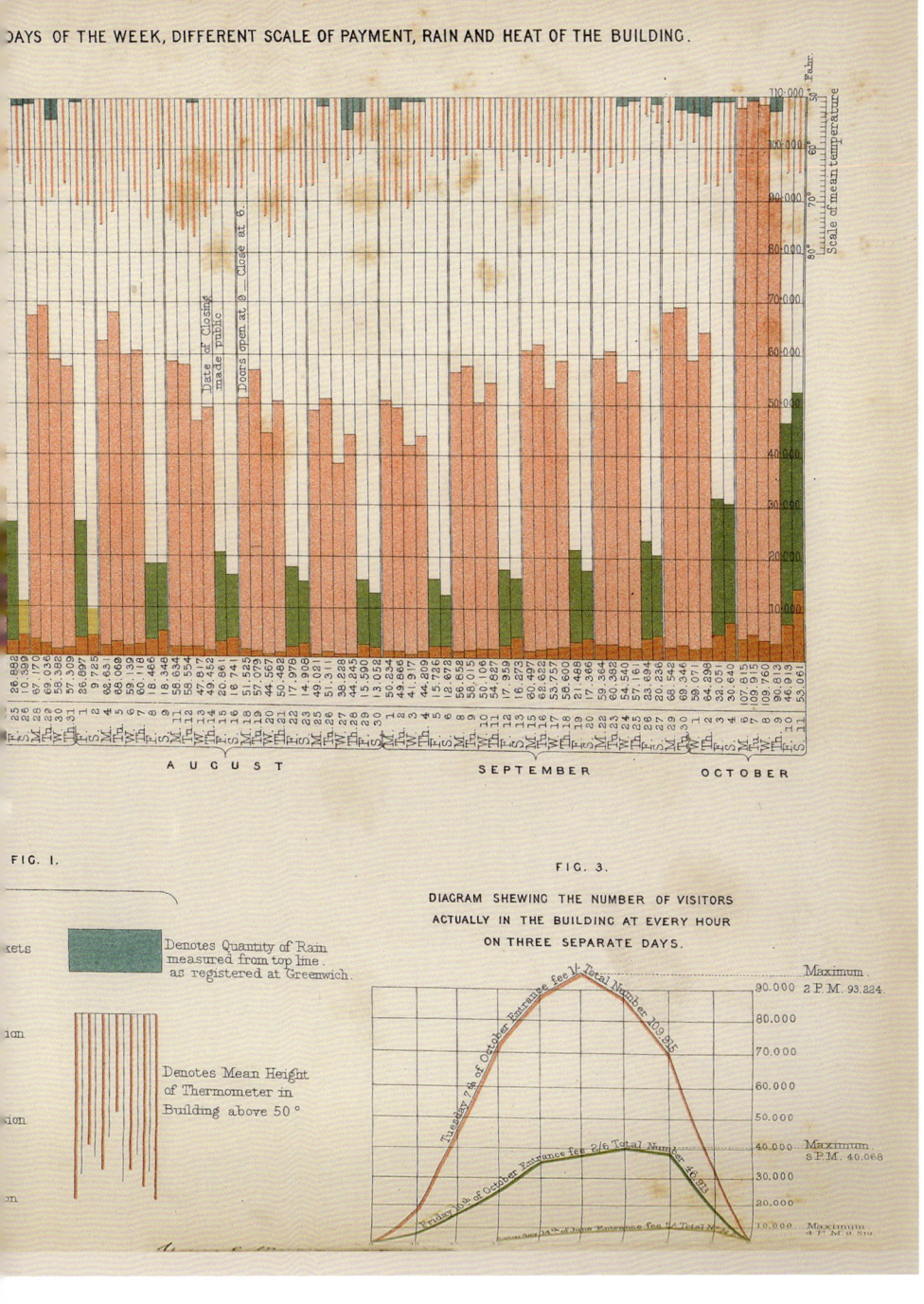

The Expo organizers documented the impact of ticket prices, rain, and temperature on visitor numbers, which provides valuable insight for future large-scale events.
Exhibition MDCCC.LI Reports of the Commissioners. 1851. World Expo Museum Collection. Print.

调整门票价格后,首届世博会的客流量激增,类似现代旅游业的相关服务应运而生印刷品,1851年,『冲向位于北端的水晶宫的世界人民』,《沙男夫妇和家人的探险》,世博会博物馆馆藏

After the adjustment of the ticket price, the number of visitors to the first Expo surged, leading to emergency of related services similar to those in the modern tourism industry.

014 All the World Going to See the Great Exhibition of 1851. *The Adventures of Mr and Mrs Sandboys and Family.* 1851. World Expo Museum Collection. Print.

EXPO 1855 PARIS

巴黎世博会

Theme:
Agriculture, Industry and Fine Arts
Location:
Paris, France
Category:
World Expo
Dates: **1855.5.15-11.15**
Area (ha): **15.2**
Visitors: **5,162,330**
Participants: **28**

Unveiling the Paris Moment

Since 1855, the city of Paris has hosted six World Expos in its history. The Palais de l'Industrie was the main building at the Expo 1855 Paris. Covering an immense area, it was still not large enough to host the 24,000 exhibitors. The Organizer had to build several annexes where large machines could be installed.

Technological Firsts

This World Expo witnessed the debut of scientific technological innovations, such as the first lawnmower, the first non-industrial sewing machine, the first speaking doll, and the first oil-powered vehicles. It is worth mentioning that the planned transatlantic telegraph cable made an appearance at Expo 1855 Paris. A few years later, this cable successfully linked Europe and North America, enabling the information transmission and opening up a new era of global communications.

The Indispensable Art

Unlike the first World Expo, this Expo put a focus not only on industrial and agricultural progress, but also on France's achievements in the arts. The exhibition at the Palais des Beaux-Arts showcased paintings, engravings, sculptures and architectural works by famous French artists. Works by French classicist painter Ingres, romanticist painter Delacroix, landscape painter Corot, and realist painter Courbet were included.

This Expo awards ceremony took place on the closing day of the Expo, and many artists, including Ingres, Delacroix, and Adolphe Sax, the inventor of the saxophone, were awarded the Legion of Honor. The ceremony ended with a concert conducted by symphonist Hector Berlioz, which also marked the first use of the electronic metronome.

主题：农业、工业和艺术
举办地：法国巴黎
类型：综合类世博会
日期：1855年5月15日至11月15日
占地（公顷）：15.2
参观者（人次）：5,162,330
参展方（个）：28

开启巴黎时刻

巴黎第一次举办世博会是在1855年，这座城市在历史上一共举办过6次综合类世博会。1855年巴黎世博会最主要的建筑是工业宫，其体量巨大，但要容纳2.4万家参展商仍显局促。组织方不得不另外搭建附属建筑，用来展示大型机械。

科技上的诸多第一

诸多科技创新出现在这一届世博会上，例如第一台割草机、第一台家用缝纫机、第一个会说话的娃娃、第一批燃油汽车等。特别值得一提的是，还在谋划中的跨大西洋电报电缆也出现在这届世博会上。几年后，这条电缆成功铺设，信息在欧美大陆间传输，开启了全球通信的新时代。

不能没有艺术

与首届世博会不同，这届世博会除了展示工农业进步，还特别强调法国在艺术方面的成就。艺术宫的展览展出了法国名家的绘画、版画、雕塑及建筑作品。法国古典主义画家安格尔、浪漫主义画家德拉克洛瓦、现实主义画家库尔贝的作品均包含其中。世博会闭幕当天举行了盛大的颁奖典礼，包括安格尔、德拉克洛瓦以及萨克斯管的发明者阿道夫·萨克斯在内的许多艺术家被授予了荣誉勋章。颁奖典礼以交响乐大师柏辽兹指挥的一场音乐会收尾，而这场音乐会也标志着电子节拍器的首次使用。

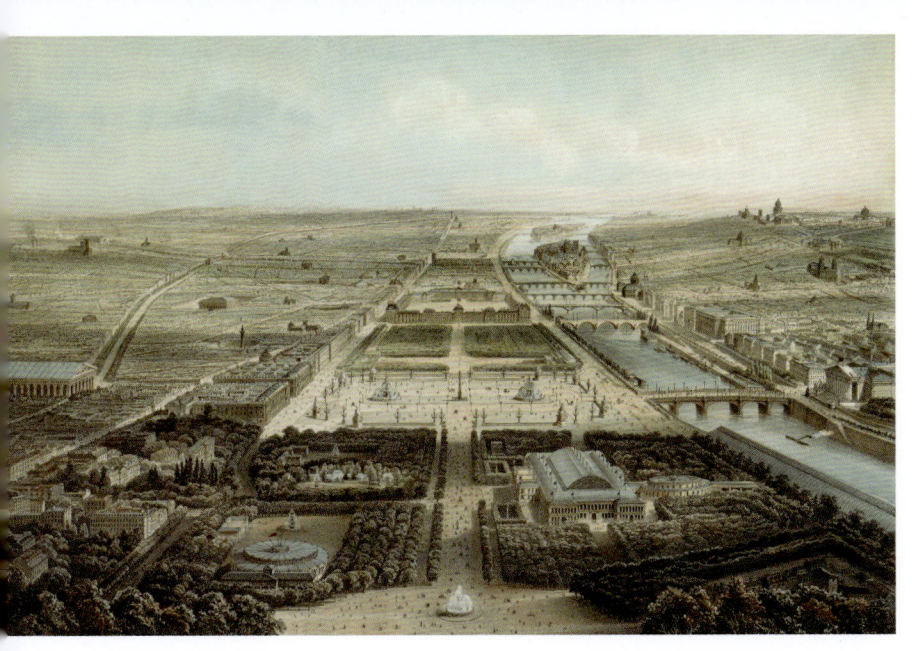

1855年巴黎世博会之后的巴黎全景印刷品，约1855年，作者：查尔斯·菲绍，美国国会图书馆印刷品与照片分部馆藏

General View of Paris after Expo 1855 Paris
Painted by Charles Fichot. c. 1855. Library of Congress Prints and Photographs Division. Print.

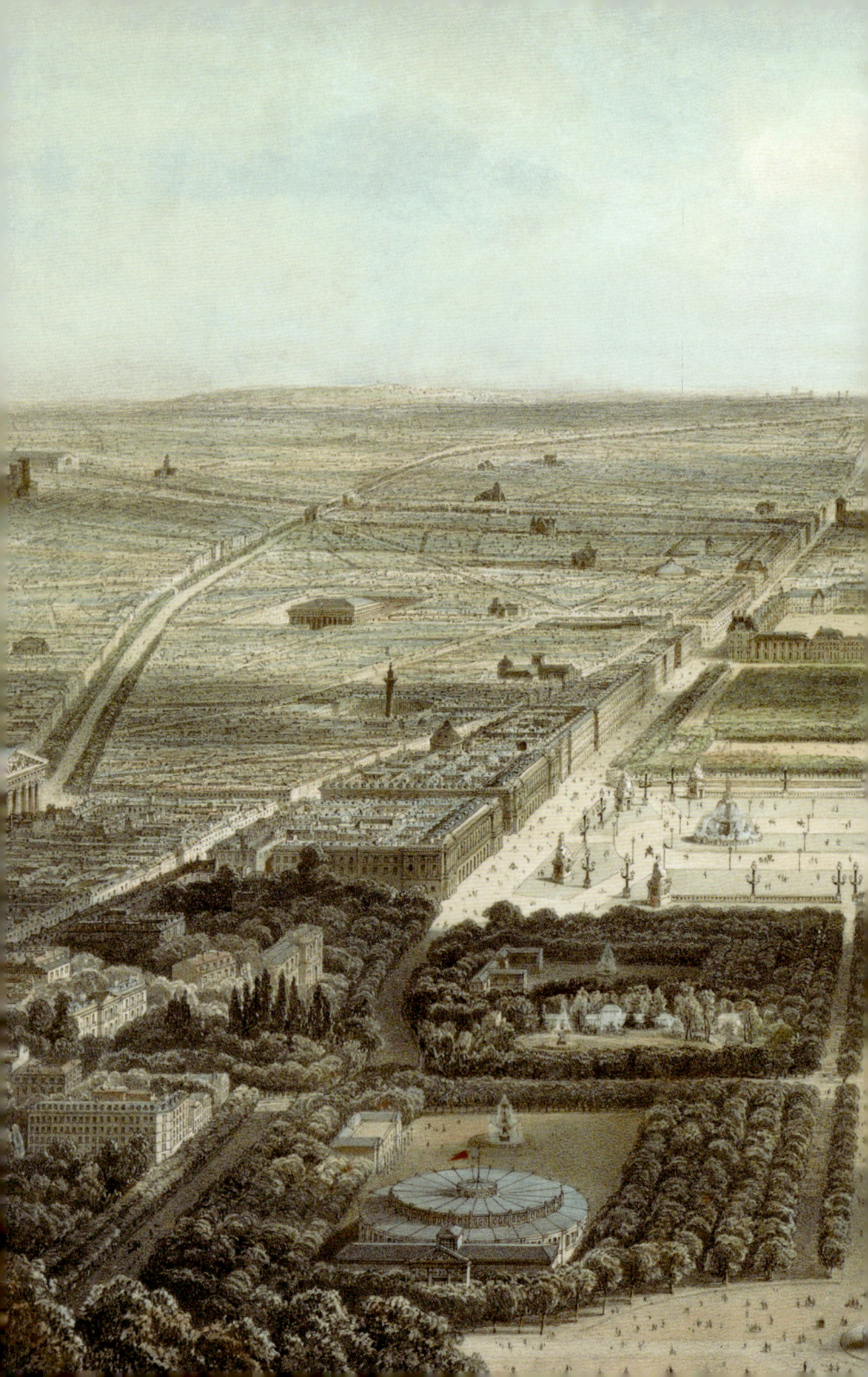

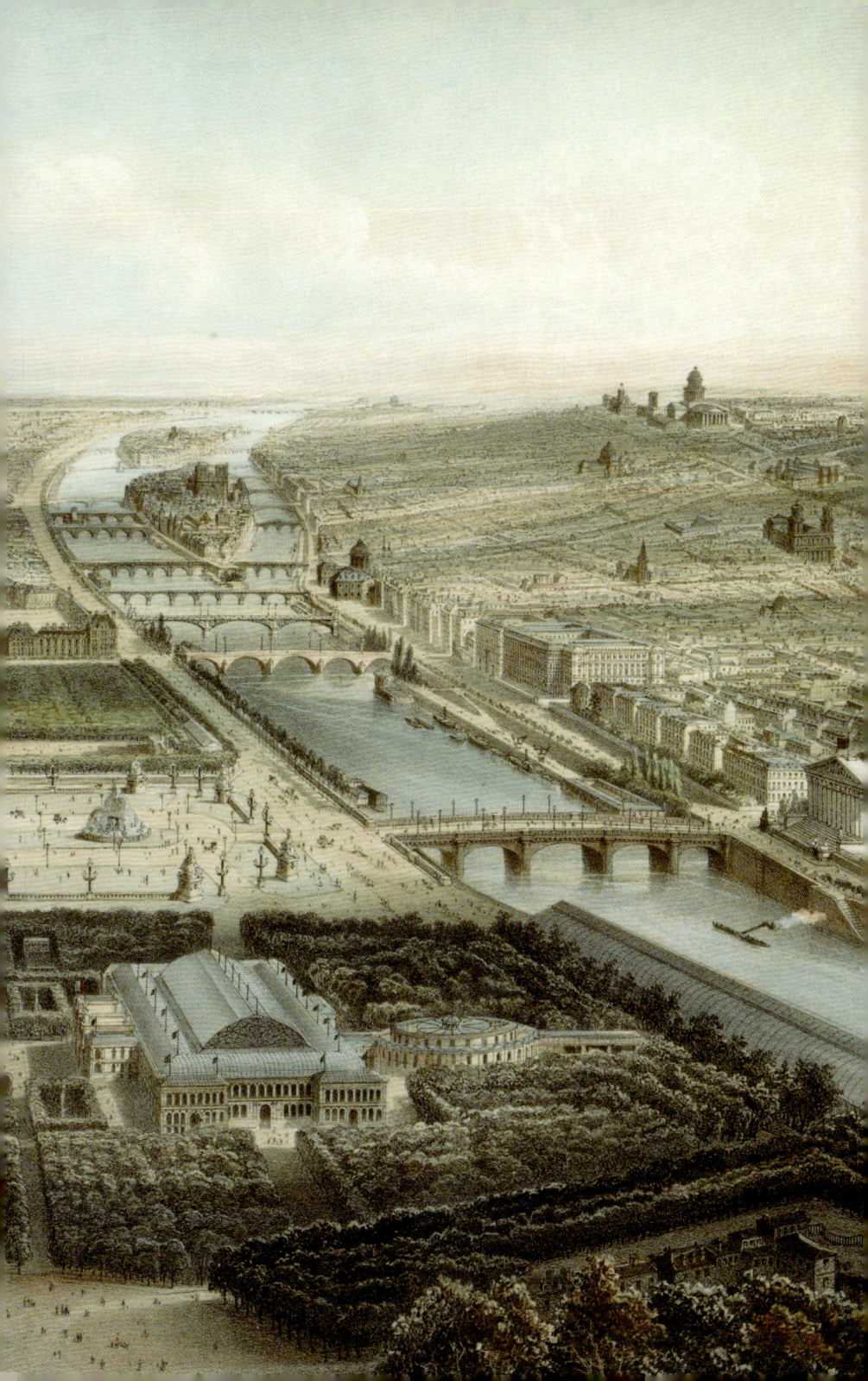

Elevation and Plan of the Palais de l'Industrie
1854. Brown University Library. Engraving.

工业宫的立面图和平面图版画，1854年，布朗大学图书馆馆藏

机械宫法国展区
印刷品,1855年,摄影:查尔斯·瑟斯顿·汤普森,国际展览局馆藏

024　The Hall of Machines: French Section
Photo by Charles Thurston Thompson. 1855. BIE Archive. Print.

EXPO 1862 LONDON

伦敦世博会

Theme: **Industry and Art**
Location: **London, United Kingdom**
Category: **World Expo**
Dates: **1862.5.1-11.1**
Area (ha): **11**
Visitors: **6,096,617**
Participants: **39**

Delayed Expo

Following the great success of the Great Exhibition in 1851, London planned to hold another event in 1861, celebrating the 10th anniversary of Expo 1851. At the time, the British had made significant advances in iron and steel production, steam engines and telegraphy. The time was considered ideal to host a new Expo to showcase the Britain's remarkable achievements in industry, technology and the arts. However, due to the death of Prince Albert, the leading patron of the Exhibition and the outbreak of international wars, the Expo was postponed for a year.

More Impressive Exhibition

The main exhibition hall featured an art gallery, which is 350 meters long that rivaled the length of the Grande Gallerie of the Louvre in Paris. The paintings were arranged in order of the nationality of the artist. The annexes displayed a variety of machinery. While only 11 years passed since the first World Expo (the Great Exhibition), the largest machine on display increased in weight from 9 tonnes in 1851 to 35 tonnes at Expo 1862.

Participation of Workers

Under the patronage of Napoleon III, the French participation included a workers' delegation, who actively engaged with their British counterparts. This meeting was a significant catalyst for the founding of the International Workingmen's Association, known as the First Internationale, two years later in 1864.

Legacy of the Expo

The Expo 1862 surpassed the previous two Expos in size and reached a new high in terms of visitor attendance. After this Expo, the Natural History Museum was built and inaugurated on the former site of the Expo, becoming one of the world's leading institutions in its field.

主题：**工业与艺术**
举办地：**英国伦敦**
类型：**综合类世博会**
日期：**1862年5月1日至11月1日**
占地（公顷）：**11**
参观者（人次）：**6,096,617**
参展方（个）：**39**

延迟召开的世博会

在首届世博会获得巨大成功的影响下，伦敦原计划在10周年之际即1861年再次举办世博会。当时，英国在钢铁生产、蒸汽机及电报等领域都取得了重大进展。组织方认为举办世博会是一个理想的时机，可以展示英国在工业、技术和艺术等方面取得的卓越成就。然而，由于首届世博会的发起人阿尔伯特亲王的离世以及国际战争的爆发，世博会的召开被推迟了一年。

不断进步的展览

世博会主展厅内设艺术画廊，其长度达350米，与巴黎卢浮宫的大画廊长度相当。画作以艺术家的国籍为序依次排列。画廊对楼则展示各种机械装置，虽然距离第一次世博会只有11年，但展出机械的最大重量，已经从9吨增长到了35吨。

工人团体的参与

在拿破仑三世的资助下，法国的参展队伍中包含了一个工人团体。他们参加世博会，与英国当地的工人开展会议交流。这次工人会议对两年后国际工人协会（即第一国际）的成立具有显著的促发作用。

世博遗产

这届世博会在规模上超过了前两届，观众参观量也达到新高。会后，自然历史博物馆在世博会原址上建造并落成，成为同领域世界领先的机构之一。

从园艺花园遥看1862年伦敦世博会展馆
石版画，1862年，1851年皇家展览委员会馆藏

The Great International Exhibition as Seen from the Horticultural Gardens
1862. RC/E/1/41, from Royal Commission for the Exhibition of 1851. Lithograph.

Agricultural Machinery Exhibited at Expo1862 London
The Illustrated London News. 1862. World Expo Museum Collection. Print.

1862年伦敦世博会上展出的农业机械印刷品,1862年,《伦敦新闻画报》,世博会博物馆馆藏

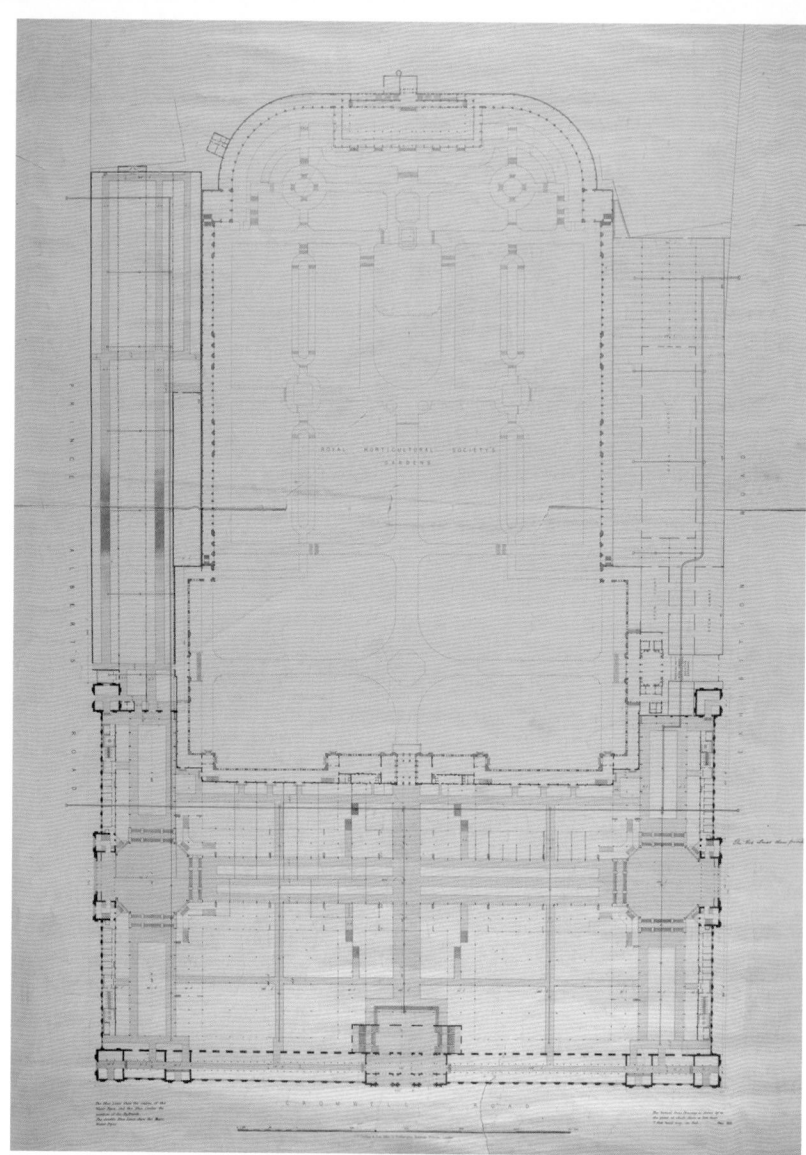

1862年伦敦世博会展馆和园艺花园的平面图图纸,1862年,1851年皇家展览委员会馆藏

034 Royal Horticultural Society Gardens and the Ground Plan of the 1862 Exhibition Building
1862. RC/E/1/40, from Royal Commission for the Exhibition of 1851.Plan.

EXPO 1867 PARIS

巴黎
世博会

Theme: **Agriculture, Industry and Fine Arts**
Location: **Paris, France**
Category: **World Expo**
Dates: **1867.4.1-11.3**
Area (ha): **68.7**
Visitors: **15,000,000**
Participants: **42**

A Symbol of Transformation

The Expo 1867 Paris took place in a context of social transformations, with the Industrial Revolution and the Baron Haussmann's renovation of Paris (the major urban renewal project of 19th-century Paris) in full swing. A new railway station was built on the Champs de Mars before the opening of the Expo; a new park, Buttes Chaumont, was inaugurated on the opening day; and the Paris Opera and the Church of St. Augustin were under construction during the Expo.

The Emergence of "Expo Architecture"

The site chosen for the Expo was the Champs de Mars, where the participants built pavilions in typical styles according to country. The agricultural and horticultural sections were located on now the Île Saint Germain, connected to the main Expo site via steamboats, the first "Bateaux-Mouches" (boats on the Seine) in Paris.

Voices of the Workers

The Expo embodied the progress of the Industrial Revolution and was a pivotal moment in the development of the French workers' movement. The Organizer of the Expo saw it as a summit of industry, training and skills, and an important exercise in education and public awareness. 400,000 workers, teachers and students were invited to participate in this Expo and 67,000 tickets were distributed to workers. Trade unions from different industries were quickly formed. Around 120 workers' reports were released during this Expo, raising questions the status of workers and industrial-era skills and calling for social reforms including for increased press freedoms, the freedom of assembly, and the legalization of trade unions.

主题：农业、工业和艺术
举办地：法国巴黎
类型：综合类世博会
日期：1867 年 4 月 1 日至 11 月 3 日
占地（公顷）：68.7
参观者（人次）：15,000,000
参展方（个）：42

变革下的世博会

1867 年巴黎世博会召开之际时值社会变革期，工业革命如火如荼地进行着，奥斯曼改造（19 世纪巴黎城市改造的重大工程）亦在持续开展中。世博会开幕前，一座新的火车站在战神广场上建成；开幕当天，一个新的公园——肖蒙山丘公园落成开放；世博会期间，巴黎歌剧院和圣奥古斯丁教堂也都在积极建设中。

世界建筑的聚会

这届世博会选址在战神广场，各个参展国依据自身特色建造风格各异的展厅。农业和园艺部分设在现在的圣日耳曼岛上，借由汽船与主会场相连，这种汽船也是巴黎最早的『苍蝇船』（塞纳河上的一种游船）。

来自工人的呼声

世博会体现了工业革命的进步。由于正值法国工人运动发展的关键时期，世博会的组织者将此次世博会视为工业、培训和技能的一次峰会，以及在教育和公众意识方面的一次重要实践。组织方邀请 40 万工人、教师和学生参与世博会，并向 6.7 万名工人发放门票。不同行业的工人委员会迅速成立，大约 120 份工人报告在世博会期间问世，对工人的地位和工业时代的技能提出质疑，呼吁进行社会改革，诉求包括提升新闻自由、集会自由、工会合法化等。

1867 年巴黎世博会鸟瞰图
石版画，1867 年，作者：尤金·西塞尔，美国国会图书馆印刷品和照片分部馆藏

Bird's Eye View of Expo 1867 Paris
Lithograph by Engène Cicéri. 1867. Library of Congress Prints and Photographs Division. Lithograph.

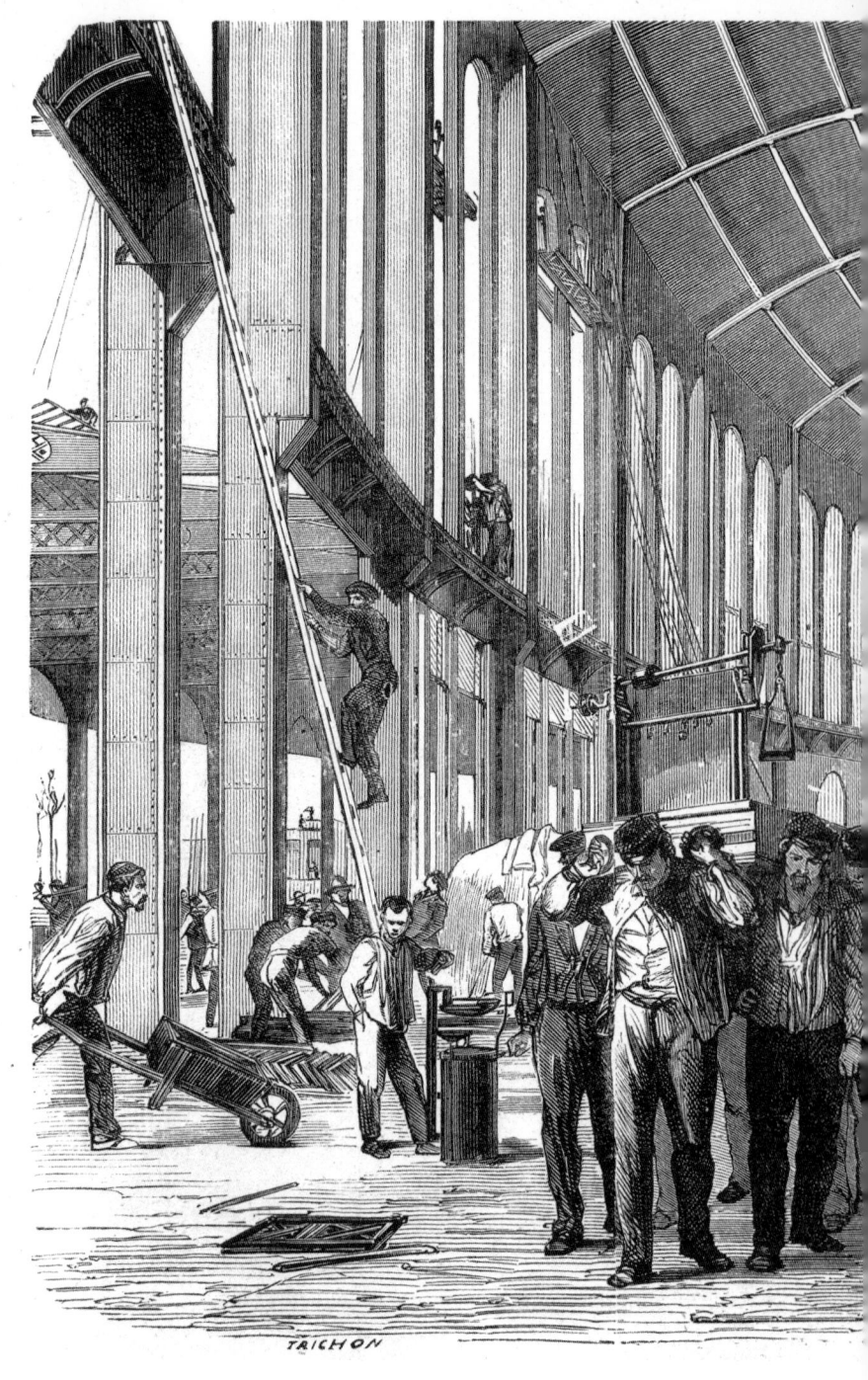

Construction of the Grand Gallery of Machines
Engraved by Trichon. 1868. Brown University Library. Engraving.

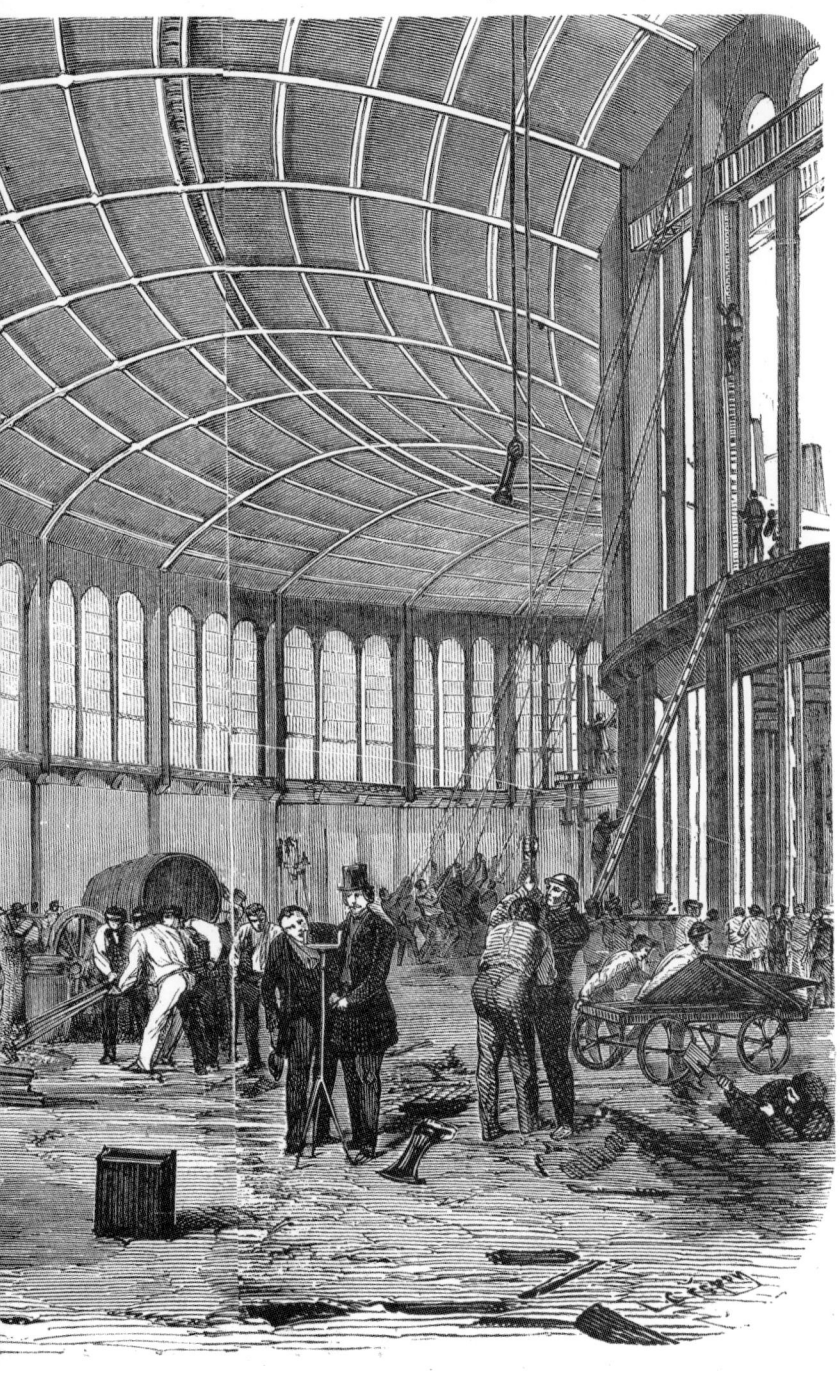

建造中的机械宫版画,1868年,作者:特里雄,美国布朗大学图书馆馆藏

莱昂·埃杜在1867年巴黎世博会上展出他设计的机械升降机,埃杜之后还为埃菲尔铁塔设计了电梯印刷品,约1867年,《1867年世界博览会图录》,世博会博物馆馆藏

Leon Edoux presented an elevator designed by him at Expo 1867 Paris, who later designed the elevator for the Eiffel Tower.
L'exposition Universelle de 1867 Illustrée. c. 1867. World Expo Museum Collection. Print.

EXPO 1873 VIENNA

维也纳世博会

Theme:
Culture and Education
Location:
Vienna, Austria
Category:
World Expo
Dates: **1873.5.1-10.31**
Area (ha): **233**
Visitors: **7,255,000**
Participants: **35**

Success in Turmoil

The Expo 1873 Vienna was supported by all sectors of Austrian society, with industrial and agricultural entrepreneurs seeing it as an opportunity to show the world the fruits of their economic success, and the Austro-Hungarian Empire wanting to use the event to establish a strong image of cosmopolitan nation. Despite the many unforeseen shocks during the preparation and organization of the Expo, such as flooding, a cholera epidemic, and the May 1873 stock exchange crash, the Expo played a significant role in the dredging and diversion of the Danube and the large-scale renovation and construction of the old city center, and succeeded in realizing the urban renewal of Vienna.

The Rotunda

The Prater Park in Vienna, once a royal hunting ground, was chosen for the Expo. The main building of the Expo, the Industrial Palace, is the architectural highlight. With a height of 83 meters and a diameter of about 110 meters, its Rotunda was the largest dome hall building in the world at that time.

Education and Science

As in previous Expos, the mechanical exhibits dominated in all sections. However, according to the press, the most interesting sections were those education-related exhibits. One of the innovative exhibits was the "History of Prices" showed the gradual increase of labor productivity and the dependency between public taste and economic development. This Expo was also the first Expo to hold an international forum of scientists: there were 12 congresses and conferences organized during the event.

主题：**文化与教育**
举办地：**奥地利维也纳**
类型：**综合类世博会**
日期：**1873年5月1日至10月31日**
占地（公顷）：**233**
参观者（人次）：**7,255,000**
参展方（个）：**35**

逆行中的世博会

1873年在维也纳举办的世博会得到了奥地利社会各界的支持，工农业将其视为向世界展现经济成果的机会，奥匈帝国君主也想借此盛会树立其强有力的国际形象。尽管这届世博会在筹办和举办的过程中遭遇了许多意想不到的冲击，例如洪水泛滥、霍乱暴发以及证券市场濒临崩溃，但是世博会的举办对多瑙河的疏浚改造以及旧城区的大规模改造和建设起到了巨大的推进作用，成功地实现了维也纳的城市更新，是城市改建的世界典范。

圆顶大厅

世博会选址在维也纳普拉特公园，这里曾是皇家狩猎场。世博会的主体建筑工业宫是所有建筑中的最大亮点，其圆顶大厅高83米，直径约110米，是当时世界上最大的圆顶类建筑。

教育与科学

与之前几届世博会一样，机械在所有展品中占据绝对的主导地位。但是，媒体认为这届世博会上与教育相关的展示更加吸引人。这届世博会上有一个颇具创意的展示内容——『价格的历史』，它展现了劳动生产率的提高以及公众趣味与经济发展之间的直接联系。这届世博会也是第一个召开科学国际论坛的世博会，会期内举办相关科学会议共计12次。

1873年维也纳世博会鸟瞰图
印刷品,约1876年,《弗兰克·莱斯利的百年纪念博览会历史记录》,世博会博物馆馆藏

Bird's Eye View of Expo 1873 Vienna
Frank Leslie's Historical Register of the Centennial Exposition.
c. 1876. World Expo Museum Collection. Print.

1873年维也纳世博会的主体建筑工业宫是当时世界上最大的圆顶大厅建筑印刷品。1876年,《美国参展1873年维也纳世博会委员会报告》,世博会博物馆馆藏

The main building of Expo 1873 Vienna, the Industrial Palace, had the world's largest Rotunda of that time.
Reports of the Commissioners of the United States to the International Exhibition Held at Vienna, 1873. 1876. World Expo Museum Collection. Print.

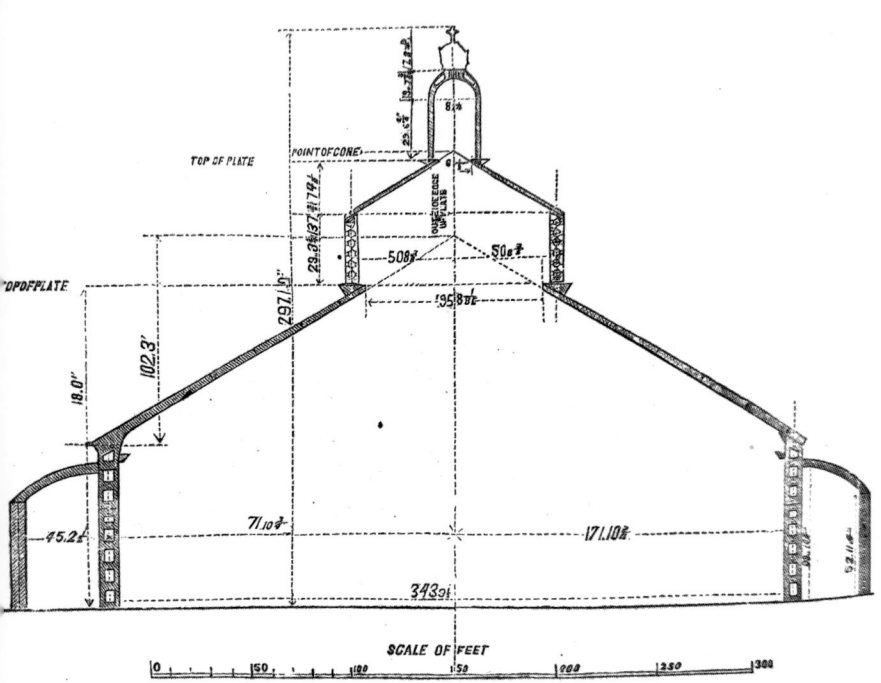

工业宫圆顶大厅的剖面图印刷品,1876年,《美国参展1873年维也纳世博会委员会报告》,世博会博物馆馆藏

Cross-section of the Rotunda of the Vienna Exhibition
Reports of the Commissioners of the United States to the International Exhibition Held at Vienna, 1873. 1876. World Expo Museum Collection. Print.

1873年维也纳世博会上展出的瑞士学校内景
印刷品，1873年，《插画周报》，国际展览局馆藏

052 **Interior of Swedish School at Expo 1873 Vienna**
Le Jounal illustré. 1873. BIE Archive. Print.

EXPO 1876 PHILADELPHIA

费城世博会

Theme: **Arts, Manufactures and Products of the Soil and Mine**
Location: **Philadelphia, United States**
Category: **World Expo**
Dates: **1876.5.10-11.10**
Area (ha): **115**
Visitors: **10,000,000**
Participants: **35**

A Special Creation

Expo 1876 Philadelphia was the first Expo held in the United States. The chief planner, Hermann Josef Schwarzmann, had a significant idea, which has been so important and adopted by the subsequent Expos: instead of concentrating the exhibits in one single building, they were distributed in five exhibition hall according to the theme: the Main Hall, the Fine Arts Pavilion, the Machinery Hall, the Horticultural Palace and the Agricultural Hall. In addition, he added nearly 200 pavilions for the U.S. states, participating countries, and private companies.

Toward the Cutting-edge Technology

Many of the technological innovations widely used in following decades were presented to the public for the first time at this Expo, such as Graham Bell's telephone, Thomas Edison's telegraph, Remington's typewriter, and Heinz tomato ketchup. The USA established itself as one of the leading industrial powers by displaying impressive exhibits and using over one third of the main building, and over 80 per cent of the Engine Hall. The Philadelphia Exposition was also distinguished for its wide use of railway transport.

Legacy of the Expo

The Fine Arts Pavilion is the only building from the Philadelphia Exposition that remains today. After the Expo, it was remodeled to accommodate the Pennsylvania Museum, and it now houses the Please Touch Museum (Philadelphia's children museum).

主题：**艺术、工业产品与土壤矿物产品**
举办地：**美国费城**
类型：**综合类世博会**
日期：**1876年5月10日至11月10日**
占地（公顷）：**115**
参观者（人次）：**10,000,000**
参展方（个）：**35**

一个特殊的创想

1876年费城世博会是美国举办的第一个世博会。总策划赫尔曼·约瑟夫·施瓦茨曼做出了一个特殊的创想，这个创想至关重要，此后举办的所有世博会都采用了他的这一做法，那就是：所有展品不再集中在某个单一的建筑中展示，而是依据主题将展品分布在五个展馆中，即主展馆、艺术宫、机械宫、园艺宫和农业宫。除此之外，他又为美国各州、其他参展国、私营企业加设了将近200个展馆。

面向科技最前沿

未来几十年里广泛运用的许多技术创新都是在费城世博会上第一次面向公众的，比如贝尔发明的电话、爱迪生发明的电报、雷明顿公司生产的打字机、亨氏公司生产的番茄酱等。美国通过这次世博会树立了工业强国的形象。美国的展品在主展馆的展示面积超过了三分之一，在发动机展厅里更是达到80%。另外，园区内供游客乘坐的列车也是费城世博会的一大特色。

世博遗产

艺术宫是费城世博会唯一保留至今的建筑。世博会结束后，它曾被改造成为宾夕法尼亚博物馆，现在它是触摸博物馆（费城儿童博物馆）的所在地。

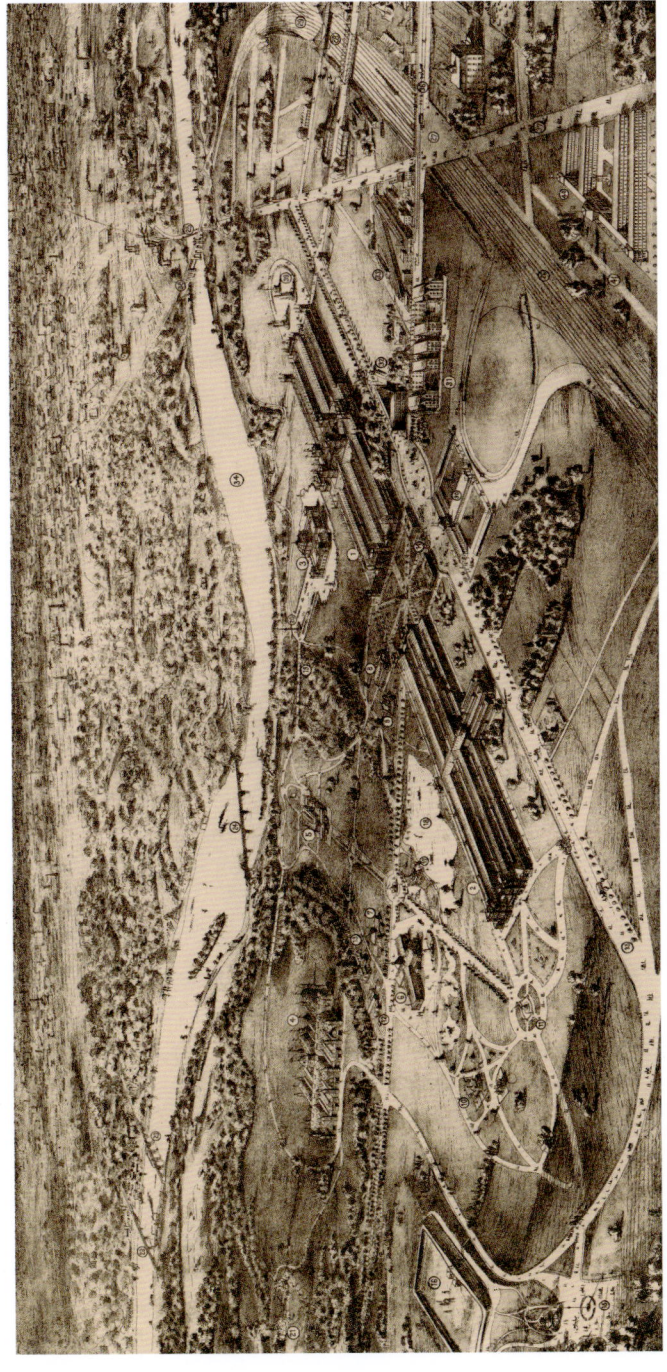

1876年费城世博会鸟瞰图地图，1876年，作者：西尼·斯默克，美国国会图书馆馆藏

Bird's Eye View, Centennial Exhibition Buildings & Grounds
Projected by Sydney Smirke. 1876. Library of Congress. Map.

小鐵筒由簷際倒垂向池闌內為遊廊多設長椅坐觀者再後則各樣吸水機器使水由筒放入池再由池底機關吸回各器水聲洶湧此吸彼放循環不斷西國凡礦內有水以此器吸取今設院內者欲使人盡知其妙用且欲加意講求尤新之法也因思中國江河之水漲落不時旱澇互患西北高原種植每艱灌溉講水利者尤以此為亟務倘得因利乘便仿而行之亦經世一助也另有小樣吸水器救火器甚多無不精巧見輪船一隻長僅五尺大小器具皆備司事者特放氣入船使各機行動與大船一式精巧不可思議美人羅直

New Travelogue Around the World, the first travelogue by a Chinese world traveler, details what Li Gui, an official of the Qing Dynasty, saw and heard at Expo 1876 Philadelphia.
Written by Li Gui. *New Travelogue Around the World.* 1878. World Expo Museum Collection. Print.

中国人环游地球的第一部游记《环游地球新录》详细描绘了清朝官员李圭在1876年费城世博会上的所见所闻印刷品，1878年，作者：李圭，《环游地球新录》，世博会博物馆馆藏

求之力製造之精他國皆不逮焉院正中置大機器一副輪徑三丈餘力抵馬一千五百匹專以輪激受他處蒸氣　院外有屋置水火二器　由鐵管宛轉達於各器所大輪動則院中各器凡需蒸氣者皆藉氣以運動其有不需蒸氣惟藉皮條扯動者各器有大小輪盤纏皮條套梁際鐵軸之輪盤亦可隨時撥動運用如吸水印字紡織鋸磨諸器咸賴焉器名哥阿力司美人哥阿力司手製故以其名名其器每日未初機動如此大器動時無甚聲響且一人即可運之是可異也院西門內有水池長十四丈寬六丈深八尺四面繚以柵闌闌上有大

The scene depicted by American illustrator Frank Leslie in his book was the same water pump that Li Gui documented in writing on the previous page.
Frank Leslie's Historical Register of the Centennial Exposition. c. 1876. World Expo Museum Collection. Print

美国插画师弗兰克·莱斯利在其著作中描画的场景,正是上一页李圭用文字记载的吸水机器印刷品,约1876年,《弗兰克·莱斯利的百年纪念博览会历史记录》,世博会博物馆馆藏

妇女执行委员会主席吉莱斯皮正在听取报告,她领导妇女团体为1876年费城世博会四处筹款,并建立了妇女馆印刷品,约1876年,《弗兰克·莱斯利的百年纪念博览会历史记录》,世博会博物馆馆藏

Elizabeth Gillespie, chair of the Women's Centennial Executive Committee, was listening to the report. She led the women's groups in fundraising for the Expo and created the Women's Pavilion. Frank Leslie's *Historical Register of the Centennial Exposition*. c. 1876. World Expo Museum Collection. Print.

自由女神像曾两次在世博会上展出,第一次是在1876年费城世博会,只展示了手臂与火炬部分照片,1876年,费城自由图书馆印刷品与图片分部馆藏

064 The Statue of Liberty was exhibited twice at the Expo, debuted at Expo 1876 Philadelphia, where only the arms and torch were displayed.
1876. Free Library of Philadelphia Print and Picture Collection. Photograph.

EXPO 1878 PARIS

巴黎世博会

Theme: **New Technologies**
Location: **Paris, France**
Category: **World Expo**
Dates: **1878.5.20-11.10**
Area (ha): **75**
Visitors: **16,156,626**
Participants: **35**

On the Banks of the Seine

The Expo site was spread out on both banks of the Seine, with pavilions on the Champs de Mars, the Esplanade des Invalides and the Chaillot hill. The main building was located on the Champs de Mars, with a central location for arts and exhibits related to the city of Paris. The international pavilions were lined up along the Rue des Nations, with unique styles and strong regional characteristics. On the right bank of the Seine, at the top of Chaillot hill, was the Trocadero Palace, the tallest building in Paris at the time.

The Beginning of the Era of Electricity

At previous Expos, the steam engine was the absolute main attraction. However, from this Expo, electrical products have made their debut, such as the Yablochkoff candle (a type of lamp used for city lighting), Bell's telephone, Hughes' microphone, and Edison's phonograph, signaling the arrival of the era of electricity. The solar generator (a predecessor of solar panels) invented by Mouchot and Pifre was also presented at this Expo, winning a gold medal.

An International Gathering

In addition to showcasing technological innovations, the Expo also provided a venue and opportunity for international forums. Two conferences on artistic and literary property rights overseen by Victor Hugo were held during the Expo, laying the foundations for the Berne Convention for the Protection of Literary and Artistic Works. In addition, an international congress dedicated to those with visual and hearing impairments reached agreement for the first time on a standardized Braille alphabet.

Legacy of the Expo

The great success of the Expo had a profound impact on the western districts of Paris, where some of the pavilions of the international participants remain until this day. The Trocadero Palace was dismantled in 1935 for the construction of the Expo 1937 Paris, and many of its iconic statues remain on display outside the present-day Musée d'Orsay.

主题：新技术
举办地：法国巴黎
类型：综合类世博会
日期：1878年5月20日至11月10日
占地（公顷）：75
参观者（人次）：16,156,626
参展方（个）：35

在塞纳河畔

这届世博会的场地分布在塞纳河两岸，在战神广场、荣军院广场和夏乐山上均设有展馆。主建筑设在战神广场，中心位置展示艺术以及与巴黎城市相关的展览。各参展国家馆沿着国家大街一路排开，风格各异，极具地域特色。特罗卡德罗宫设在塞纳河的右岸、夏乐山的山顶上，是当时巴黎最高的建筑。

开启电气时代

在往届的世博会上，蒸汽机是绝对的主角，然而从这届世博会开始，电气产品纷纷亮相，例如雅布洛奇科夫蜡烛（一种灯具，可用于城市照明）、贝尔发明的电话、休斯发明的麦克风、爱迪生发明的留声机等，意味着电气时代的到来。穆肖和皮弗雷发明的太阳能发动机（太阳能电池板的前身）也在这届世博会上展出，并荣获金奖。

全世界的聚会

除了展现技术创新，世博会也为国际论坛提供了场所和机会。在维克多·雨果的主持下，世博会期间举行了两次关于艺术和文学产权的会议，为《保护文学和艺术作品伯尔尼公约》奠定了基础。另外，一场专门为视听障碍人士举行的国际大会首次就统一盲文字母标准达成协议。

世博遗产

世博会的巨大成功深刻影响了巴黎西部地区，部分参展国国家馆保留至今。为建设1937年巴黎世博会，特罗卡德罗宫在1935年被拆除，其多个标志性雕像被移至如今的奥赛博物馆。

1878年巴黎世博会全景
印刷品，1878年，卡纳瓦莱巴黎历史博物馆馆藏

Panoramic View of Expo 1878 Paris
1878. Musée Carnavalet, Histoire de Paris. Print.

发明家亨利·吉法尔在杜伊勒里宫废墟上升起系留气球，游客可乘坐气球俯瞰巴黎全景印刷品，1878年，《环球画报》，世博会博物馆馆藏

Inventor Henri Giffard raised a tethered balloon over the ruins of the Tuileries Palace, offering visitors a panoramic view of Paris.
L'Univers Illustré. 1878. World Expo Museum Collection. Print.

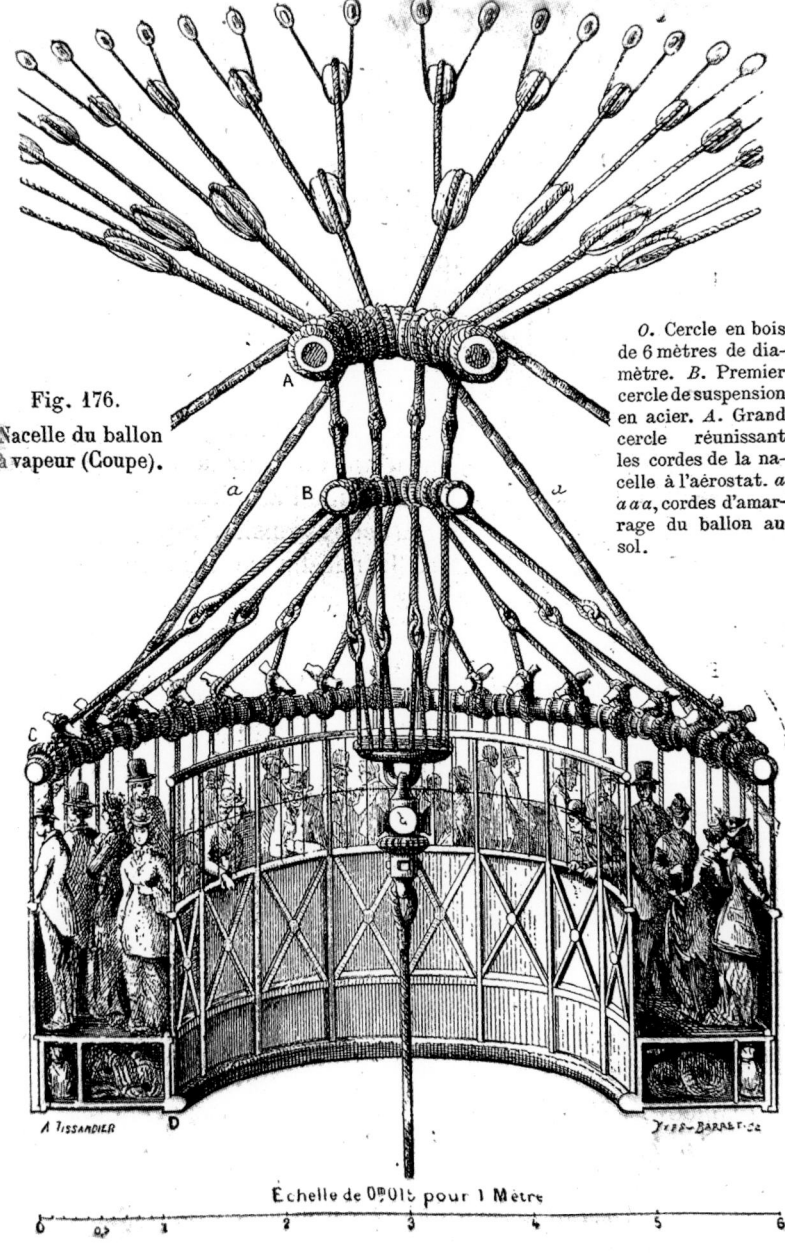

Fig. 176.
Nacelle du ballon à vapeur (Coupe).

O. Cercle en bois de 6 mètres de diamètre. B. Premier cercle de suspension en acier. A. Grand cercle réunissant les cordes de la nacelle à l'aérostat. a a a, cordes d'amarrage du ballon au sol.

Echelle de 0^m015 pour 1 Mètre

During the Expo, many visitors were brought to 500 meters into the air in balloons, an event that ushered in a new era of flying experiences for the general public. *Causeries Scientifiques*. 1879. World Expo Museum Collection. Print.

1878年巴黎世博会期间，众多游客乘坐气球升至500米高空，这一事件开启了公共飞行体验的新时代印刷品，1879年，《科学漫谈》，世博会博物馆馆藏

自由女神像第二次出现在世博会，这一次展示的是女神的头部，游客可进入内部参观印刷品，1878年，《环球画报》，世博会博物馆馆藏

The Statue of Liberty made its second appearance at the Expo, this time displaying the head of the Statue of Liberty, which visitors could access inside.
L'Univers Illustré. 1878. World Expo Museum Collection. Print.

游客在自由女神像内部参观
印刷品,1878年,《世界画报》,世博会博物馆馆藏

Visitors taking a tour inside the Statue of Liberty.
Le Monde Illustré. 1878. World Expo Museum Collection. Print.

法国发明家穆肖预见到未来对可再生能源的需求,在1878年巴黎世博会上展示了他发明的太阳能发动机(太阳能电池板的前身)印刷品,1878年,《环球画报》,世博会博物馆馆藏

In response to the future need for renewable energy, French inventor Augustin Mouchot demonstrated his invention of the solar engine at Expo 1878 Paris.
L'Univers Illustré. 1878. World Expo Museum Collection. Print.

EXPO 1880 MELBOURNE

墨尔本世博会

Theme:
Arts, Manufactures and Agricultural and Industrial Products of all Nations
Location:
Melbourne, Australia
Category:
World Expo
Dates:
1880.10.1-1881.4.30
Area (ha): **25**
Visitors: **1,330,000**
Participants: **33**

Expo legacy as World Heritage

The Melbourne Exhibition Building and the Carlton Gardens were built specifically for this Expo. The Melbourne Exhibition Building was inspired by the Basilica of Santa Maria del Fiore in Florence and incorporates elements of Byzantine, Romanesque, Lombardy and Italian Renaissance styles. After the Expo, the Melbourne Exhibition Building was further extended to host the Melbourne Centennial Exhibition in 1888. The first Federal Parliament of Australia was also held here, and in 2004 the Melbourne Exhibition Building and Carlton Gardens were listed as a UNESCO World Heritage Site.

Boosting Urban Development

This Expo was an opportunity for Melbourne to develop its infrastructure and industry. Electricity, telephones, elevators and tram systems were implemented in the city for the Expo. Australia's international links were also significantly enhanced, with a direct steamboat line introduced between Australia and the European cities of Marseille and Bremen, and direct trade relationships established between Australia, European and American continents.

The Expo attracted 1.3 million visitors at a time when the entire population of Australia was only 2.2 million. In the following decade after the Expo, Melbourne's population doubled to 500,000, and the success of the Expo gave a boost to the rapidly growing city.

主题：**各国艺术、制造、农业和工业产品**
举办地：**澳大利亚墨尔本**
类型：**综合类世博会**
日期：**1880年10月1日至1881年4月30日**
占地（公顷）：**25**
参观者（人次）：**1,330,000**
参展方（个）：**33**

世博遗产也是世界遗产

皇家展览馆和卡尔顿园林都是专为举办这次世博会而建造的。皇家展览馆的设计灵感来自佛罗伦萨圣母百花大教堂，风格上融合了拜占庭式、罗马式、伦巴第式以及意大利文艺复兴时期的多种元素。世博会闭幕后，皇家展览馆进一步扩建，用于举办1888年墨尔本百年纪念展。第一次澳大利亚联邦会议后来也在这里召开。2004年，皇家展览馆和卡尔顿园林被联合国教科文组织列为世界遗产。

城市发展的催化剂

世博会是墨尔本发展基础设施与工业的一次契机。电灯、电话、电梯、有轨电车系统因世博会的举办在城市里被安装和铺设。澳大利亚的国际联系也得到显著提升，法国马赛、德国不来梅这些欧洲城市纷纷与澳大利亚开通船运，澳大利亚与欧美大陆之间建立起直接的贸易关系。

世博会召开期间吸引了130万游客，而当时整个澳大利亚的人口也只有220万。在世博会结束之后的十年里，墨尔本的人口翻了一番，达到50万，世博会的成功举办给这个快速发展的城市注入了一剂催化剂。

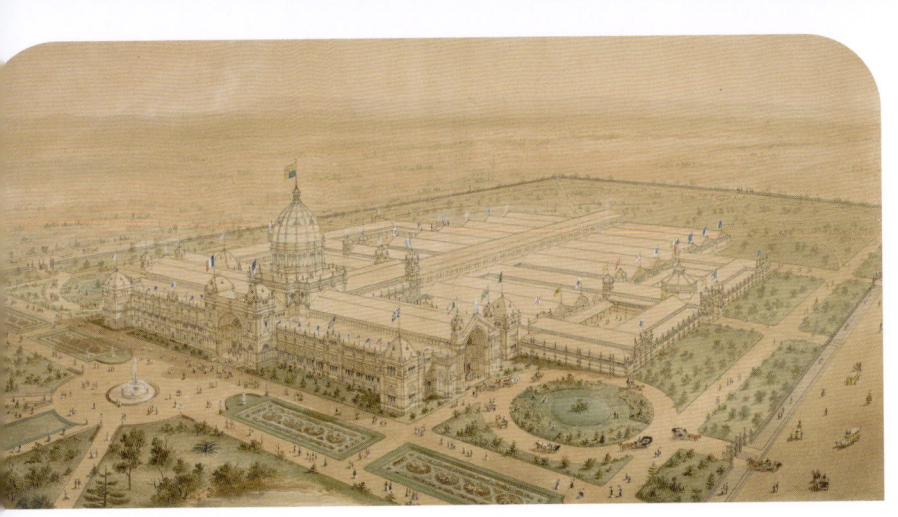

皇家展览馆
水彩画，1880年，作者：约瑟夫·里德，维多利亚博物馆馆藏

The Royal Exhibition Building
Watercolor by Joseph Reed. 1880. Museum Victoria. Watercolor.

The Machinery Court: Victorian Section
Publisher, David Syme and Co. 1880. The State Library of Victoria. Print.

机械馆维多利亚部分
印刷品,1880年,出版:大卫·赛姆公司,维多利亚州立图书馆馆藏

开幕式上的康塔塔声乐表演
印刷品，1880年，维多利亚州立图书馆馆藏

The Cantata at the Opening Ceremony
1880. The State Library of Victoria. Print.

EXPO 1888 BARCELONA

巴塞罗那世博会

Theme:
Fine and Industrial Art
Location:
Barcelona, Spain
Category:
World Expo
Dates: **1888.4.8-12.10**
Area (ha): **46.5**
Visitors: **2,300,000**
Participants: **30**

Transformation of Urbanization

To celebrate the achievement of urbanization and the successful transformation to an industrial, commercial and cultural center, Barcelona hosted this Expo in 1888. The Expo was an opportunity for Spain, and in particular Catalonia in the northeast of Spain, to demonstrate its industrial and technological strength. In order to allow visitors to explore Barcelona at night, two of the city's major streets, La Rambla and Gran Via, were illuminated for the first time with electric lights.

The main building of the Expo was the Palace of Industry, which was 120 meters long and 34 meters wide, with a central hall hosting exhibits from Spain, and the pavilions of the participants and the Spain's regions located in 24 adjoining galleries. The Palace of Fine Arts, the Machine Gallery, the Scientific Palace and the Marine Pavilion are also located in the Expo site.

Legacy of the Expo

The famous architect Montaner, whose buildings were listed as UNESCO World Heritage Sites, designed the neo-Gothic Castell dels Tres Dragons for the Expo. The Castle was used as a café-restaurant during the Expo and is now home of Barcelona's Museum of Zoology. The Columbus Monument was also built for the Expo, commemorating Columbus' return voyage from the Americas to Spain. The Arc de Triomf, the main entrance of the Expo, is still one of Barcelona's landmarks.

主题：**美术与工业艺术**
举办地：**西班牙巴塞罗那**
类型：**综合类世博会**
日期：**1888年4月8日至12月10日**
占地（公顷）：**46.5**
参观者（人次）：**2,300,000**
参展方（个）：**30**

城市化的进程

为庆祝实现城市化，成功向工业、商业和文化中心转型，巴塞罗那于1888年举办了世博会。这届世博会为西班牙，特别是西班牙东北部的加泰罗尼亚地区，提供了一个展示工业科技实力的机会。为了让参观世博会的游客夜间也能游览巴塞罗那，两条城市主干道——兰布拉大街和加泰罗尼亚议会大道首次被安装了电灯照明。

这届世博会的主建筑是工业宫，其长120米、宽34米，中心展区展示来自西班牙的展品，国际参展方以及西班牙各地区的场馆设在相邻的24个长廊中。世博园区内同时还设有艺术宫、机械宫、科学宫、航海宫等场馆。

世博遗产

著名建筑师蒙塔内尔设计的多个建筑被联合国教科文组织列为世界遗产，他为这届世博会设计了新哥特式建筑——三龙城堡。三龙城堡在世博会期间被用作咖啡餐厅，如今是巴塞罗那动物学博物馆的所在地。哥伦布纪念碑也是因这届世博会而建造的，用以纪念哥伦布从美洲返航登陆西班牙。世博会的主入口凯旋门至今仍是巴塞罗那标志性建筑之一。

机械宫施工现场
印刷品,1888年,《博览会》,世博会博物馆馆藏

The Machine Gallery under Construction
Exposicion. 1888. World Expo Museum Collection. Print.

Panoramic view of Barcelona and the squadrons, taken on the occasion of Expo 1888 Barcelona. 1888. Museu Marítm de Barcelona. Engraving.

1888年巴塞罗那世博会期间的城市全景，以及停泊在港口的各参展国军舰版画，1888年，巴塞罗那海事博物馆馆藏

工业宫的中庭
印刷品,1888年,《博览会》,世博会博物馆馆藏

Atrium of the Palace of Industry
La Exposicion. 1888. World Expo Museum Collection. Print.

EXPO 1889 PARIS

巴黎世博会

Theme: **Celebration of the Centenary of the French Revolution**
Location: **Paris, France**
Category: **World Expo**
Dates: **1889.5.6-10.31**
Area (ha): **96**
Visitors: **32,250,297**
Participants: **35**

The Eiffel Tower

Building the tallest building in the world has been a long-standing dream of mankind, and the Organiser of Expo 1876 Philadelphia had planned to build a 1,000-foot-tall (about 300 m) tower, but the project never came to fruition. In 1886, the French government launched a competition to study the feasibility of building a 300-meter-tall tower. The design of the Eiffel Tower was selected from 107 competing proposals. It then took about 150 to 300 workers two years, two months and five days to assemble the 18,000 components of the tower. The Eiffel Tower was completed two months before the opening of the Expo and received more than two million visitors during the six months of the Expo period.

Modernity as the Center of Progress

At the time of the Second Industrial Revolution, the Expo reflected not only the technical progress, but of the social impact of progress and modernity. For example, in architecture, the Eiffel Tower and the Gallery of Machines were built with steam-powered equipment such as hydraulic cranes and steam cranes; in electricity, Aristide Bergès proposed the concept of hydroelectricity, and Thomas Edison demonstrated his invention of the incandescent lamp and the gramophone; in transportation, Armand Peugeot, the founder of the Peugeot, and the expert in steam power, Léon Serpollet, demonstrated the first steam-powered tricycle; automobile industry pioneers Gottlieb Daimler and Wilhelm Maybach demonstrated steel-wheeled automobiles powered by petrol engine; in the textile industry, Herminie Cadolle demonstrated her design of a corselet-gorge model for woman, a precursor to the modern bra; and, with the increase in awareness of hygiene, the Expo featured several pavilions dedicated to healthcare and hygiene.

- 主题：**庆祝法国大革命 100 周年**
- 举办地：**法国巴黎**
- 类型：**综合类世博会**
- 日期：**1889 年 5 月 6 日至 10 月 31 日**
- 占地（公顷）：**96**
- 参观者（人次）：**32,250,297**
- 参展方（个）：**35**

埃菲尔铁塔

建造世界上最高的建筑是人类由来已久的梦想。1876 年费城世博会的组织者曾计划建造一座高 1,000 英尺（约 300 米）的高塔，但未能实现。1886 年，法国政府发起一项竞赛，研究建造 300 米高塔的可行性。埃菲尔铁塔的设计方案从 107 份竞选方案中脱颖而出。之后，大约 150 至 300 名工人用两年两个月零五天，完成了 1.8 万个铁塔部件的组装。埃菲尔铁塔在世博会开幕前两个月完工，半年会期内共接待游客超过 200 万。

现代性是进步的核心

时值第二次工业革命时期，这届世博会充分体现了当时最先进的技术以及现代化进程对社会层面的影响。例如，在建筑方面，埃菲尔铁塔和机械宫在建造时运用了液压起重机和蒸汽汽吊车等蒸汽动力装备；在电力方面，阿里斯蒂德·贝格斯提出了水力发电的概念，爱迪生展示了他发明的白炽灯和留声机；在交通方面，标致创始人阿尔芒·标致和蒸汽汽动力专家莱昂·戈特利布·戴姆勒和威廉·迈巴赫展示了由汽油发动机驱动的钢轮汽车，汽车工业先驱埃尔米妮·卡多勒展示了她设计的紧身胸衣，即现代胸罩的前身；随着卫生意识的增强，世博会上还专门设立了多个场馆以展示医疗与卫生。

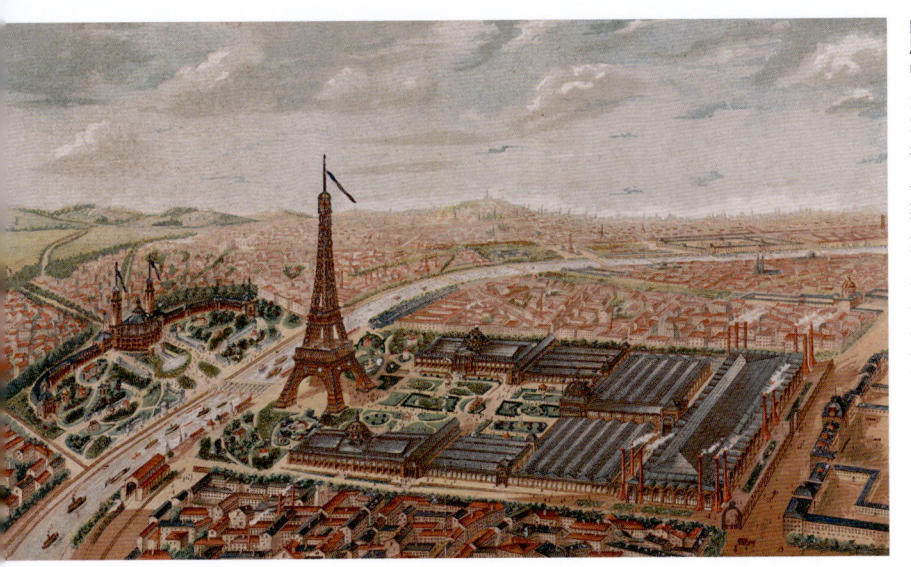

1889年巴黎世博会全景
印刷品，1889年，卡纳瓦莱巴黎历史博物馆馆藏

Panoramic View of Expo 1889 Paris
1889. Musée Carnavalet, Histoire de Paris. Print.

The Start of the Erection of the Metal Work of the Eiffel Tower
1888–1889. Bibliothèque nationale de France. Photo Print.

埃菲尔铁塔的钢架结构搭建过程照片，1888—1889年，法国国家图书馆馆藏

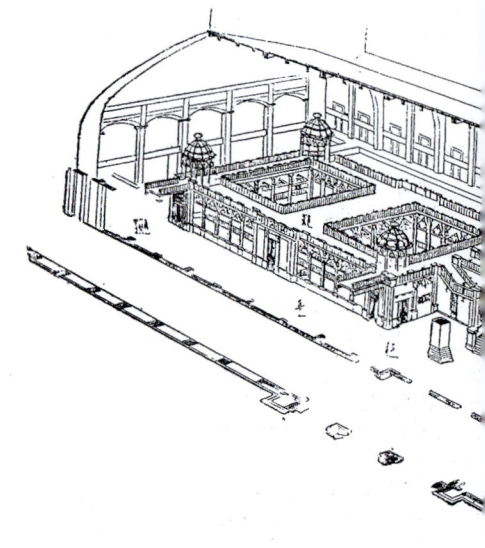

机械宫内景
染色照片，1889年，美国国会图书馆印刷品与照片分部馆藏

Interior View of the Gallery of Machines
1889. Library of Congress Prints and Photographs Division. Photochrom Print.

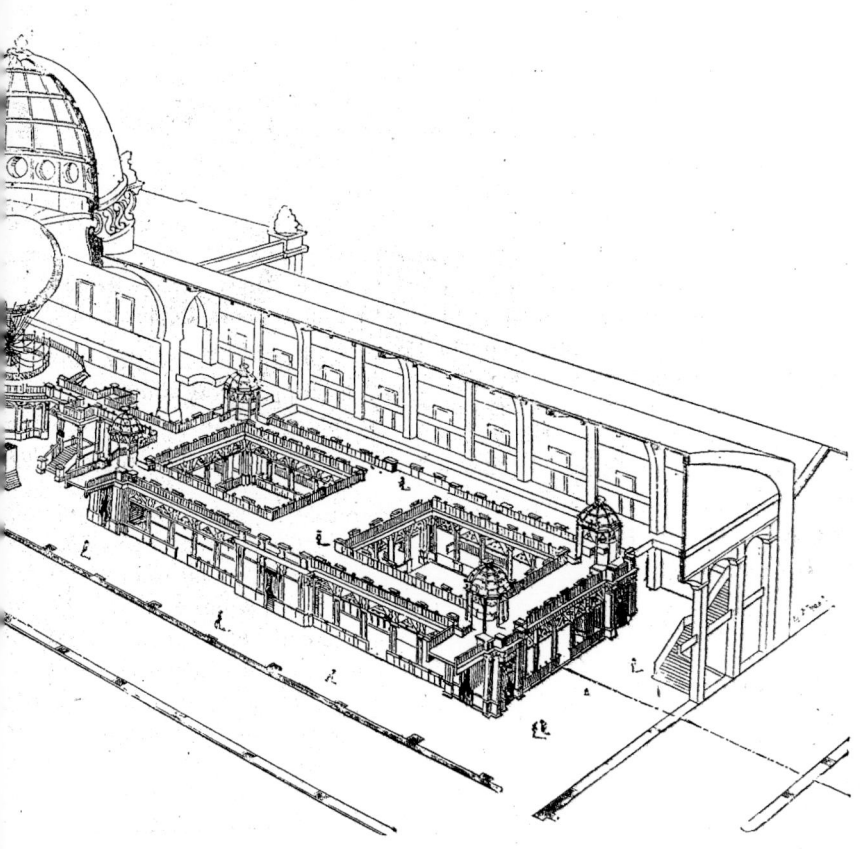

人文宫的建筑剖视图位于穹顶下方的展区介绍了气球、飞艇等航空器的发展历史,中心展品是一只热气球印刷品,1889年,《1889年世博会:足不出户的观展体验》,世博会博物馆馆藏

Cross section of the Palais des Arts Libéraux. The hot air balloon under the dome was part of the exhibit on the "Histoire de l'aérostation".
L'Exposition Chez Soi 1889. 1889. World Expo Museum Collection. Print.

在1889年巴黎世博会上,人们争相排队试听爱迪生发明的留声机印刷品,1889年,《1889年世博会:足不出户的观展体验》,世博会博物馆馆藏

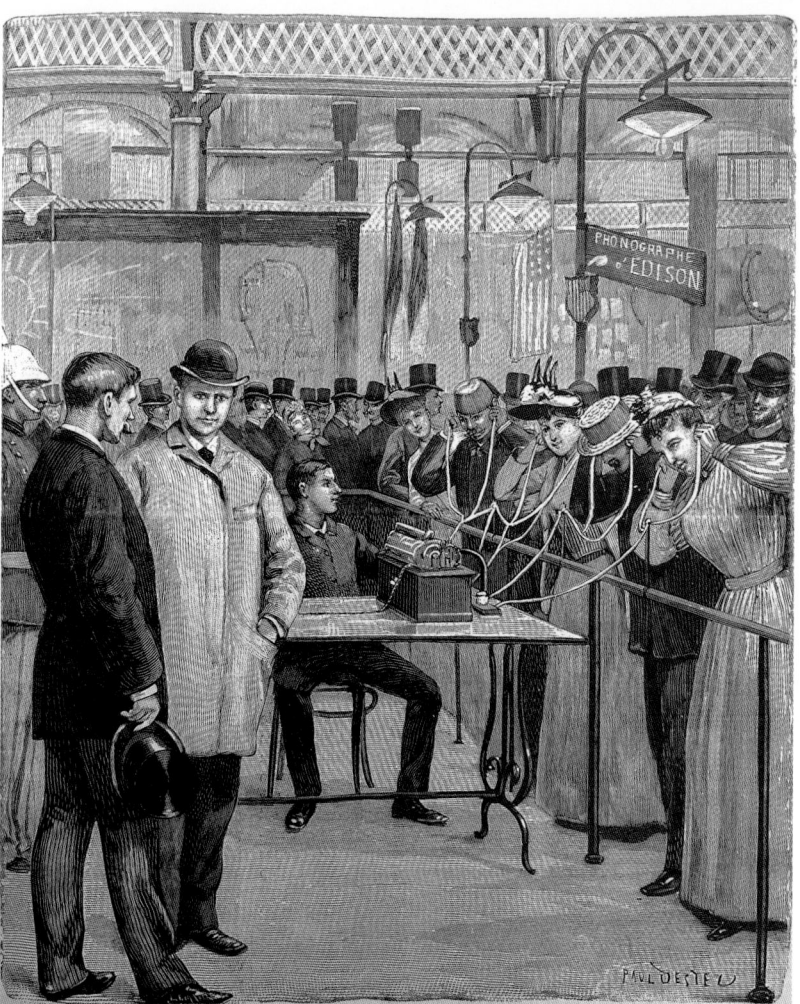

People line up to try out Edison's phonograph at Expo 1889 Paris.
L'Exposition Chez Soi 1889. 1889. World Expo Museum Collection. Print.

EXPO 1893 CHICAGO

芝加哥世博会

Theme: **Fourth Centenary of the Discovery of America**
Location: **Chicago, United States**
Category: **World Expo**
Dates: **1893.5.1-10.3**
Area (ha): **290**
Visitors: **27,500,000**
Participants: **19**

The White City

Frederick Law Olmsted, one of America's foremost landscape architects and the designer of New York's Central Park, chose the site of this expo on the shores of Lake Michigan. Olmsted was ambitious with his project, not only draining the lake to turn it into land, but also creating canals and lagoons all along the site. As a result, the Expo covered a far larger area than any previous Expos and the landscape was wonderful. The 14 main pavilions were designed and constructed in the Classical architectural style. As white stucco glowed with nighttime illumination, the Expo was also nicknamed as the "White City".

Women's Pavilion

From a cultural and technological point of view, the Expo 1893 was an event of a number of "firsts": it featured Edison's Kinetoscope, the first elevated intramural railway, the first movable sidewalk, the first set of scenic postcards, and the first set of commemorative stamps and coins. One of the most important innovations was the creation of Women's Pavilion. The Women's Pavilion was designed and operated entirely by women, and featured women's achievements in a variety of fields.

First Ferris Wheel

The biggest attraction of this Expo was the Midway Plaisance, a mile-long strip land dedicated to an amusement park. Major amusement parks such as Coney Island and even Disneyland were largely influenced by it. The park's most popular attraction was the George Ferris' "Big Wheel", the world's first Ferris wheel. To catch up with the height of the Eiffel Tower at the Expo 1889 in Paris, the George Ferris' "Big Wheel" reached a height of 76 meters in diameter and became the symbol of Expo 1893 Chicago.

主题：发现美洲 400 周年
举办地：美国芝加哥
类型：综合类世博会
日期：1893 年 5 月 1 日至 10 月 3 日
占地（公顷）：290
参观者（人次）：27,500,000
参展方（个）：19

白色之城

美国最重要的景观设计师之一、纽约中央公园的设计者奥姆斯特德将这届世博会选址在密歇根湖岸。奥姆斯特德对这个项目是有野心的，他不仅抽干湖水将其变成陆地，还引导湖水围绕世博园区形成河道和湖泊。因而这届世博会的占地面积远超之前任何一届，并且风景极其优美。14 个主要场馆遵循古典主义建筑风格进行设计与建造，其外立面均施以白色，在夜间照明的渲染下熠熠生辉，因此得名『白色之城』。

妇女馆

从文化和技术的角度来说，1893 年的世博会创造了诸多『第一』：它展示了爱迪生的活动电影放映机、第一条高架铁路、第一条自动人行道、第一套风景明信片、第一套纪念邮票和纪念币。不过，这届世博会在展示方面最重要的创新之一是妇女馆。妇女馆完全由女性设计和运营，馆内展现了女性在各个领域的成就。

第一座摩天轮

这届世博会最大的亮点是大道乐园，它长达 1 英里（1,609 米），是一个专属的娱乐场地。后来的美国大型游乐场所康尼岛甚至迪士尼乐园都深受其影响。乐园最受欢迎的项目是菲利斯摩天轮，它是世界上第一座摩天轮。为了追赶 1889 年巴黎世博会上埃菲尔铁塔的高度，菲利斯摩天轮的直径高度达到了 76 米，成为 1893 年芝加哥世博会的象征。

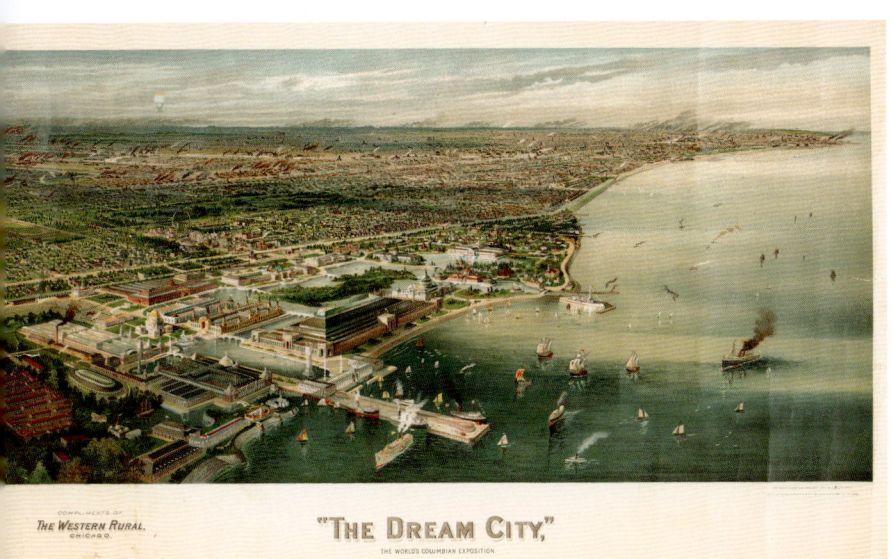

1893年芝加哥世博会鸟瞰图
印刷品，1893年，出版：美国艺术公司，耶鲁大学贝内克古籍善本图书馆馆藏

he DREAM City, a Bird's-eye View of Expo 1893 Chicago
ublished by American Fine Arts. 1893. Beinecke Rare Book and Manuscript Library,
ale University. Print.

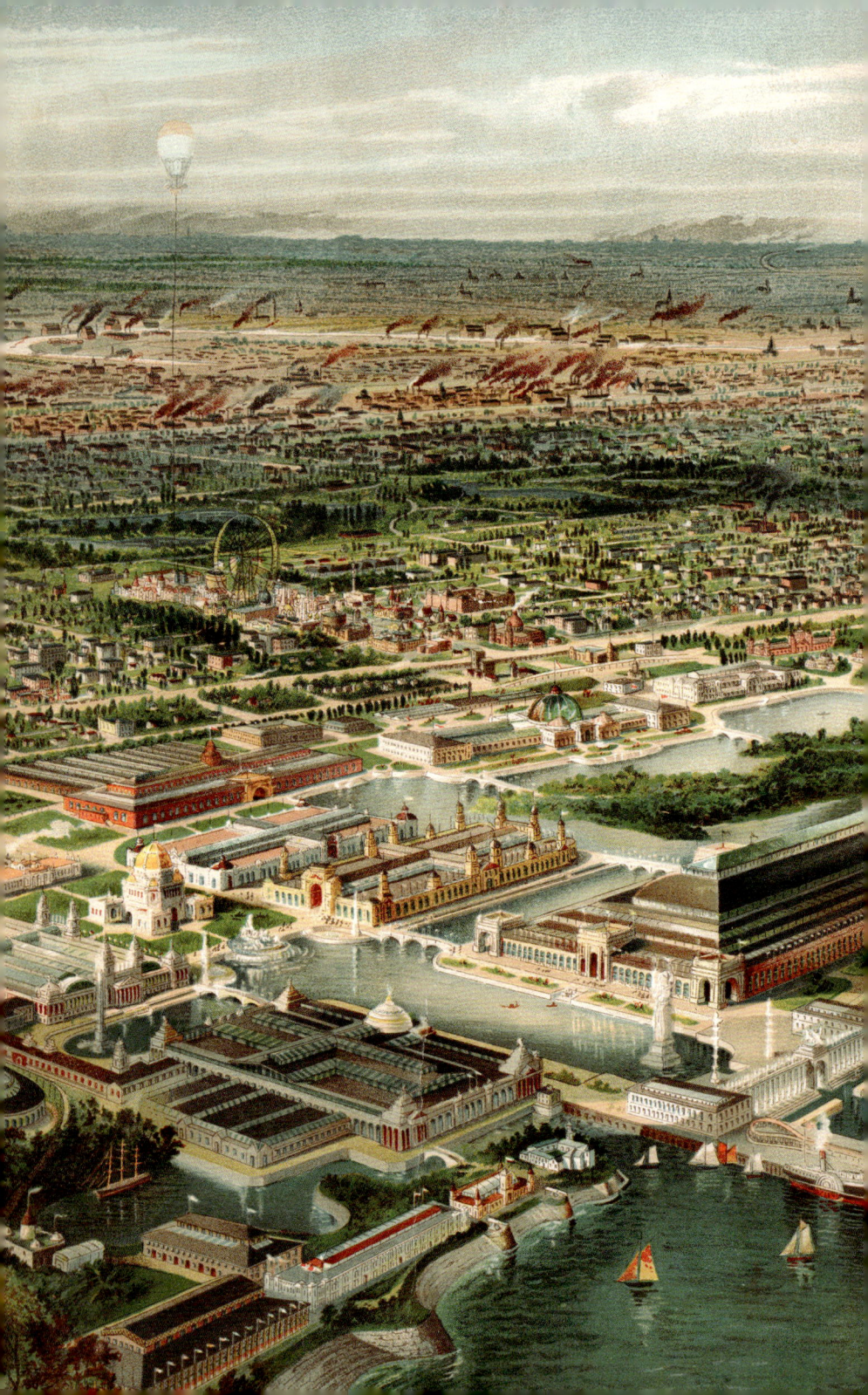

George Ferris' "Big Wheel", the world's first Ferris wheel, was a landmark at Expo 1893 Chicago.
Shepp's World's Fair Photographed. 1893. World Expo Museum Collection. Print.

世界上第一座摩天轮——菲利斯摩天轮是1893年芝加哥世博会的地标性建筑印刷品,1893年,《谢普的世博会摄影集》,世博会博物馆馆藏

受1889年巴黎世博会启发,1893年芝加哥世博会也提供了乘坐系留气球的服务,气球一次可承载16人

印刷品,1893年,《谢普的世博会摄影集》,世博会博物馆馆藏

Inspired by Expo 1889 Paris, Expo 1893 Chicago also offered tethered balloon rides, which could carry 16 people at a time.
Shepp's World's Fair Photographed. 1893. World Expo Museum Collection. Print.

EXPO 1897 BRUSSELS

布鲁塞尔世博会

Theme: **Modern Life**
Location: **Brussels, Belgium**
Category: **World Expo**
Dates: **1897.5.10-11.8**
Area (ha): **36**
Visitors: **6,000,000**
Participants: **27**

Art Nouveau

This Expo demonstrated Belgium's modernity and was a milestone in the development of the Art Nouveau movement, featuring many modernist works by Belgian architects, furniture designers, and artists. For example, the 'Temple of Human Passions' was a work built especially for the Expo. It was designed by the young Belgian architect Victor Horta, who later grew to become a pioneer of the Art Nouveau movement. The 'Temple of Human Passions' is the only building from this Expo that remains today.

Influence beyond Borders

On the threshold of the 20th century, the Expo 1897 Brussels spread its aesthetic concepts around the world through a new artistic expression. The Austrian architect Otto Wagner, a pioneer of the Viennese Secession, was influenced by the early Art Nouveau movement, and in particular by the geometric style of the Belgian architects Paul Hankar, when he visited the Expo. In other words, the artistic exchange platform provided by the Expo also played a role in promoting the development of the aesthetics of the 'Viennese Secession'.

Continuous Technological Innovation

In anticipation of the Expo, the rail and road infrastructure were greatly expanded to accommodate the transportation of more than six million visitors. The technological innovations section was very popular among the visitors. The Machine Gallery featured state-of-the-art apparatus and equipment, such as power converters, ventilation systems, and an "Electric Sun" consisting of 4,500 light bulbs.

主题：**现代生活**

举办地：**比利时布鲁塞尔**

类型：**综合类世博会**

日期：**1897年5月10日至11月8日**

占地（公顷）：**36**

参观者（人次）：**6,000,000**

参展方（个）：**27**

新艺术运动

这届世博会展现出比利时的现代性，其举办也成为新艺术运动发展过程中的里程碑事件。世博会展出了许多比利时建筑师、家具设计师、艺术家的现代主义作品。例如，人类激情之庙，就是为世博会专门建造的作品。它的设计者是年轻的比利时建筑师维克多·霍塔，霍塔后来成长为新艺术运动的先锋。人类激情之庙是这届世博会唯一保留至今的建筑。

影响超越国界

在20世纪即将到来之际，1897年布鲁塞尔世博会通过一种新的艺术表达，将其美学概念传播至世界各地。奥地利建筑师，维也纳分离派先驱人物奥托·瓦格纳在参观这届世博会时，就受到了早期新艺术运动，特别是比利时建筑师保罗·汉卡尔的几何风格的影响。因而可以说，世博会提供的艺术交流平台对推动维也纳分离派美学的发展也起到了一定的作用。

技术持续创新

为了迎接世博会，铁路和公路基础建设得到了极大扩展，承载了600多万游客的交通运输。技术创新展区依然很受游客欢迎。机械展区展示了当时最先进的器械设备，例如电力转换器、通风系统，以及一个由4,500个灯泡组成的『电力驱动的太阳』。

EXPO 1900 PARIS

巴黎世博会

Theme:
19th Century: an Overview
Location:
Paris, France
Category:
World Expo
Dates: **1900.4.15-11.12**
Area (ha): **120**
Visitors: **50,860,801**
Participants: **40**

The Best of Paris

The Expo 1900 was the largest and most successful Expo ever held in Paris, attracting nearly 51 million visitors at that time when the entire population of France was just 41 million. The success of the Expo 1900 Paris was largely due to the rapid economic growth, optimistic expectations for the future, and emerging various forms of entertainment, reflecting the technological advances during this period, as well as the Art Nouveau movement, photography, cinema, and other artistic developments.

City Transformation

With the building of several infrastructures and cultural landmarks, Paris revitalized its city appearance. Thanks to the Expo, the Palais de l'Industrie, which had been built for the Expo 1855 Paris, was demolished and replaced by two striking new buildings: the Petit Palais and the Grand Palais. Not far away, the Pont Alexandre III bridge was built, connecting the right bank of the Seine with the Esplanade des Invalides. The Palais du Trocadéro, which had been built for the Expo 1878, was remodeled to a 4,000-seat concert hall for performances. Three new train stations were built to welcome tourists and the first metro line was opened.

A Road to the Future

To make it easier for visitors to access various pavilions at the Expo, the Organiser of the Expo built a moving walkway, called the "Rue de l'Avenir". American engineers Joseph Lyman Schmidt and Max E. Silsbee had designed and built the first ever moving walkway at the Expo 1893 Chicago. This 3.5-kilometer-long walkway in Paris had an instantaneous capacity of 14,000 people.

The Palace of Electricity was particularly impressive, providing all electrical power for the entire site. The Expo also featured a large celestial globe, a telescope, the first Cinéorama, and a variety of other innovative technologies and inventions.

主题：19世纪的总结
举办地：法国巴黎
类型：综合类世博会
日期：1900年4月15日至11月12日
占地（公顷）：120
参观者（人次）：50,860,801
参展方（个）：40

巴黎之最

1900年巴黎世博会是巴黎有史以来规模最大、最成功的世博会，吸引了将近5,100万游客，而当时整个法国的人口也不过4,100万。社会经济增长迅猛，人们对未来抱有乐观的预期，新兴娱乐方式更是层出不穷，世博会正是反映了这一时期人类在科技方面取得的进步，以及新艺术运动、摄影、电影等艺术方面的发展。

城市改造

世博会为巴黎带来了新的城市面貌，多项城市基础设施和文化地标因世博会而兴起。1855年巴黎世博会建造的工业宫被拆除，取而代之的是两座引人注目的新建筑：小皇宫和大皇宫。不远处，亚历山大三世桥建成，连接了塞纳河右岸和荣军院广场。1878年巴黎世博会建造的特罗卡德罗宫被改建，增设了一个可容纳4,000人的音乐厅，用来举办文化表演。巴黎为迎接游客新建了三个火车站，还开通了第一条地铁线路。

未来之路

为方便游客往返世博会各个场馆，世博会组织者还铺设了一条自动人行道，称其为「未来之路」。「未来之路」的设计者美国工程师施密特和希尔斯比曾在1893年芝加哥世博会上设计建造了第一条自动人行道。巴黎的这条自动人行道全长3,500米，瞬时承载量为1.4万人。
世博会上还展出了大型天体地球仪、望远镜、第一个环幕影院等各种创新科技与发明。电力宫尤为光彩夺目，它为整个世博会提供电力支持。

1900年巴黎世博会全景图
印刷品，1900年，作者：吕西安·贝拉克，美国国会图书馆印刷品与照片分部馆藏

Panoramic View of Expo 1900 Paris
Created by Lucien Baylac. 1900. Library of Congress Prints and Photographs Division. Print.

电力宫为 1900 年巴黎世博会所有场地供电,因此,整个园区灯火通明,并设有多个喷泉和水景项目印刷品,1900 年,卡纳瓦莱巴黎历史博物馆馆藏

he Palace of Electricity provided all the electrical power for the Expo site, which was entirely lit up
nd featured numerous fountains and water features.
900. Musée Carnavalet, Histoire de Paris. Print.

自动人行道『未来之路』方便游客往返 1900 年巴黎世博会的各个场馆,全长 3,500 米,瞬时承载量为 1.4 万人照片,1900 年,美国布朗大学图书馆馆藏

128 Organisers also installed a moving walkway dubbed 'Rue de l'Avenir'. The walkway spanne 3.5km and could transport up to 14,000 people at any given moment.
1900. Brown University Library. Photograph.

发明家桑松展示了他发明的环幕电影系统,他用十台放映机同步放映,为观众模拟了一次热气球之旅。版画,约1900年,作者:路易·波耶,《科学美国人》增刊

Raoul Grimoin-Sanson demonstrated his invention of the Cinéorama. He simulated a hot air balloon ride for the audience using 10 projectors in synchronisation. Created by Louis Poyet. *Scientific American Supplement.* c. 1900. Engravings.

1900年巴黎世博会光学宫内展出的大型天文望远镜照片，1902—1903年，《1900年巴黎世博会》第3卷，法国国家图书馆馆藏

130　Great Telescope in the Palace of Optics at Expo 1900 Paris
L'Exposition de Paris (1900), tome 3, 1902-1903. Bibliothèque nationale de France. Photo Print.

EXPO 1904 ST. LOUIS

圣路易斯
世博会

Theme:
Celebration of the Centennial of the Louisiana Purchase
Location:
St. Louis, United States
Category:
World Expo
Dates: **1904.4.30-12.1**
Area (ha): **500**
Visitors: **19,694,855**
Participants: **60**

The Large Expo site

Spanning over 500 hectares, this Expo was one of the three largest Expos to date (the other two being the Expo 1939 New York and the Expo 2010 Shanghai). A complete tour of the Expo site of St. Louis would take a week to see all. 1,500 buildings were built around the site and 75 kilometers of walkways and railways were laid. To increase visit, St. Louis also adjusted the price of train tickets and improved hotel and accommodation facilities so that it had the largest capacity in the United States during the Expo period.

Edible Sculptures

The Palace of Agriculture, the largest building at this Expo, hosted many statues or monuments made of edible products, such as a Louisiana statue made of sugar, a statue of President Roosevelt made of butter, and a nearly six-meter-tall lighthouse made of salt. The agricultural resources of each state were displayed on a 2-hectare map that shows at a glance how crops grow in each state.

Three Scientific Achievements

Automobiles, wireless technology and aeronautics were the three main scientific achievements showcased at Expo 1904 St. Louis. The most popular exhibit was the De Forest Wireless Telegraph Tower named after the father of radio and an American inventor, where visitors clamored to line up to send telegrams to friends and relatives as far away as Chicago. The Expo also featured a five-hectare aeronautic field, featuring the most advanced aeronautical equipment, including balloons, airplanes, gliders and airships.

Legacy of the Expo

The only building from this Expo that has preserved to this day is the Palace of Visual Arts, currently serves as the Museum of Arts of St. Louis, one of the largest art museums in the United States.

主题：纪念路易斯安那购地100周年
举办地：美国圣路易斯
类型：综合类世博会
日期：1904年4月30日至12月1日
占地（公顷）：500
参观者（人次）：19,694,855
参展方（个）：60

超大的世博会园区

这届世博会占地500公顷，是迄今为止园区面积最大的三届世博会之一（另外两届是1939年纽约世博会和2010年上海世博会）。完整游览世博园区需要一周的时间。园区周围建起1,500座建筑，铺设了75千米的人行道和铁路。为增加参观量，圣路易斯还调整了火车票的价格，改善了酒店和住宿设施，使其在世博会举办期间拥有全美国最大的接待能力。

可食用的雕塑

农业宫是这届世博会上最大的建筑，展示了许多用食物制作的雕像或纪念碑，例如用糖制作的路易斯安那州纪念碑、用黄油制作的罗斯福总统雕像，以及一个近6米高的用盐制作的灯塔。美国各个州的农业资源都展示在一张2公顷大的地图上，各州农作物生长状况一目了然。

三大科学成果

汽车、无线电技术和航空技术是这届世博会最主要的三个科学成果展示。最受欢迎的项目是无线电之父、美国发明家李·德·福雷斯特发明的无线电报塔，游客们争相排队向远在芝加哥的亲友发送电报。世博会上还有一个5公顷的航空展览场地，气球、飞机、滑翔机和飞艇等当时最先进的航空设备在此展开竞赛。

世博遗产

这届世博会唯一保存至今的建筑是视觉艺术宫，目前它是美国最大的艺术博物馆之一圣路易斯艺术博物馆的所在地。

模范城市设计示意图
1904年圣路易斯世博会的模范城市展区向游客展示了理想化的城市设施和机构
印刷品，1903年，《世界博览会通信》，世博会博物馆馆藏

Proposed diagram of Model City. The Model City, designed for the Expo 1904 St. Louis, showed visitors an idealised design of urban facilities and institutions.
World's Fair Bulletin. 1903. World Expo Museum Collection. Print.

无线电之父李·德·福雷斯特在园区里安装了无线电报塔，游客排队向芝加哥发送电报印刷品，1904年，作者：威廉·李，《纪念购置路易斯安那博览会及著名的派克乐园掠影》，世博会博物馆馆藏

The De Forest Wireless Telegraph Tower, where visitors queued up to send wireless telegraph messages to Chicago.
Created by William H. Lee. *Glimpses of the Louisiana Purchase Exposition and the Famous Pike in Colors*. 1904. World Expo Museum Collection. Print.

德国建筑展区：柏林阿尔诺·科尔尼格设计的儿童卧室印刷品，1904年，《大都会》，世博会博物馆馆藏

German Architectural Exhibit: a Child's Bedroom Designed by Arno Kornig, of Berlin
The Cosmopolitan. 1904. World Expo Museum Collection. Print.

模范游乐场位于模范街区,展现了一个理想化的游乐场,来自不同国家的孩子们聚集在这里印刷品,1904年,《世界的工作》,世博会博物馆馆藏

Children from different countries gathering at the Model Playground. Located in the Model City, it was an idealised playground.
The World's Work. 1904. World Expo Museum Collection. Print.

EXPO 1905 LIEGE

列日
世博会

Theme:
Commemoration of the 75th Anniversary of Independence
Location:
Liege, Belgium
Category:
World Expo
Dates: **1905.4.27-11.6**
Area (ha): **70**
Visitors: **7,000,000**
Participants: **35**

Massive Construction

Since the site of the Expo 1905 Liège was the flood-prone area, a significant amount of infrastructure work, including building new bridges and paving roads, needed to be done. Inspired by Pont Alexandre III Bridge at the Expo 1900 Paris, the Organiser constructed Fragnée bridge over the River Meuse. The Expo also transformed around 100 the Walloon style houses, as well as the Saint Lambert Church, which became part of the "Vieux Liège" exhibition, which was a big hit with visitors when it opened.

Continuous Technological Progress

This Expo showcased the excellent achievements of scientists, doctors and engineers. 17,004 exhibitors took part in the Expo, with a particularly large number of French exhibitors. The Paris police demonstrated a fingerprint identifying magnifier at the Expo. French inventor and film pioneer Léon Gaumont demonstrated his invention of Chronophone projector, one of the world's first sound and picture synchronization devices.

Let's Go to Liège

The Expo Organiser made great efforts to attract international exhibitors and visitors. Brochures for the Expo were distributed to hotels and trains all over the world. While the Expo was still under preparation, the Organiser invited journalists to visit the site and report on it. After the opening of the Expo, many foreign dignitaries were invited to visit the Expo, even from far away as Russia, Persia and Japan.

主题：**纪念独立 75 周年**
举办地：**比利时列日**
类型：**综合类世博会**
日期：**1905 年 4 月 27 日至 11 月 6 日**
占地（公顷）：**70**
参观者（人次）：**7,000,000**
参展方（个）：**35**

大兴土木

1905 年列日世博会选址在一个常受洪水侵袭的地区，这意味着会前需要完成大量基础建设工程，比如新建桥梁、铺设道路。受 1900 年巴黎世博会上亚历山大三世桥的启发，列日世博会的组织者在默兹河上新建了弗朗涅桥。世博会还改造了大约 100 座具有瓦隆地区风格特色的建筑以及圣拉姆伯特教堂，这些老建筑成为『老列日』展区的一部分，一经开放便广受游客欢迎。

持续进步的技术

这届世博会展现了科学家、医生和工程师的卓越成就。17,004 家参展商参加了这次世博会，其中法国参展商的数量尤为众多。巴黎警方在世博会上展示了指纹识别放大器。法国发明家、电影先驱莱昂·高蒙展示了他发明的同步声放映机，这是世界上最早的声画同步设备之一。

走，去列日

世博会的组织方为吸引国外参展商和游客做出了极大努力。世博会的宣传手册被分发到世界各地的酒店和火车上。在世博会筹备建设时，组织方就邀请记者到现场参观和报道。世博会开幕后，组织方又邀请众多外国政要参观世博会，甚至包括远在俄罗斯、波斯和日本的政要。

机械展区印刷品,1905年,《1905年世界博览会金色纪念册》,世博会博物馆馆藏

Machinery Section
Liver D'orde L'Exposition Universelle et Internationale de 1905.
1905. World Expo Museum Collection. Print.

交通展区
印刷品,1905年,《1905年世界博览会金色纪念册》,世博会博物馆馆藏

Transportation Section
Le Liver D'orde L'Exposition Universelle et Internationale de I905.
1905. World Expo Museum Collection. Print.

EXPO 1906 MILAN

米兰
世博会

Theme:
Transportation
Location:
Milan, Italy
Category:
World Expo
Dates: **1906.4.28-11.11**
Area (ha): **100**
Visitors: **1,000,000**
Participants: **40**

More than Just Transportation

In 1906, to celebrate the inauguration of the Simplon Tunnel, Italy hosted its first Expo. The Simplon Tunnel project was not only an engineering achievement, but also a perfect example of the application of science in practice. Similarly, the theme of this Expo was not limited to the initial focus on transportation, but expanded to how science and technology were applied to production and life.

Train and car engineering as well as aeronautics and maritime transport were the highlights of Expo 1906 Milan. The Expo featured signaling and communication systems, equipment for railroad facilities, and the use of electricity to power trains. A building dedicated to the motor cars appeared for the first time at the Expo, and prototypes of early aircraft were also on display.

One Expo, Two Venues

The Expo was held in two venues at the same time, the Sempione Park and the Piazza d'Armi, about a few kilometers apart. Visitors travel between the two venues by raised electric railway. In the Piazza d'Armi, the Fiat petro-powered tramway took visitors to the different pavilions. These innovations in transportation greatly facilitated for visitors to visit the Expo.

Legacy of the Expo

Of 200 temporary buildings constructed for the Expo, the only one that remains until this day is the Civic Aquarium, a typical Italian Art Nouveau building, bombed during World War II and reopened in 1963. Today it is the home to the hydro-biological section of the Natural History Museum.

主题：交通运输
举办地：意大利米兰
类型：综合类世博会
日期：1906年4月28日至11月11日
占地（公顷）：100
参观者（人次）：1,000,000
参展方（个）：40

不局限于交通

1906年，为庆祝辛普朗隧道贯通，意大利第一次举办了世博会。辛普朗隧道工程不仅是一次工程建设上的成就，还是一个将科学应用于实践的完美实例。同样，这届世博会的主题也没有局限在最初设定的交通运输上，而是扩展到科技如何应用于生产与生活。

火车、汽车、航空和海运是这届世博会的亮点。世博会上展出了信号与通信系统、铁路设施设备，以及电力在火车动力方面的运用。汽车馆第一次出现在世博会上，早期飞机的原型也在这届世博会上被展出。

一个世博会，两个园区

这届世博会同时在两个园区举行。这两个园区分别是森皮奥内公园和阿尔米广场。在阿尔米广场的园区内，菲亚特燃油电车可以带游客去往不同的展馆。这些交通方面的创新技术为游客参观世博会带来极大便利。

世博遗产

这届世博会建造了200座临时性建筑，唯一保存至今的是市民水族馆。它是一座典型的意大利新艺术风格建筑，"二战"期间曾被炸毁，1963年又重新开放。如今，它是米兰自然历史博物馆的水生生物分馆。

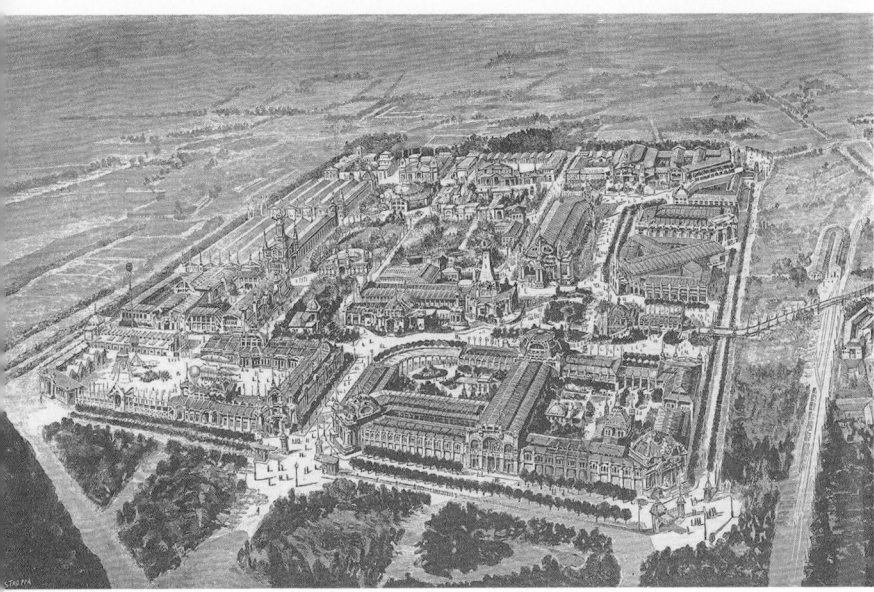

1906年米兰世博会阿尔米广场园区
印刷品，1906年，《1906年米兰世博会法国展区总报告》，国际展览局馆藏

The Piazza d'Armi at Expo 1906 Milan
Exposition Internationale de Milan 1906 Rapport Général de la Section Française.
1906. BIE Archive. Print.

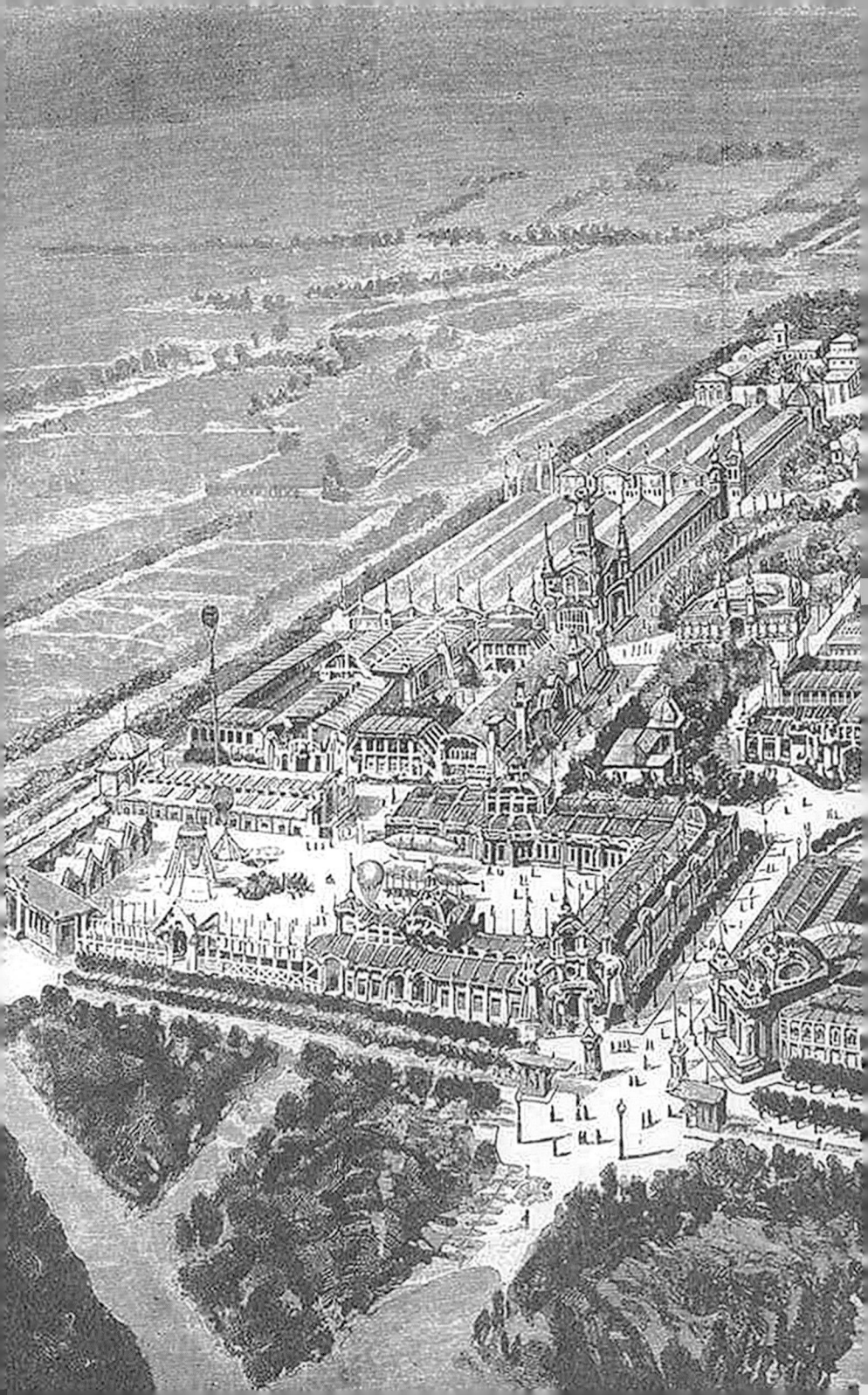

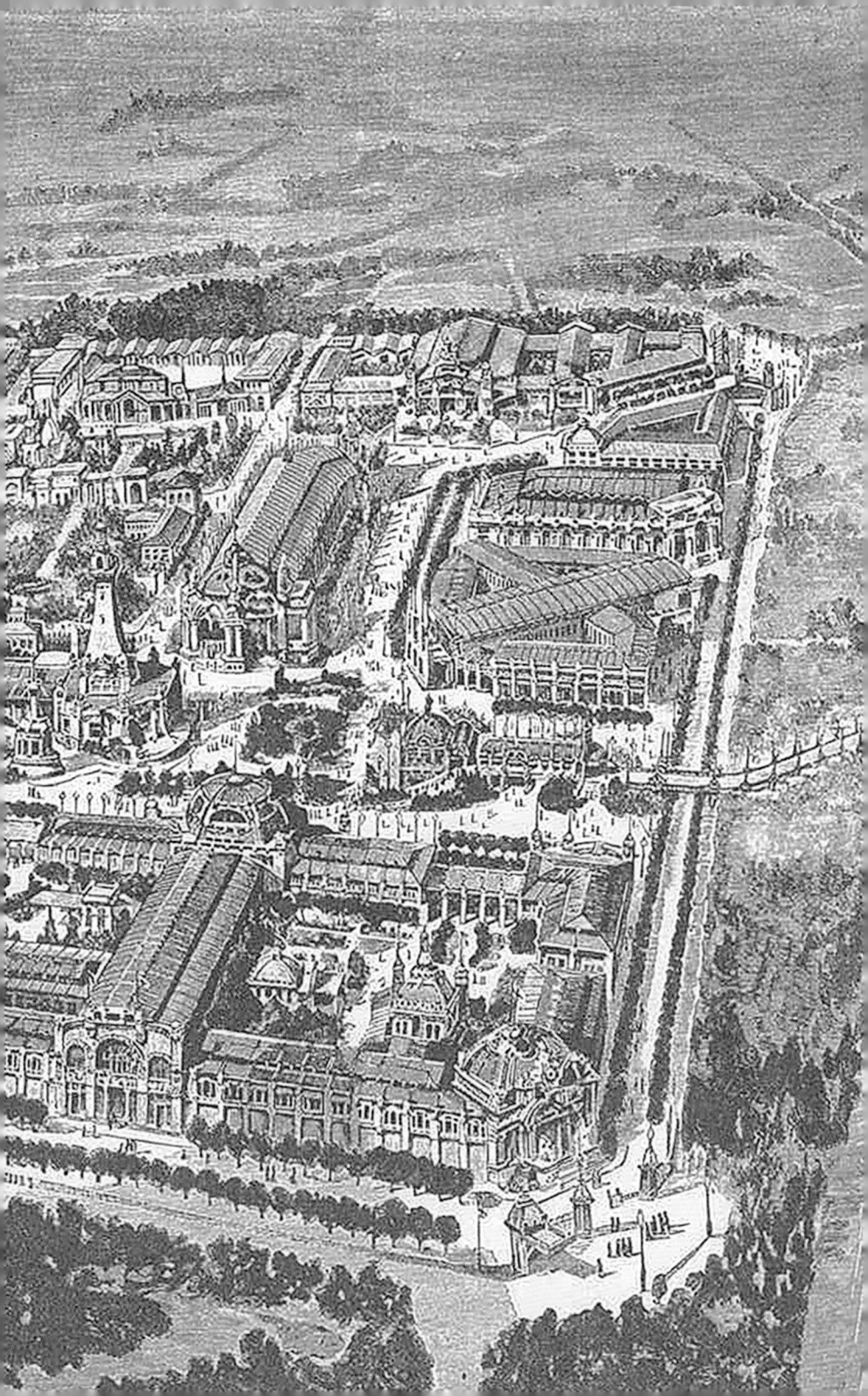

1906年米兰世博会森皮奥内公园园区
印刷品，1906年，《1906年米兰世博会法国展区总报告》，国际展览局馆藏

The Parco Sempione at Expo 1906 Milan
Exposition Internationale de Milan 1906 Rapport Général de la Section Française.
1906. BIE Archive. Print.

EXPO 1910 BRUSSELS

布鲁塞尔世博会

Theme:
Works of Art and Science, Agricultural and Industrial Products of All Nations

Location:
Brussels, Belgium

Category:
World Expo

Dates: **1910.4.23-11.7**
Area (ha): **90**
Visitors: **13,000,000**
Participants: **26**

Belgium, Again

At the turn of the 20th century, several Belgian cities hosted large-scale expositions. For example, Antwerp in the northwest of Belgium hosted two major international exhibitions in 1885 and 1894, while Brussels and Liège hosted Expos in 1897 and 1905 respectively. The hosting of Expos has extended Belgium's international influence and, together with its growing industrial development, has led to the country's rising international standing.

Entertainment and Forum

The Brussels Kermess, located near the entrance to the Expo site, was one of the highlights of the Expo. The "Water chutes" and the "Scenic Railway" ride were popular among visitors. In addition, the Expo offered relaxation areas and garden landscapes for visitors to explore.

In terms of academic and international exchanges, Brussels held various conferences and forums for experts, scholars and the general public on topics ranging from horticulture and astronomy to intellectual property and international associations.

The Road to the Expo

The Expo has contributed significantly to Brussels' development plans. The Expo site covers an area of 90 hectares on the Solbosch Plateau. In order to make it easier for visitors to reach the site by tramway, Brussels built a new railroad line connecting the Solbosch Plateau with the city roads. In addition, the avenue des Nations was built as another major connection to the site. In the 1920s, the Université Libre de Bruxelles was inaugurated on the Solbosch Plateau, the site of Expo 1910 Brussels. The avenue des Nations was renamed Franklin Roosevelt Avenue.

主题：各国的艺术与科技成就、农业和工业产品
举办地：比利时布鲁塞尔
类型：综合类世博会
日期：1910年4月23日至11月7日
占地（公顷）：90
参观者（人次）：13,000,000
参展方（个）：26

再见比利时

19世纪末20世纪初,比利时有多个城市举办过大型的博览会,例如比利时西北部城市安特卫普在1885年和1894年两次举办重要的国际性展览,布鲁塞尔和列日则分别在1897年和1905年举办过世博会。多次举办世博会扩展了比利时的国际影响力,加之工业发展日益壮大,比利时的国际地位也在不断提高。

游乐与论坛

"布鲁塞尔市集"位于世博园区的入口附近,是这届世博会的一大亮点。水上滑梯和观光列车等娱乐项目受到游客欢迎。此外,世博会还提供了休闲场所和花园景观供游客休憩和游览。而在学术与国际交流方面,布鲁塞尔面向专家学者和普通公众召开各类会议与论坛,议题涉及园艺、天文、知识产权、国际协会等多个层面。

通往世博的大道

世博会极大地促进了布鲁塞尔的发展规划。世博园区占地90公顷,位于索博施高地。为了让游客能够方便地搭乘有轨电车到达园区,布鲁塞尔新修了一条铁路线,连接索博施高地和城区道路。另外,布鲁塞尔又修建了国家大道,将其作为园区另一条主要的连接通路。20世纪20年代,布鲁塞尔自由大学在这届世博会的原址索博施高地上落成。国家大道则更名为富兰克林·罗斯福大道。

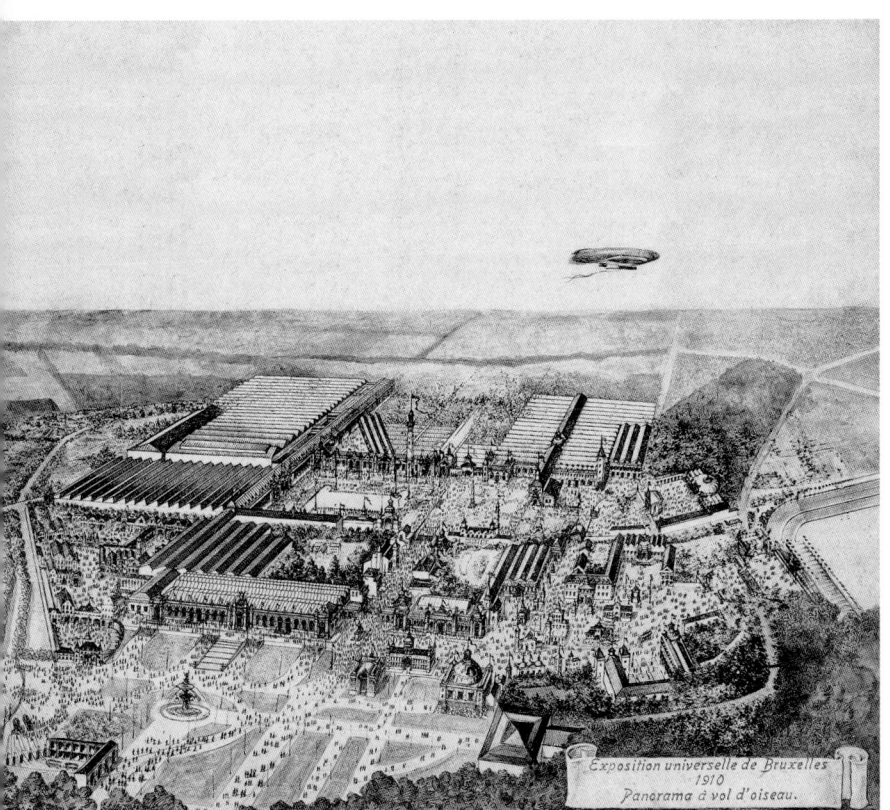

1910年布鲁塞尔世博会全景
印刷品，1910年，布鲁塞尔自由大学馆藏

Panoramic View of Expo 1910 Brussels
1910. Université Libre de Bruxelles. Print.

The Belgian Machinery Hall
1910. Université Libre de Bruxelles. Photo.

比利时机械宫照片，1910年，布鲁塞尔自由大学馆藏

英国展区的中庭
印刷品,1910年,《1910年布鲁塞尔世博会官方影集》,布鲁塞尔自由大学馆藏

The Central Gallery of the Britain Section
Album official de l'Exposition Universelle et Internationale de Bruxelles 1910.
1910. Université Libre de Bruxelles. Print.

EXPO 1913 GHENT

根特
世博会

Theme:
Peace, Industry and Art
Location:
Ghent, Belgium
Category:
World Expo
Dates: **1913.4.26-11.3**
Area (ha): **130**
Visitors: **9,503,419**
Participants: **24**

A City Decorated with Flowers

The Expo provided an opportunity to transform Ghent's city center, and in particular the Graslei (grass quay). The Graslei dates back to the 18th century and is still the city's most famous attraction. The Sint-Pieters Railway Station as well as the Flandria Palace Hotel was built for this Expo. Designed in a style typical of the late Art Nouveau, the hotel overlooked the Expo site. In conjunction with the Expo, the city's best-known Floralies floral exhibitions, was also taking place at the same time, with flowers and greenery transforming the city center.

The New and the Old

Like the "Brussels Kermesse" at the Expo 1910 Brussels, "Old Flanders" was one of the most popular exhibits for visitors (Flanders is the region where Ghent is located, in the north of Belgium). "Old Flanders" was designed by the Belgian architect Valentin Vaerwyck, who also designed the Modern Village at the Expo. The "Old Flanders" was based on the paintings of Belgian artist Armand Heins and showcased typical Flemish architecture. The "Modern Village" has a symmetrically layout of houses and modern farms featuring the latest technology. The old and the new were presented at the same time, so visitors could experience the contrast between the past and the present.

Legacy of the Expo

The Expo was bigger than any other Expos ever held in Belgium and was the last Expo held in European countries before the outbreak of the First World War. After the Expo, the Flandria Palace Hotel was subsequently used as offices by the Belgian National Rail Company NCB and part of the "Modern Village" was transformed into the Sint Geradus School.

主题：**和平、工业和艺术**

举办地：**比利时根特**

类型：**综合类世博会**

日期：**1913 年 4 月 26 日至 11 月 3 日**

占地（公顷）：**130**

参观者（人次）：**9,503,419**

参展方（个）：**24**

开满花的城市

这届世博会为根特的市中心，特别是香草河岸的改造提供了一次机会。香草河岸的历史可以追溯到 18 世纪，至今它仍是这座城市最著名的景点。圣彼得火车站以及弗朗德里亚宫殿酒店都是为这届世博会而建造的。弗朗德里亚宫殿酒店的设计风格具有典型的新艺术运动晚期特点，游客入住酒店可俯瞰世博园区。为配合世博会，根特最为人熟知的根特花展也在同期举办，鲜花和绿植将市中心装扮一新。

一个新，一个旧

同 1910 年布鲁塞尔世博会上的『布鲁塞尔市集』一样，『老弗兰德斯』是广受游客欢迎的展区之一（弗兰德斯是根特所在的地区，位于比利时北部）。『老弗兰德斯』的设计者是比利时建筑师瓦伦丁·瓦埃维克，他同时也是世博园区内『现代村』的设计者。『老弗兰德斯』以比利时艺术家阿曼德·瓦恩维克的绘画作品为蓝本，展示了典型的弗兰德斯地区的建筑。而『现代村』则拥有对称布局的房屋以及运用最新技术的现代化的农场。新旧两个展区同时呈现，游客可在此间体会过去与现在的差异。

世博遗产

这届世博会的规模超过了之前在比利时举办过的任何一届世博会，也是『一战』爆发前欧洲举办的最后一届世博会。会后，弗朗德里亚宫殿酒店成为比利时国家铁路公司的办公场所，『现代村』的其中一部分被改造为圣杰拉德学校。

1913年根特世博会海报,海报上绘制的是这届世博会上广受欢迎的"老弗兰德斯"区域印制品,1913年,作者:让·德·昂普廷

This poster showcases the region's historical charm with a picturesque depiction of the "Old Flanders" district, one of the most popular sections of the Expo 1913 Ghent. Illustrated by Jean de Hemptinne. 1913. Print.

弗朗德里亚宫殿酒店
照片，约 1913 年

Flandria Palace Hotel
c. 1913. Photo

EXPO 1915 SAN FRANCISCO

旧金山世博会

Theme: **Celebrating the Opening of the Panama Canal**
Location: **San Francisco, United States**
Category: **World Expo**
Dates: **1915.2.20-12.4**
Area (ha): **254**
Visitors: **18,876,438**
Participants: **41**

Rebirth

In 1906, a sudden earthquake and subsequent fire hit San Francisco in the United States nearly destroyed the city. The need to rebuild reinforced San Francisco's original desire to host a World Expo, which opened successfully in 1915, boosting the morale of the San Francisco Bay Area and proving once again the city's value.

The Domed City

It took three years to build the entire Expo site, and the most recognised buildings were the Tower of Jewels and the Domed City. Thanks to the use of "indirect lighting", the silhouettes and colors of the buildings seem to shimmer in the reflection of the lights at night. This exposition was also the first to make extensive use of "indirect lighting".

New Forms of Presentation

The main attraction at the Expo was the 2-hectare model of the Panama Canal. Surrounding the model was a movable platform, 139 meters long, consisting of 144 connected carriages, which could accommodate 1,200 people at the same time. Visitors paid 50 cents to ride this special "train". The ride around the model took 23 minutes. More than two decades later, in 1939, New York hosted the World Expo, which featured a popular exhibit called "Futurama," which was modeled after the Panama Canal at the Panama Pacific International Exposition 1915. In addition, the Liberty Bell, a symbol of American independence, traveled from Philadelphia to San Francisco and was on display in the Pennsylvania Pavilion for four months during the Expo. This was the last time the Liberty Bell left Philadelphia for exhibition.

主题：**庆祝巴拿马运河通航**
举办地：**美国旧金山**
类型：**综合类世博会**
日期：**1915 年 2 月 20 日至 12 月 4 日**
占地（公顷）：**254**
参观者（人次）：**18,876,438**
参展方（个）：**41**

重生

1906 年，一场突如其来的地震和火灾侵袭了美国旧金山，几乎摧毁了这座城市。重建的需求越发坚定了旧金山原本就想举办世博会的想法。1915 年，旧金山世博会顺利开幕，鼓舞了旧金山湾区的士气，再次证明了旧金山的价值。

圆顶之城

整个世博园区的建设花费了三年时间，园区里最知名的建筑是珠宝塔和圆顶城。由于采用反射照明，建筑物的轮廓和颜色在夜间灯光的反射下仿佛闪烁着光芒。这届世博会也是第一个广泛运用反射照明的世博会。

新的展览形式

世博会上最大的亮点是占地 2 公顷的巴拿马运河的模型。围绕模型四周的是一个可移动的平台，长 439 米，由 144 节相连的车厢组成，可容纳 1,200 人同时参观。游客支付 50 美分就可以乘坐这列特殊的『列车』。环绕模型一圈需要 23 分钟。20 多年后的 1939 年，纽约举办世博会，这届世博会上的巴拿马运河模型广受游客欢迎的参项『未来世界』，它的参观模式就和 1915 年旧金山世博会非常相似。除此之外，象征美国独立的自由钟也从费城来到旧金山，世博会期间在宾夕法尼亚馆展出了四个月。这也是自由钟最后一次离开费城外出展示。

Aeroplane View Main Group of Exhibit Palaces Panama-Pacific International Exposition

1915年旧金山世博会在园区里建造了许多圆顶结构的建筑，因此园区又被称为圆顶之城印刷品（半色调照片），1915年，作者：加布里·穆兰，国际展览局馆藏

The many domed structures built at the Expo 1915 San Francisco earned it the name of "The Domed City."
Created by Gabriel Moulin. 1915. BIE Archive. Photo-mechanical Print (Halftone).

171

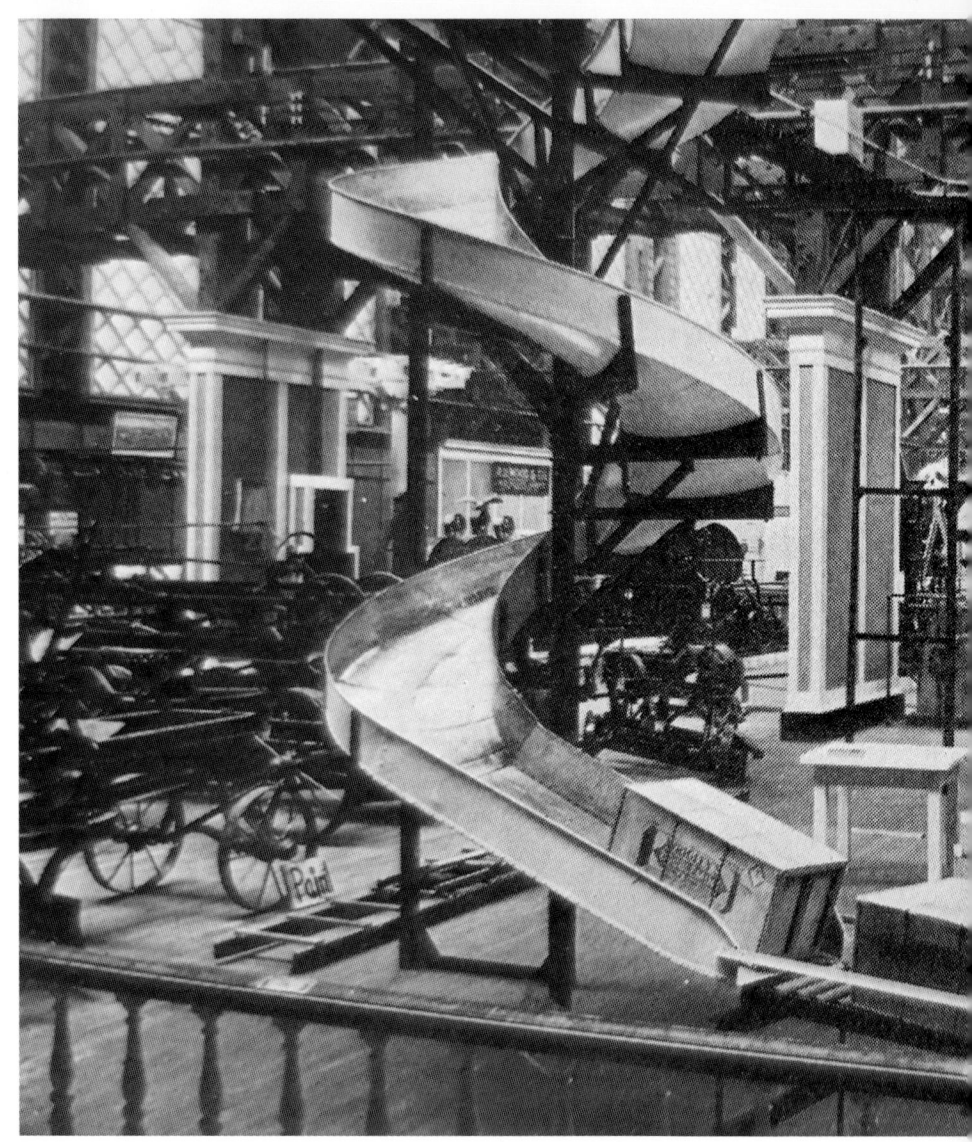

Conveyer System for a Modern Factory at Expo 1915 San Francisco
Written by Frank Morton Todd. *The Story of the Exposition*. 1921. World Expo Museum Collection. Print.

1915年旧金山世博会上展示的现代工厂传送系统印刷品，1921年，作者：弗兰克·莫顿·托德，《博览会的故事》，世博会博物馆馆藏

1915年旧金山世博会上展示的无线电话设备印刷品，1921年，作者：弗兰克·莫顿·托德，《博览会的故事》，世博会博物馆馆藏

Sets for Wireless Telephony at Expo 1915 San Francisco
Written by Frank Morton Todd. *The Story of the Exposition.* 1921.
World Expo Museum Collection. Print.

美国著名特技飞行员林肯·比奇在1915年旧金山世博会上驾驶单翼飞机向人群挥手致意

银盐感光照片，1915年，小艾德温·鲍尔和琳达·利斯康赠与旧金山博物馆

Lincoln Beachey, the famous American stunt flyer, waved to the crowd in his monoplane at the Expo.

1915. SFO Museum. Gift of Edwin I. Power, Jr. and Linda L. Liscom. Gelatin Silver Print.

汽车制造商在1915年旧金山世博会上展示汽车装配过程印刷品,1921年,作者:弗兰克·莫顿·托德,《博览会的故事》,世博会博物馆馆藏

Demonstration of car assembly process by an automobile assembling plant at the Expo.
Written by Frank Morton Todd. *The Story of the Exposition*. 1921.
World Expo Museum Collection. Print.

EXPO 1929 BARCELONA

巴塞罗那世博会

Theme: **Industry, Art and Sport**
Location: **Barcelona, Spain**
Category: **World Expo**
Dates: **1929.5.20-1930.1.15**
Area (ha): **118**
Visitors: **5,800,000**
Participants: **29**

Transforming Barcelona

After 1888, Barcelona hosted the World Expo for the second time in 1929. In fact, as early as 1905, architects and political activists called for a new wave of modernization of Barcelona city by hosting another World Expo. This initiative was carried out to good effect, including the redevelopment of the Gothic Quarter and Plaça de Catalunya in the city center, the reconstruction of França railway station, the introduction of modern tarmac and street lighting, and the operation of Barcelona's first metro line.

Expo on A Slope

In order to accommodate all the pavilions, the Expo area covered more than 100 hectares and was located in the Montjuïc Park, situated on a slope, making the Expo 1929 the first to be built on a non-flat surface.

A Modern Metropolis

Many famous architects were involved in the design of the pavilions, which were built in a variety of styles, including classicism, modernism, and avant-garde, and became a model for 20th-century architecture. After the Expo, many of the pavilions were preserved and together they changed the image of the city. For example, the Palau Nacional, which later became the Museo Nacional de Arte de Cataluña (MNAC); the Montjuic Stadium, which later became the venue for the 1992 Olympic Games in Barcelona; the Poble Espanyol (Spanish Town), consisting of 117 Spanish buildings, and the Greek Theater, which was converted from an ancient quarry, have all been preserved and have become favorite attractions. The German Pavilion, designed by modernist architect Mies van der Rohe, was one of the most important buildings of this Expo and was demolished afterwards. However, as it was one of the most important early works of the modernist movement, it attracted much attention from the architectural community and was rebuilt in the 1980s.

主题：**工业、艺术和体育**
举办地：**西班牙巴塞罗那**
类型：**综合类世博会**
日期：**1929年5月20日至1930年1月15日**
占地（公顷）：**118**
参观者（人次）：**5,800,000**
参展方（个）：**29**

改造巴塞罗那

继1888年之后，1929年巴塞罗那第二次举办了世博会。其实，早在1905年就有建筑师和政治活动家呼吁，通过再次举办世博会对巴塞罗那进行新一轮的现代化改造。这一倡议得到很好的贯彻，市中心的哥特区和加泰罗尼亚广场被重新整修，法兰西亚火车站获得重建，现代柏油马路和路灯照明铺设到位，巴塞罗那的第一条地铁线路也投入使用。

斜坡上的世博会

为了容纳所有展馆，世博园区面积超过了100公顷，地点位于蒙特惠奇公园。蒙特惠奇公园位于一个斜坡上，1929年的世博会因而成为第一个在非水平面上建造的世博会。

一个现代化的大都市

许多著名的建筑师参与了场馆的设计，使这些建筑呈现出古典主义、现代主义以及先锋派等多种风格，成为20世纪建筑典范。会后，不少场馆得以保留，共同改变了这座城市的面貌。例如，西班牙馆后来成为加泰罗尼亚国家艺术博物馆，蒙特惠奇体育场之后成为1992年巴塞罗那奥运会的场馆，由117栋西班牙建筑组成的西班牙小镇，以及由古代采石场改造而成的希腊剧院，都被保留下来，成为最受欢迎的景点。现代主义建筑大师密斯·凡·德罗设计的德国馆是这届世博会最重要的建筑之一，会后被拆除。然而，由于它是现代主义运动早期最重要的作品之一，备受建筑界关注，在20世纪80年代时被复建。

1929年巴塞罗那世博会园区手绘图
印刷品，1928年，巴塞罗那市政档案馆馆藏

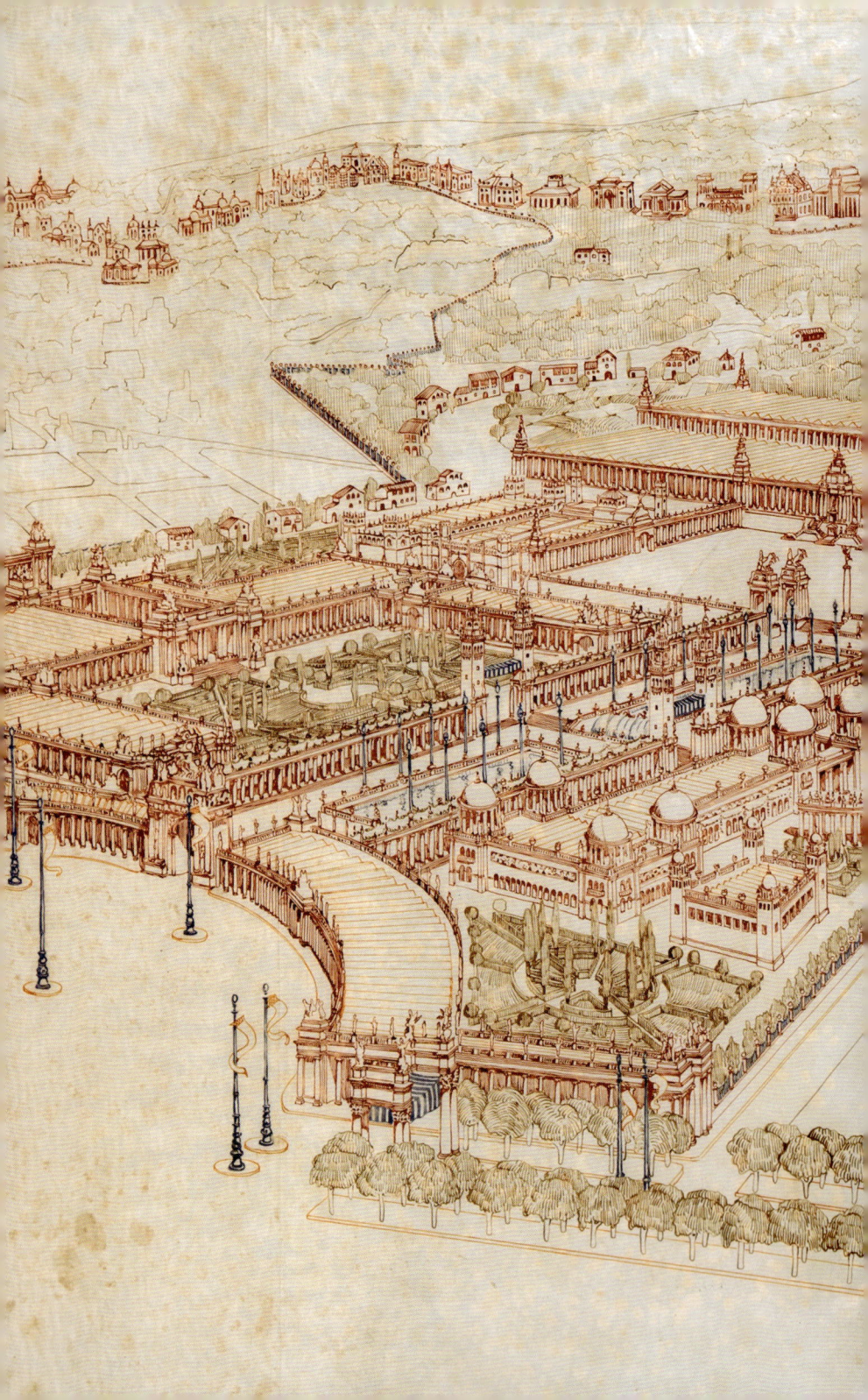

施工方在园区建造过程中运用电力进行吊装作业
印刷品，1929年，《1929年巴塞罗那国际博览会官方日志》，世博会博物馆馆藏

Electricity was used for lifting operations during construction.
Diario Oficialdela Exposición Internacional Barcelona 1929.
1929. World Expo Museum Collection. Print.

安装在国家馆顶部的泛光灯为夜色中的建筑增添光彩印刷品，1929年，《1929年巴塞罗那国际博览会官方日志》，世博会博物馆馆藏

Floodlighting on the Palacio Nacional illuminated the building at night.
Diario Oficialdela Exposición Internacional Barcelona 1929.
1929. World Expo Museum Collection. Print.

通信馆内同时展示了现代化的有轨电车和传统的「公共马车」，体现人类交通的进步与发展印刷品，1929年，《1929年巴塞罗那国际博览会官方日志》，世博会博物馆馆藏

Ayer y hoy - En el Palacio de Comunicaciones aparece, junto al tranvía modernísimo, la vieja "carrozza di tutti" tirada por mulas. - Foto Maymó -

The Palace of Communications and Transport showcased both modern trams and traditional "public carriages", reflecting the progress and development of human transportation.

188

Diario Oficialdela Exposición Internacional Barcelona 1929.
1929. World Expo Museum Collection. Print.

EXPO 1933 CHICAGO

芝加哥世博会

Theme:
The Independence among Industry and Scientific Research
Location:
Chicago, United States
Category:
World Expo
Dates: **1933.5.27-11.12 1934.6.1-10.31**
Area (ha): **170**
Visitors: **38,872,000**
Participants: **21**

A Century of Progress

In the 1920s, Chicago had a poor reputation for law and order. In order to improve the city's image, Chicago decided to organize its second World Expo. The title "A Century of Progress" was incorporated into the official name of the Expo 1933, defining the direction in which the organizers hoped to showcase Chicago's strengths and prestige in a themed exposition.

One Expo with Two Openings

The Great Depression, which began in 1929, severely affected this Expo, resulting in a much fewer number of participants than the previous Expo held in San Francisco. However, after the opening of the Expo on May 27, it welcomed 22.3 million visitors in six months. The unexpected success made the Organizer decide to reopen the Expo next year and 16 million people visited the "second edition" of the Expo. The two Expos not only allowed the organizers to pay off their debts, but also to make a profit.

Entertainment

The most popular attraction of the Expo was the Sky Ride, which provided visitors with a 191-meter-high view of the entire Expo site. Especially at night, with the light show, the carriages of the cable car looked like rockets in the sky. In this Expo, Belgium built the world's first amusement park, which inspired Walt Disney who later built the Disneyland in California.

主题：工业科技研究的独立性
举办地：美国芝加哥
类型：综合类世博会
日期：1933年5月27日至11月12日
1934年6月1日至10月31日
占地（公顷）：170
参观者（人次）：38,872,000
参展方（个）：21

一个世纪的进步

20世纪20年代，芝加哥因治安问题声誉不佳。为了改善城市形象，芝加哥决定第二次举办世博会。"一个世纪的进步"这个标题被纳入1933年世博会的官方名称中，明确了世博会的展示方向，组织者希望通过这个主题鲜明的博览会展现出芝加哥的实力与声望。

两次开幕的世博会

1929年开始的经济大萧条严重影响了这届世博会，参展方数量远不及上一次美国旧金山世博会。然而，5月27日世博会开幕后，半年会期里竟迎来2,230万游客。出人意料的成功让组织者决定在闭幕后的第二年又一次开放了世博会，1,600万人参观了这届世博会的『下半场』。连开两次的世博会不仅让组织者偿清了债务，还让其赚取了一定的利润。

娱乐项目

这届世博会最受欢迎的项目是空中缆车，方便游客从191米的高空俯瞰整个世博园区。特别是晚上，配合灯光表演，空中缆车的车厢在夜色下如同一艘火箭。比利时参展这届世博会时，建造了世界上最早的游乐园。沃尔特·迪士尼受此启发，后来在加利福尼亚建立了迪士尼乐园。

1933年芝加哥世博会园区的北岛泻湖印刷品，1933年，美国芝加哥历史博物馆馆藏

Northerly Island and Lagoon at the Expo Site
1933. Chicago History Museum. Print.

空中缆车形似火箭,游客乘坐缆车可在191米的高空俯瞰整个世博园区印刷品,1933年,《一个世纪的进步博览会官方图集》,世博会博物馆馆藏

...haped like a rocket, visitors could overlook the whole Expo site within a cable car from a height of
91 meters.
Official Pictures of a Century of Progress Exposition. 1933. World Expo Museum Collection. Print.

1933年芝加哥世博会展示了一个电气化的厨房,配备了洗碗机等家用电器,显现出现代化的生活方式

印刷品,1934年,《1934年世博会官方指南》,世博会博物馆馆藏

Leading a modern lifestyle, the Expo showcased an electrical kitchen, equipped with dishwashers and other household appliances.
Official Guide Book of the World's Fair of 1934. 1934. World Expo Museum Collection. Print.

斯特兰钢屋是1933年芝加哥世博会上展出的一种创新的预制钢结构住宅，具有防火、造价低廉、搭建便捷等特点。印刷品，1933年，《官方指南：1933年博览会之书》，世博会博物馆藏

Fireproof, inexpensive and easy to erect, the Stran-Steel House was an innovative prefabricated steel house exhibited at the Expo. *Official Guide: Book of the Fair, 1933*. 1933. World Expo Museum Collection. Print.

手指壁画的人正是壁画的创作者希尔德里思·梅耶，壁画里的女性"注视"着画家，体现女性一个世纪的进步印刷品，1933年，《世博会官方周刊》，世博会博物馆馆藏

The person pointing at the mural was its creator, Hildreth Meiere. The women in the mural were as if "looking" at the artist, reflecting a century of progress for women.
Official World's Fair Weekly. 1933. World Expo Museum Collection. Print.

EXPO 1935 BRUSSELS

布鲁塞尔
世博会

Theme:
Transport
Location:
Brussels, Belgium
Category:
World Expo
Dates: **1935.4.27-11.3**
Area (ha): **152**
Visitors: **20,000,000**
Participants: **25**

Convenient Transportation

Expo 1935 Brussels was the first World Expo organized after the establishment of the Bureau International des Expositions (BIE). The planning of the Expo site was carried out by the famous Belgian architect Joseph van Neck, who designed to transform the originally undulating ground into 152 hectares of plateau, requiring the removal of 700,000m^3 of earth. Transportation facilities, including bridges, tramways and a train station, were also put in place to ensure that the Expo site would be an easily accessible hub.

A Triumph of Technology

The Exhibition Palaces, and in particular the Halle Centrale, utilized the latest design and construction techniques and became the landmark of this Expo. The Halle Centrale was 31 meters high and 150 meters long and was constructed entirely of reinforced concrete. Supporting the building was an 86-meter-long parabolic arch (a type of arch structure in engineering architecture), and there were no columns in the space, providing an extremely open space for exhibitions. The construction of the Exhibition Palaces was completed by using the most modern technology in a short period of time, proving to the world the feasibility of a new type of architectural structure.

Offer a Place for a Worried World to Find its Bearings

In times of economic crisis, the development of the Expo site and the construction of the city's infrastructure was undoubtedly a bold decision. The Expo 1935 inspired optimism and created job opportunities, and the Organizer made it clear that they wanted the Expo to "offer a place for a worried world to find its bearings". The Expo closed with more than 20 million visitors, equivalent to two-and-a-half-times the population of Belgium at the time. The Expo created a new exhibition complex and paved the way for the development of the Laeken region in northwestern Belgium, which later became the site of Expo 1958 Brussels.

主题：**交通运输**
举办地：**比利时布鲁塞尔**
类型：**综合类世博会**
日期：**1935年4月27日至11月3日**
占地（公顷）：**152**
参观者（人次）：**20,000,000**
参展方（个）：**25**

便捷的交通

1935年布鲁塞尔世博会是国际展览局成立后举办的第一届世博会。世博园区的规划由比利时著名建筑师约瑟夫·范·内克负责，他设计将原本高低起伏的地面规整为152公顷的平地，这意味着需要转移70万立方米的土方。包括桥梁、有轨电车和火车站在内的各项交通设施也一一到位，以确保世博园区成为一个方便到达的枢纽体，为展览提供了一个极为开阔的场地。布鲁塞尔在短时间内使用最现代的技术建世博会的展馆，向世界证明了新型建筑结构的可行性。

技术的胜利

主建筑展览宫，特别是它的中央大厅，运用了最新的设计与建造技术，成为这届世博会的标志性建筑。中央大厅高31米，长150米，完全由钢筋混凝土建造。支撑建筑的是长达86米的抛物线拱（工程建筑上的一种拱形结构），空间内没有任何柱

为世界找到方向

在经济危机时期，开发世博园区以及进行城市基础设施建设无疑是一个大胆的决定。这届世博会鼓舞了乐观的社会情绪，并为就业创造机会，组织者明确表示希望世博会「为一个忧虑重重的世界找到方向」。世博会闭幕时，参观量超过2,000万，相当于当时比利时人口的2.5倍。这届世博会创造了新的展览建筑群，也为比利时西北部的拉肯地区的发展铺平了道路，而拉肯后来成为1958年世博会的举办地。

1935年布鲁塞尔世博会概貌
印刷品，1935年，国际展览局馆藏

Overview of Expo 1935 Brussels
1935. BIE Archive. Print.

铁路馆
印刷品,1935年,国际展览局馆藏

Grand Palais of Railroad
1935. BIE Archive. Print.

EXPO 1936 STOCKHOLM

斯德哥尔摩世博会

Theme:
Aviation
Location:
Stockholm, Sweden
Category:
Specialised Expo
Dates: **1936.5.15-6.1**
Participants: **8**

The First Specialised Expo

Expo 1936 Stockholm was the first Specialised Expo to be recognized by the BIE.

Centered on the theme of aviation, this Expo was aim to demonstrate the achievements of the participating countries in the field of aircraft manufacturing and the need to develop modern air services.

The Expo was held at two different locations: Lindarängen seaplane airport and Bromma airport. The Lindarängen Water Airport was used as an exhibition venue, mainly for displaying airplanes, engines and aircraft materials. Bromma Airport was where air races and air shows took place between air forces and airlines from eight countries participated, including Germany, England, Finland, Poland, Czechoslovakia, Switzerland, Canada and the Netherlands. Bromma Airport was officially put into operation after the opening of the Expo and was the first airport in Europe with paved runways.

主题：**航空**

举办地：**瑞典斯德哥尔摩**

类型：**专业类世博会**

日期：**1936年5月15日至6月1日**

参展方（个）：**8**

第一个专业类世博会

1936年斯德哥尔摩世博会是国际展览局认可的第一个专业类世博会。这届世博会以"航空"为主题，旨在展示各参展国在飞机制造领域的成就，以及发展现代航空服务的必要性。

世博会的会场设在两个不同的地点：林达伦水上机场和布罗马机场。林达伦水上机场作为展览场地，主要展示飞机、发动机以及飞机材料。布罗马机场则用来开展飞行竞赛与表演，来自德国、英国、芬兰、波兰、捷克斯洛伐克、瑞士、加拿大和荷兰等8个国家的空军和航空公司的飞机在此驰骋翱翔。布罗马机场是在世博会开幕后才正式启用的，是欧洲第一个铺设飞机跑道的机场。

展览场地：布罗马机场
照片，1936 年

Exhibition Area: Bromma Airport
1936. Photo.

观众参观利延塔尔滑翔翼
照片,1936年

Lilienthal Slider at Expo 1936 Stockholm
1936. Photo.

EXPO 1937 PARIS

巴黎
世博会

Theme: **Arts and Technology in Modern Life**
Location: **Paris, France**
Category: **World Expo**
Dates: **1937.5.25-11.25**
Area (ha): **105**
Visitors: **31,040,955**
Participants: **45**

...or the People

...po 1937 Paris was a reflection of the cultural policy of the ...ont Populaire government. The Organizer of the Expo hoped to ...emocratize access to culture, the media and science. The Ministry of ...ational Education and Fine Arts invited artists to contribute to the ...:po through cultural creation programs, such as the French Cubist ...ainter Fernand Léger, who created the large-scale mural *Transport ...es Forces* for the Palais de la Découverte, and French modernist artist ...aoul Dufy, who created the 60-meter-long mural *La Fée Électricité* for ...e Electricity pavilion. The display of various technologies in the Palais ...e la Découverte brought ordinary people closer to science, and the ...se of mass media, such as movies and radio, in a number of pavilions ...lso allowed visitors to understand the role of communication. The ...:po also featured a series of temporary pavilions whose themes were ...e focus of the Front Populaire's ideas, such as the Peace Pavilion, ...e Education Pavilion, the National Solidarity Pavilion, the Hygiene ...avilion and the Labor Pavilion.

...xpo on the Eve of World War II

...rganized just between the two world wars, the Expo 1937 was ...evitably affected. The Germany Pavilion and the Soviet Union ...avilion, facing each other, seemed to symbolize the confrontation ...etween the two powers. The Spain Pavilion was also politically ...fluenced by the Spanish Civil War, with the most famous exhibit ...eing Picasso's *Guernica*, which was commissioned especially for this ...xpo. Nevertheless, the Organizer wanted to focus on human progress, ...novation, and art. Edmond Labbé, the Commissioner General, ...escribed the exposition as "a beneficial oasis, an oasis of peace".

主题：**现代生活中的艺术与科技**
举办地：**法国巴黎**
类型：**综合类世博会**
日期：**1937 年 5 月 25 日至 11 月 25 日**
占地（公顷）：**105**
参观者（人次）：**31,040,955**
参展方（个）：**45**

为了人民

1937 年巴黎世博会充分反映了当时的执政者『人民阵线』的一系列文化政策。世博会的组织者希望借由世博会实现文化、传媒与科学的民主化。国家教育与艺术部通过文化创作项目邀请艺术家为世博会进行艺术创作，例如法国立体主义画家费尔南德·莱热为探索发现宫创作了大型壁画《力的传递》，法国现代主义艺术大师拉乌尔·杜菲为电力宫创作了 60 米长的巨型壁画《电气'精灵》。探索发现宫里各种技术的展示拉近了普通人与科学的距离，多个展馆内电影、广播等大众媒介的运用也让游客了解到传播的作用。世博会上还设置了一系列临时展馆，这些展馆，比如和平馆、教育馆、国家团结馆、卫生馆和劳动馆，它们的主题正是『人民阵线』关注的重点。

『二战』前夕的世博会

这届世博会的举办时间正好介于两次世界大战之间，战争无可避免地影响着这届世博会。德国馆与苏联馆面对面分立两侧，似乎象征着两种权力的对抗。而受内战影响，西班牙馆的展示也颇具政治意味，其中最出名的展品是毕加索为这届世博会专门创作的《格尔尼卡》。尽管如此，世博会的组织者仍希望将展示的重点放在人类的进步、创新以及艺术上。组委会主席埃德蒙·拉贝认为这届世博会是『一个有益大众的绿洲、一个和平的绿洲』。

1937年巴黎世博会地图
印刷品，2013年，作者：让－皮埃尔·戴贝哈

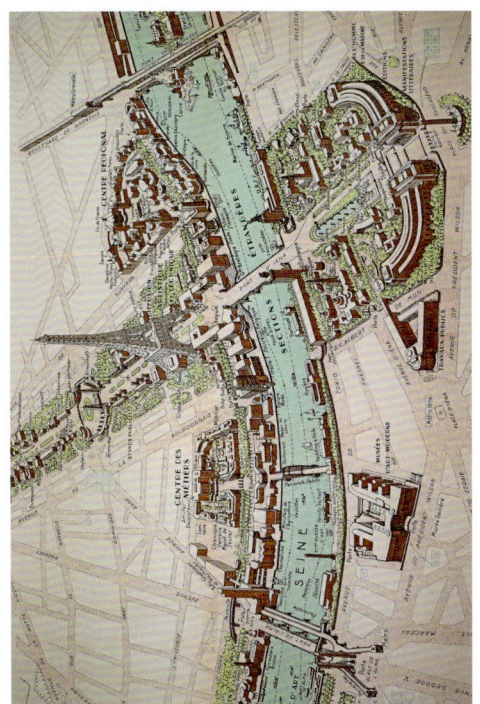

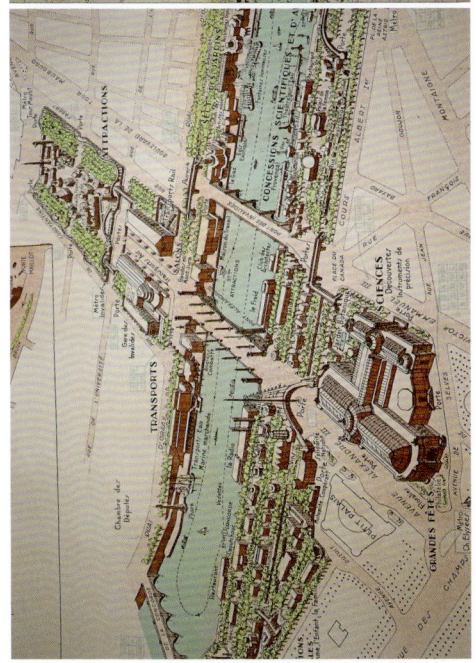

The Detail Map of Expo 1937 Paris
Created by Jean-Pierre Dalbéra. 2013. Print.

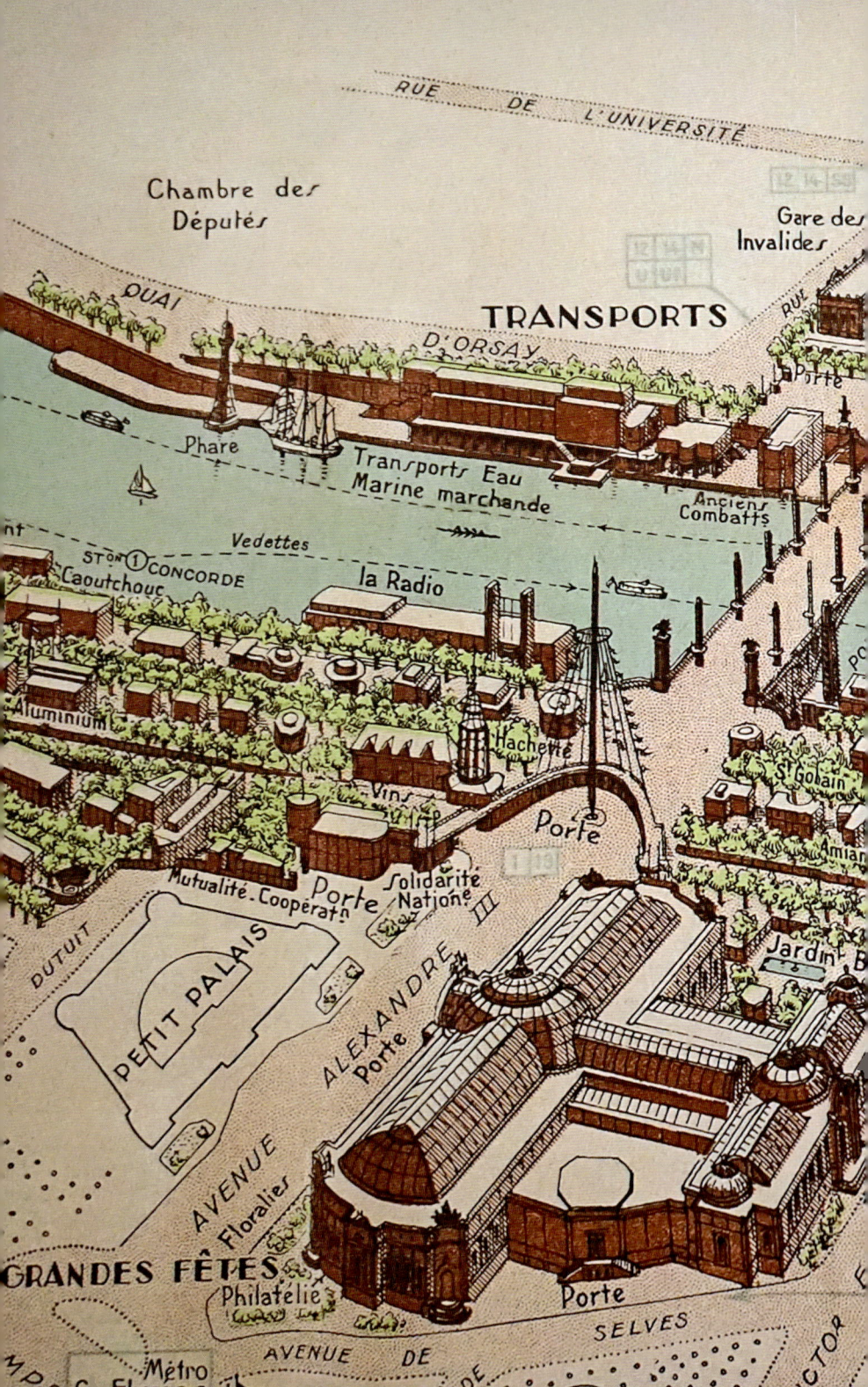

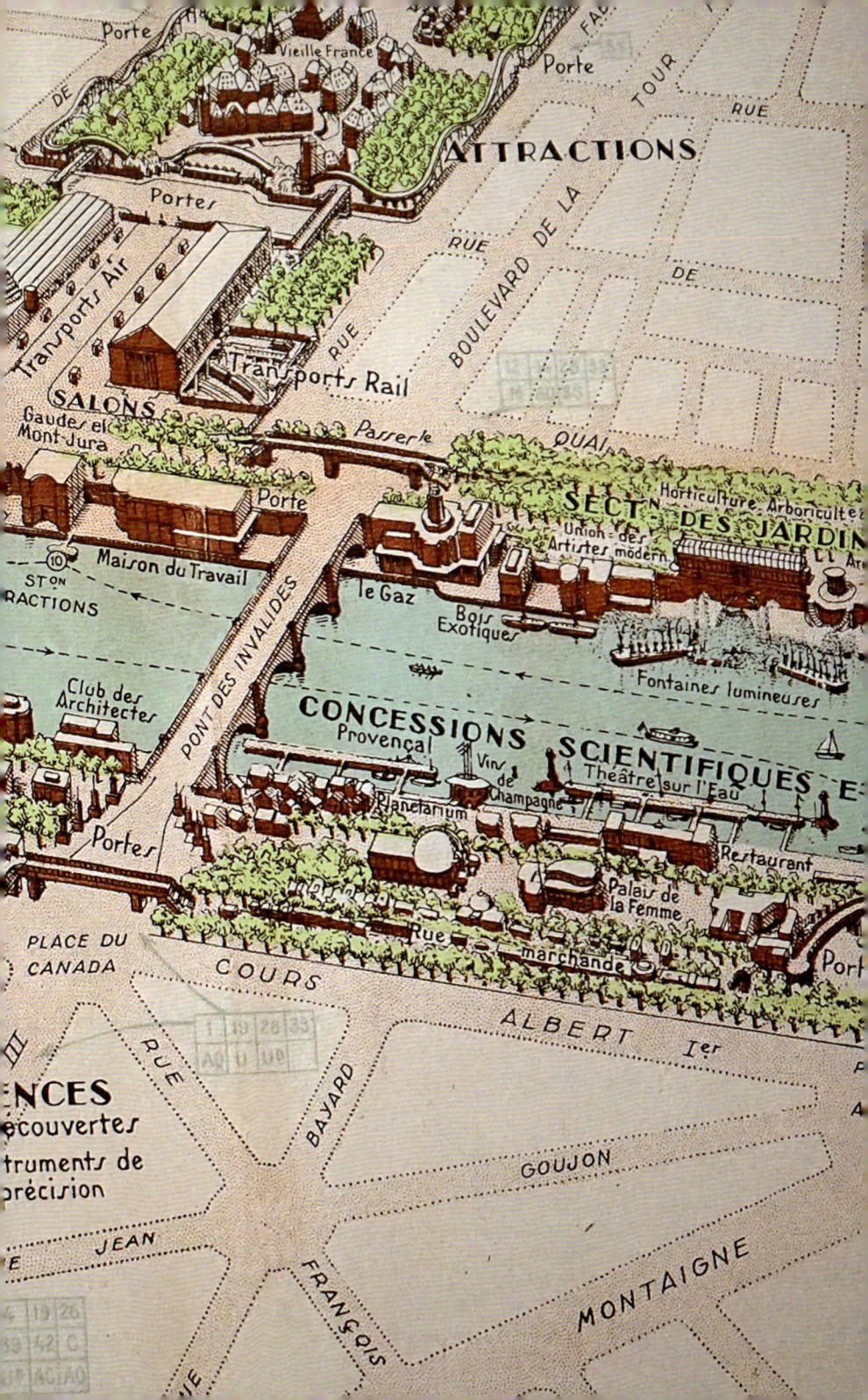

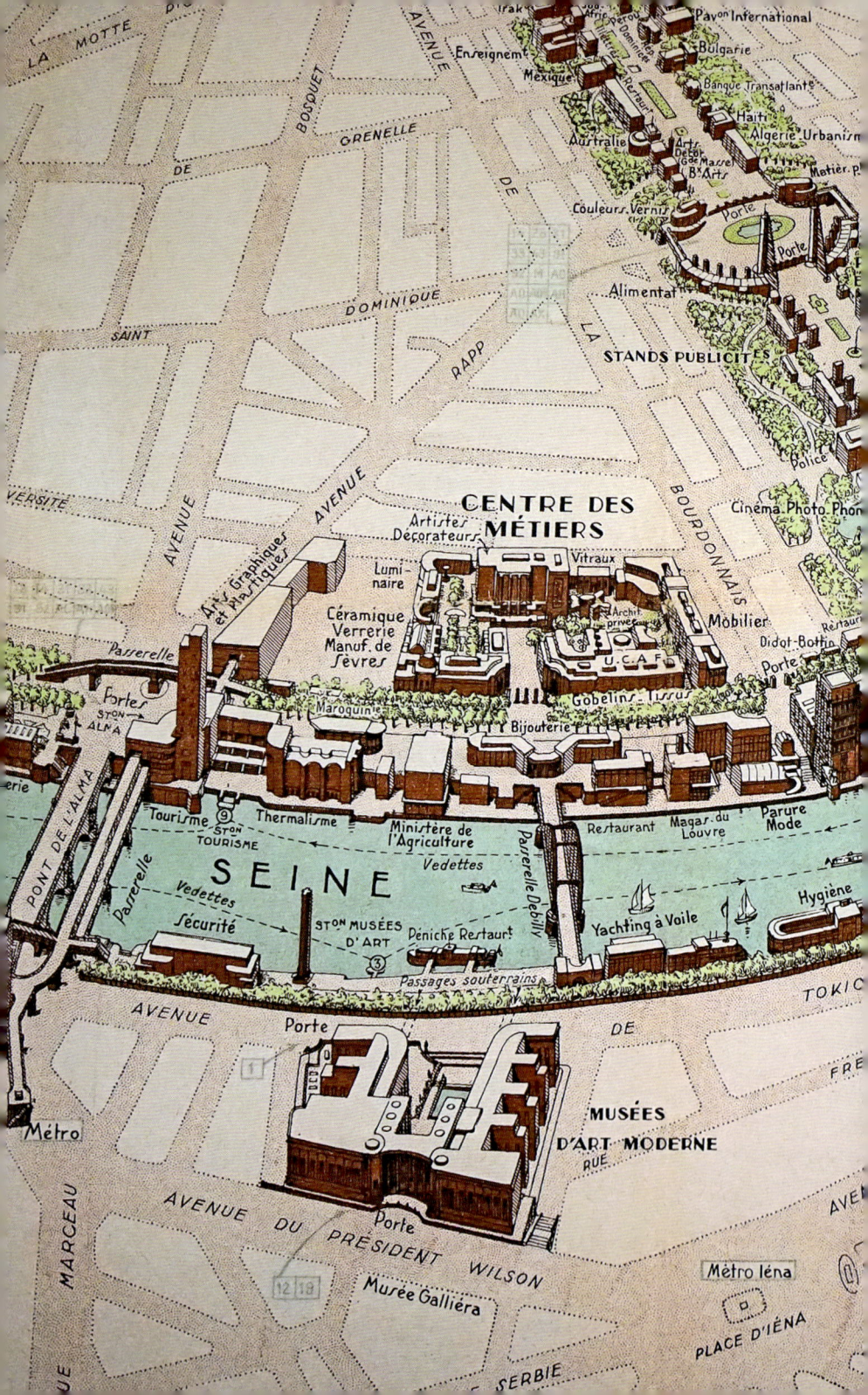

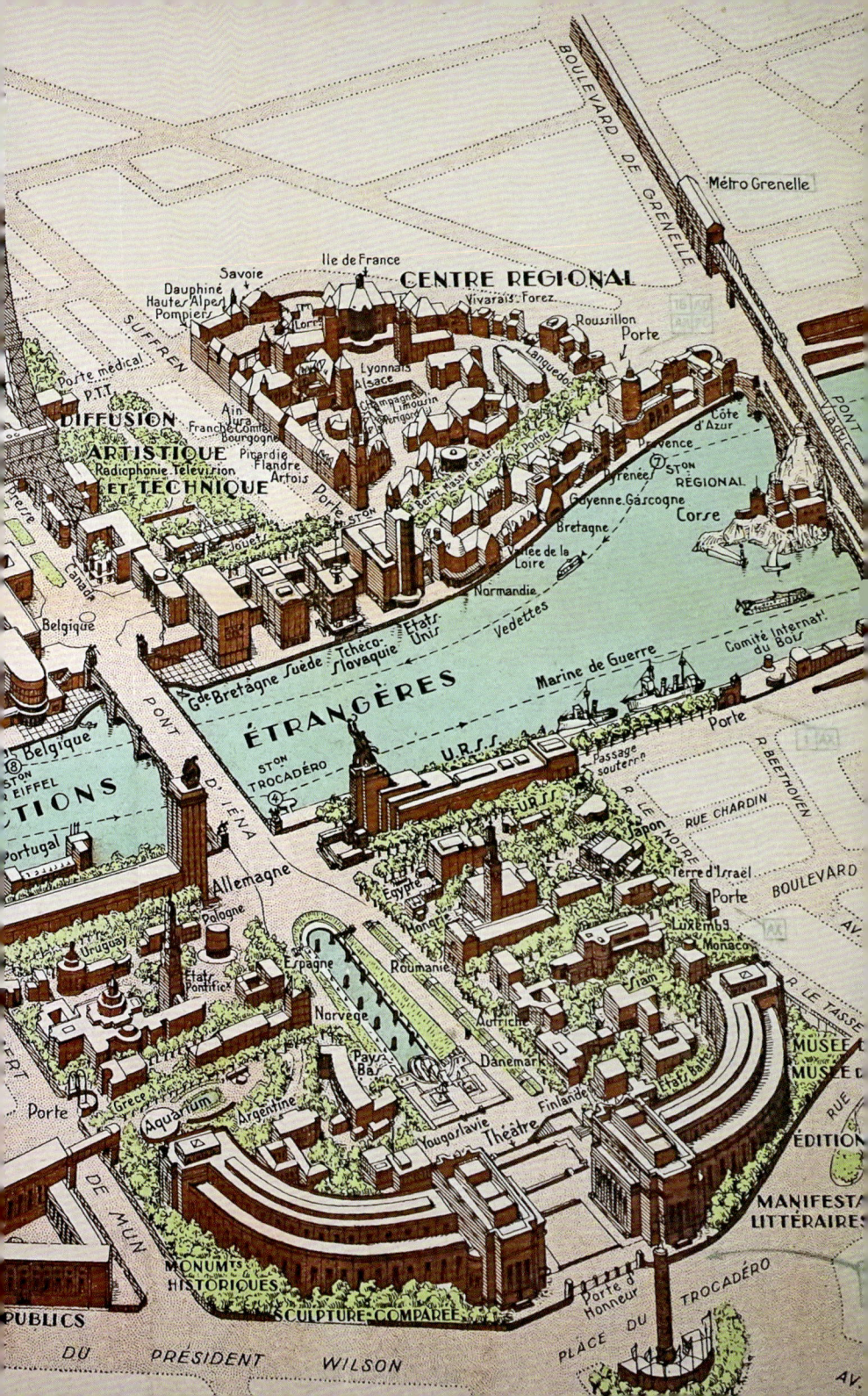

《格尔尼卡》创作记录照片，1937年，摄影师：朵拉·马尔，索菲娅王后国家艺术中心博物馆馆藏

Photo Report of the Evolution of *Guernica*
Photography by Dora Maar. 1937. Museo Nacional Centro de Arte Reina Sofia. Photo.

航空馆
印刷品，1937年，《1937年巴黎现代生活中的艺术与技术国际博览会官方实录》，世博会博物馆馆藏

lais de l'Air
re D'or Officiel de L'Exposition Internationale des Arts et Techniques dans la Vie Moderne Paris 1937.
37. World Expo Museum Collection. Print.

重达28吨的蒸汽涡轮机低压转子锻件的背后是现代主义艺术大师拉乌尔·杜菲的名作《电气精灵》印刷品，1937年，《1937年巴黎现代生活中的艺术与技术国际博览会官方实录》，世博会博物馆馆藏

A low-pressure rotor for steam turbine, weighing 28 tons, with the famous *La Fée Électricité* by modernist artist Raoul Dufy in the background.
Livre D'or Officiel de L'Exposition Internationale des Arts et Techniques dans la Vie Moderne Paris 1937. 1937. World Expo Museum Collection. Print.

EXPO 1938 HELSINKI

赫尔辛基世博会

Theme: **Aerospace**
Location: **Helsinki, Finland**
Category: **Specialised Expo**
Dates: **1938.5.14-5.22**
Participants: **25**

Flying to Helsinki

Due to its geographical location, air transport is of vital importance to Finnish transportation. The Finnish aviation industry is strong and internationally renowned, and in 1938 Helsinki hosted the International Aeronautical Exhibition of 1938, a specialised exposition on the theme of aviation. Helsinki Malmi Airport, completed and opened before the Expo, was one of the first airports in the world designed to deal with international air routes, making it easier for tourists to visit the Expo.

The main venue for the Expo was the Messuhalli Exhibition Hall. The pavilion displayed a range of aviation-related exhibits including civil and military aircraft, communications, aviation science, and aviation literature. The UK pavilion displayed the first two-speed supercharger with auxiliary drives. The France pavilion featured the most powerful engine at the Expo, the Gnome-Rhône, an 18-cylinder engine, produced 1,650 horsepower at takeoff.

First Expo, and then Olympics

The Messuhalli Exhibition Hall and Helsinki Malmi Airport remain to this day. The Messuhalli Exhibition Hall was later transformed into a stadium, and in 1952 the Summer Olympics were held in the same stadium.

主题：**航空**
举办地：**芬兰赫尔辛基**
类型：**专业类世博会**
日期：**1938 年 5 月 14 日至 5 月 22 日**
参展方（个）：**25**

飞向赫尔辛基

受地理条件影响，航空运输对芬兰交通而言至关重要。芬兰航空工业实力强大，在国际上享有盛誉。1938 年，芬兰赫尔辛基举办了以"航空"为主题的专业类世博会。为了方便游客参观世博会，赫尔辛基马尔米机场在世博会开幕前完工并启用，是世界上第一批为接入国际航线而设计的机场之一。

这届世博会的主场馆是梅苏哈利展览馆。展馆内展示了包括民用和军用飞机、通信、航空科学以及航空文献等一系列与航空相关的展品。法国展区展示了这届世博会上最强大的带有辅助驱动装置的双速增压器。英国展区展示了第一个带有姆－罗纳 18-P 发动机，作为一台 18 缸发动机，起飞时它的功率可达 1650 马力。

是世博，也是奥运

梅苏哈利展览馆和赫尔辛基马尔米机场一直保留至今。梅苏哈利展览馆后来经过改造成为体育馆。1952 年，还是在梅苏哈利展览馆，在世博会曾经举办过的地方又举办了夏季奥运会。

Aerospace Themed Poster
1938. Print.

EXPO 1939 NEW YORK

纽约世博会

Theme:
Building the World of Tomorrow
Location:
New York, United States
Category:
World Expo
Dates: **1939.4.30-10.31 1940.5.11-10.27**
Area (ha): **500**
Visitors: **44,955,997**
Participants: **54**

The World of Tomorrow

The theme of Expo 1939 New York was a clear reference to the future, and sought to demonstrate the importance of technology to the future by "Building the World of Tomorrow".

The landmarks of Expo 1939 were the Trylon and the Perisphere. The Trylon was a 212-meter-high triangular tower, while the Perisphere was a massive 65-meter-diameter sphere. Inside the Perisphere was a giant diorama of the "Democracity", a futuristic city of 2039. Visitors can experience a day in the life of the future in five minutes. In the General Motors Pavilion there was also a city model "Futurama", showing a future city in 1960. The "city" was filled with modern infrastructure such as highways and beautiful gardens on the roofs of buildings.

Another worth-mentioning highlight was Westinghouse's time capsule, which was buried underground and waiting to be reopened in 6939. The capsule contained both everyday objects, such as a toothbrush and ruler, as well as samples of different media, such as text, images and music. The initiators hoped that humans 5,000 years from now would be able to use the capsule to read about the present era.

From Dump to Park

The site of Expo 1939, the Corona Dumps, was referred to the "Valley of Ashes" by American writer F. Scott Fitzgerald in his famous book *The Great Gatsby*. However, this Expo succeeded in transforming the dumps into the Flushing Meadows Corona Park, where the U.S. Open is held, and the New York Pavilion of the Expo 1937 is preserved and currently housing a museum.

主题：构建明日世界
举办地：美国纽约
类型：综合类世博会
日期：1939年4月30日至10月31日
1940年5月11日至10月27日
占地（公顷）：500
参观者（人次）：44,955,997
参展方（个）：54

明日世界

1939年纽约世博会的主题非常明确，直指未来，力图通过『构建明日世界』体现技术对未来的重要影响。

这届世博会的标志性建筑是特赖龙和佩里球。特赖龙是一个高达212米的三角锥塔，佩里球则是一个直径65米的巨大球体建筑。佩里球内有一座巨大的立体模型——『民主城市』，它是幻想中的2039年的城市。游客在这里只需要5分钟就可以感受未来一天的生活。而在通用汽车馆也有一座城市模型——『未来世界』，不过它指向的未来锁定在1960年。在这座『城市』里，遍布高速公路等现代化基础设施，建筑的屋顶上是美丽的花园。

另外值得一提的是西屋公司的时间胶囊，它被埋在地下，等待6939年再次开启。胶囊内既有日常生活用品，比如牙刷、计算尺等，也有不同媒介的样本，比如文本、影像和音乐。发起者希望5000年后的人类可以借由这颗胶囊，读懂现在这个时代。

从垃圾场到大公园

世博会当年选址在科罗娜垃圾场，美国作家菲茨杰拉德在名作《了不起的盖茨比》里把这个垃圾场称为『灰烬之谷』。然而，世博会成功地改造了它。这个地方如今已成为法拉盛草原可乐娜公园，美国网球公开赛的举办地就设在这里。纽约馆会后也未拆除，目前是一家博物馆的所在地。

1939年纽约世博会园区鸟瞰图，园区中心位置为地标性建筑特赖龙和佩里球照片，1939年，1939年至1940年纽约世博会档案，纽约公共图书馆手稿档案部馆藏

The emblematic monuments of the Expo, Trylon and Perisphere, as well as an aerial view of Fair site. 1939. New York World's Fair 1939-1940 Records. Manuscripts and Archives Division. The New York Public Library. Photo.

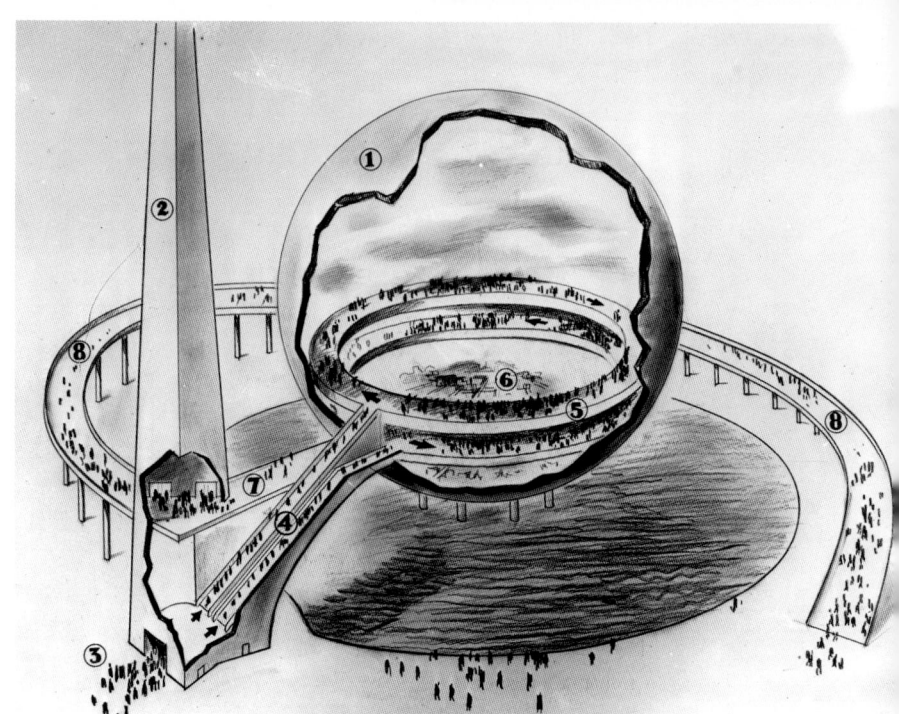

Cutaway Drawing of Trylon and Perisphere
1939. New York World's Fair 1939-1940 Records. Manuscripts and Archives Division. The New York Public Library. Photo.

特赖龙和佩里球的剖面图照片,1939年,1939年至1940年纽约世博会档案,纽约公共图书馆手稿档案部馆藏

在通用汽车馆里,观众坐在移动座椅上观看"未来世界"照片,1939年,1939年至1940年纽约世博会档案,纽约公共图书馆手稿档案部馆藏

sitors in moving chairs were viewing exhibit "Futurama" in General Motors. 39. New York World's Fair 1939-1940 Records. Manuscripts and Archives Division. e New York Public Library. Photo.

「未来世界」向观众呈现的是幻想中的1960年照片,1939年。1939年至1940年纽约世博会档案,纽约公共图书馆手稿档案部馆藏

The "Futurama" presented the visitors with a fantastical view of the year 1960. 1939. New York World's Fair 1939-1940 Records. Manuscripts and Archives Division. The New York Public Library. Photo.

西屋公司将时间胶囊埋入地下，等待6939年再次开启照片，1939年，1939年至1940年纽约世博会档案，纽约公共图书馆手稿档案部馆藏

Westinghouse's time capsule was buried underground, waiting to be reopened the year 6939.

39. New York World's Fair 1939-1940 Records. Manuscripts and Archives Division. e New York Public Library. Photo.

239

放入时间胶囊的物品关于物品的选择标准，记录中写道："我们不放过任何东西，既不放过我们的智慧，也不放过我们的愚蠢"照片，1939年，1939年至1940年纽约世博会档案，纽约公共图书馆手稿档案部馆藏

Objects placed in the time capsule. Regarding the criteria for the selection of the items, it quoted that "we spare nothing, neither our wisdom nor our foolishness." 1939. New York World's Fair 1939-1940 Records. Manuscripts and Archives Division. The New York Public Library. Photo.

EXPO 1939 LIEGE

列日世博会

Theme: **Art of Water**
Location: **Liege, Belgium**
Category: **Specialised Expo**
Dates: **1939.5.20-9.2**
Area (ha): **50**
Participants: **8**

Urbanization

In 1936, the "Greater Liège" movement was launched in order to expand the influence of Liège and the Walloon region, and in 1939, Liège hosted a specialised Expo, marking the development of the region. Planned by the modernist architect Georges Dedoyard, the Expo site adopted the principle of urbanization and took into account technical, social and cultural aspects in its design. The famous French architectural magazine *Architecture d'aujourd'hui* praised him for his success in creating a completely new area and described the buildings as reflecting a sense of "organized grandeur".

The Art of Water

In line with the Expo's water theme, this Expo highlighted the significance of water for energy supply, development, and international cooperation. The site featured a 'water theatre', where visitors could appreciate an illuminated 60-metre waterfall and a water jet rising to 100 metres. It was also the venue of several sports competitions including water polo, water jousting, water ski, water skateboarding, speedboat and yachting regatta.

An Early End to the Expo

As a result of the war, the Expo, which was originally scheduled to close in November, ended early, in September. After the event, the Expo site was transformed into the Droixhe residential area. It was the fact that the Expo area was designed with greenery, roads, parks and other facilities in mind that resulted in a smooth post-Expo transformation and urbanization process of the area.

主题：水的艺术
举办地：比利时列日
类型：专业类世博会
日期：1939年5月20日至9月2日
占地（公顷）：50
参展方（个）：8

城市化

1936年，为了拓展列日及其所在的瓦隆地区的影响力，当地发起大列日运动。1939年，列日举办专业类世博会，由此掀开瓦隆地区发展的序幕。现代主义建筑师乔治·德多亚尔规划了世博园区。他以城市化为原则，在设计时考虑到技术、社会、文化等各个层面。法国著名建筑杂志《今日建筑》称赞他成功打造了一个全新的区域，并认为其中的建筑体现出一种『有秩序的宏伟』之感。

水的艺术

1939年列日世博会以水资源管理为主题，展现了水在供给能源、促进发展、开展合作等方面的重要作用。为契合水的主题，园区里设有一座『水上剧场』，游客可以欣赏到60米高的瀑布以及射程100米的水射流。这届世博会还举办了许多与水有关的体育比赛，比如水球、水战、水上滑板、快艇和帆船赛等。

提前结束的世博会

受战争影响，原本计划11月闭幕的世博会提前至9月结束。会后，世博园区被改造为德鲁克斯住宅区。正是因为世博园区在设计之初就将绿化、道路、公园等设施规划其中，使得后世博的改造极为便利，在这一区域轻松地实现了城市化。

1939年列日世博会的中心区域
照片，1939年

246 The Heartland of Expo 1939 Liege
1939. Photo.

EXPO 1947 PARIS

巴黎
世博会

Theme: **Urbanism and Housing**
Location: **Paris, France**
Category: **Specialised Expo**
Dates: **1947.7.10-8.15**
Area (ha): **6.35**
Participants: **14**

Post-war Challenges

After the end of the Second World War, the challenges of post-war reconstruction, especially the housing challenges, became increasingly urgent. In 1947, Paris organized a Specialized Expo in the theme of Urbanism and Housing, trying to find solutions to the housing problems.

This Expo was held in the Grand Palais, one of the venues of Expo 1900 Paris. French architect and urban planner André Herman designed a master plan for the exhibition in the Grand Palais, under which the international participants presented examples of national architecture and interiors, including housing complexes, models of furnished homes, and mass-produced furniture. In the gardens outside the pavilion, French construction-related companies also displayed prefabricated buildings.

Gathering Architecture Masters

The 14 countries participating in the Expo presented their own research and design plans on the theme of Urbanism and Housing. France presented the "Immeubles d'Etat", a model of a state-owned housing project, which was being carried out in several French cities at the time. Most of France's leading architects were participating in the Expo: modernist architect Le Corbusier presented one of his most important works, Unité d'Habitation in Marseille, and Auguste Pellet, a pioneer of modern architecture, presented his plans for a housing project in the French port city of Le Havre. In addition, Sweden exhibited prefabricated wooden houses, and Belgium presented a model of a five-bedroom apartment.

The Expo 1947 Paris promoted the development of functional architecture, where architects and urban planners from different countries exchanged experiences, shared their research results and inspired each other with innovative solutions that can be applied in the future.

主题：**城市与住房**

举办地：**法国巴黎**

类型：**专业类世博会**

日期：**1947 年 7 月 10 日至 8 月 15 日**

占地（公顷）：**6.35**

参展方（个）：**14**

战后的挑战

"二战"结束后，战后重建面临诸多挑战，随之引发的住房问题也愈发严重。1947 年，巴黎举办了一届以"城市与住房"为主题的专业类世博会，试图为此提出解决方案。

这届世博会的举办地点设在大皇宫，它曾经是 1900 年巴黎世博会的场馆之一。法国建筑师和城市规划师安德烈·赫尔曼对大皇宫内的展示做出总体规划，各参展方在此规划下展示建筑与室内装修案例，包括住房建筑群、配备家具的住宅模型，以及量产化的家具等。在馆外花园里，法国建筑相关企业还展示了预制建筑。

建筑大师云集

14 个参展方围绕城市与住房这一主题提出各自的研究成果和设计规划。法国展示了国有住宅项目的模型，这个项目当时正在多个法国城市开展。法国顶尖的建筑师大都参加了这届世博会：现代主义建筑大师勒·柯布西耶展示了他最重要的作品之一——马赛公寓，现代建筑先驱奥古斯特·佩雷展示了他设计的法国港口城市勒阿弗尔的住宅项目规划。另外，瑞典展示了预制木屋，比利时展示了五居室公寓模型。

1947 年巴黎世博会推动了功能性建筑的发展，不同国家的建筑师与城市规划师通过世博会的平台交流经验、分享研究成果，彼此激发可以在未来应用的创新方案。

展区主要结构

照片,1947年,法国重建与城市规划部(1944年至1958年)档案

Main Construction of Exhibition Area
1947. France. Ministère de la Reconstruction et de l'Urbanisme (1944–1958). Photo

EXPO 1949 STOCKHOLM

斯德哥尔摩世博会

Theme: **Sport and Physical Culture**
Location: **Stockholm, Sweden**
Category: **Specialised Expo**
Dates: **1949.7.27-8.13**
Participants: **14**

Non-competitive Expo

To commemorate the 110th anniversary of the death of Pehr Henrik Ling, the founder of Swedish gymnastics and an advocate of physical education, Stockholm hosted a Specialized Expo in 1949.

Unlike the Olympic Games, Expo 1949 was an event that did not aim at competition and emphasized collective participation in gymnastics. It was opposed to the popular concept of the sport at the time, which emphasized competition and was dominated by elitism. In an era of technological development, especially the invention of the automobile which made people increasingly lacking in sports, the organizer hoped that this Expo could stimulate people's interest in sports, promote their health, and allow sports to play a positive role in sharing, communicating, and promoting unity.

World Gymnastics Festival

The site of the Expo was the Stockholm Stadium, which was built for the 1912 Olympic Games. Shortly after the opening of the Expo, a four-day World Gymnastics Festival was held, with 14,000 gymnasts from all over the world performing a series of group demonstrations and performances.

Inspired by the Expo, the FIG held a congress during the Expo, at which the Dutch delegates proposed the idea of organizing an international gymnastics festival on a regular basis. The following year, the FIG approved this proposal, and in 1953, the first World Gymnaestrada was held in Rotterdam, the Netherlands, and since then it has been held every four years. In a way, the World Gymnaestrada succeeded the original intention of the Expo 1949 Stockholm, which was to focus on collective participation rather than winning medals.

主题：**运动和体育文化**

举办地：**瑞典斯德哥尔摩**

类型：**专业类世博会**

日期：**1949年7月27日至8月13日**

参展方（个）：**14**

不为奖牌的比赛

为纪念瑞典体操创始人、体育教育倡导者佩尔·亨里克·林逝世110周年，斯德哥尔摩在1949年举办了一届专业类世博会。

与奥运会不同，1949年世博会是一个不以竞争为目的、重在集体参与的体操的盛会。它反对当时流行的强调竞争，以精英化为主导的运动理念。科技的发展，特别是汽车的发明让人们越来越缺乏运动，组织者希望这届世博会能够激发人们对运动的兴趣，促进人们的健康，让体育发挥分享、沟通、增进团结的积极作用。

世界体操节

这届世博会的会址设在斯德哥尔摩体育场，它是为1912年奥运会兴建的场馆。世博会开幕不久后便举行了为期四天的世界体操节，来自世界各地的1.4万名体操运动员进行了一系列的集体展示和表演。

国际体操联合会在世博会期间召开了代表大会，在会上提出定期举办国际性的体操节的想法。第二年，国际体操联合会批准了这一提议。1953年，第一届世界体操节在荷兰鹿特丹举办，之后每四年举办一次。从某种程度上说，世界体操节继承了1949年斯德哥尔摩世博会，它依旧保持1949年时的初心，重在集体参与，而非赢得奖牌。

体操选手在 1949 年斯德哥尔摩世博会上进行展示和表演照片,1949 年

he gymnasts put on a range of collective displays and performances at Expo.
949. Photo.

257

1949年斯德哥尔摩世博会开幕式
照片，1949年

Opening Ceremony of Expo 1949 Stockholm
1949. Photo.

EXPO 1949 LYON

里昂世博会

Theme: **Rural Habitat**
Location: **Lyon, France**
Category: **Specialised Expo**
Dates: **1949.9.24-10.9**
Area (ha): **110**

Better Rural Area and Agriculture

In 1949, Lyon hosted a Specialised Expo on the theme of "Rural Habitat and Agricultural Machinery." On the opening day of the Expo, a number of dignitaries from the Netherlands, the United Kingdom, the United States and other countries attended the opening ceremony. Édouard Herriot, President of the French Council of Ministers, delivered a speech at the opening ceremony with the keynote of the future of agriculture in a technological world.

The Expo is located in the famous grounds of "Foire de Lyon", covering an area of 110,000m^2 The "Foire de Lyon" is one of the oldest trade fairs in France, dating back to the Middle Ages, and has attracted traders from all over Europe for centuries.

In response to the challenges, the Expo offered solutions in various areas, such as agricultural firefighting, new ways to increase agricultural yields, agriculture in the age of industrialization, and advances in weather forecasting. The Expo also featured a number of theme days and a series of conferences to discuss the related topics. The highlights of this Expo were the helicopter show in the center of the site, the French Wine Pavilion, and displayed a replica of modern farms, reflecting the latest technological innovations in agriculture at the time.

主题：**农村人居环境**
举办地：**法国里昂**
类型：**专业类世博会**
日期：**1949 年 9 月 24 日至 10 月 9 日**
参展方（个）：**110**

更好的农村和农业

1949 年，法国里昂举办了一届以农村人居环境和农业机械为主要展示内容的专业类世博会。世博会开幕当天，荷兰、英国、美国等多国政要出席了开幕式。法国部长理事会主席爱德华·赫里欧在开幕式上以技术世界中农业的未来为主旨发表致辞。世博会选址在著名的里昂博览会场馆内，占地 12 万平方米。里昂博览会是法国最古老的商贸集会地之一，它的历史可追溯至中世纪，数百年来一直吸引着欧洲各地的商人。

为应对农业面临的挑战，这届世博会从各个不同的方面提出解决方案，比如农业消防、提高农业产量的新方法、工业化时代的农业以及天气预报方面的进展。世博会同时还设立了若干主题日，举办系列会议共同讨论相关议题。这届世博会上的亮点是位于场地中心的直升机表演、法国葡萄酒馆以及有关现代农场的展示，体现了当时最新的农业技术创新。

1949年里昂世博会选址在里昂博览会场馆内,这是法国最古老的商贸集会地之一,其历史可追溯至中世纪

照片,1949年

The Expo site was located on the grounds of the 'Foire de Lyon', one of France's oldest marketplaces, dating back to the Middle Ages.
1949. Photo.

EXPO 1949 PORT-AU-PRINCE

太子港世博会

Theme:
The Festival of Peace
Location:
Port-au-Prince, Haiti
Category:
World Expo
Dates:
1949.12.8-1950.6.8
Area (ha): **24**
Visitors: **250,000**
Participants: **18**

Travel to Haiti

To celebrate the bicentennial anniversary of the founding of Port-au-Prince, Haiti hosted the Expo in 1949, giving the country an opportunity to attract international attention and develop the country's tourism industry, as well as to modernize the city and transform the area of Port-au-Prince (known as the Gonave Bay area). In preparation for this Expo, Haiti created its Department of Tourism in 1947 and launched a massive promotional campaign for the United States and across Latin America. At the same time, more than a dozen new hotels were built, and the city was sanitized and cleaned in preparation for visitors.

Palm Trees and Modernist Architecture

The site of the Expo was located in the Gonave Bay area, covering an area of 24 hectare. New York-based architect August Schmiedigen, who had worked at Expo 1937 Paris and Expo 1939 New York, was responsible for the construction of the Expo site. On the boulevard full of palm trees, named in honour of the United State President Harry Truman, Art Nouveau buildings were erected with colorful murals depicting life in Haiti. These pavilions were preserved as government offices and became permanent structures in Port-au-Prince.

The Expo eventually welcomed 250,000 visitors, with the Botanical Gardens, the Tropical Aquarium, and the "Les Palmistes" Park popular with tourists. The Haitian National Folklore Troupe performed in the outdoor Voodoo amphitheater, and Haitian artifacts were on display at the Expo, all of which are unique and proud of Haiti's culture.

主题：**和平的节日**
举办地：**海地太子港**
类型：**综合类世博会**
日期：**1949年12月8日至1950年6月8日**
占地（公顷）：**24**
参观者（人次）：**250,000**
参展方（个）：**18**

去海地旅游

为庆祝太子港建立200周年，1949年，海地举办了世博会。这届世博会为海地提供了一个吸引国际社会关注以及发展海地旅游业的机会，海地也借此实现了城市现代化以及太子港所在的戈纳夫湾地区的改造。为筹办世博会，海地在1947年成立了旅游部，面向美国和整个拉丁美洲开展大规模的宣传活动。同时，海地新建十多家酒店，完善城市卫生与清洁，做好迎接游客的准备。

棕榈树与现代主义建筑

世博会选址在戈纳夫湾海滨，占地24公顷。来自纽约的建筑师奥古斯特·施密迪根负责园区的建造，他曾参与过1937年巴黎世博会和1939年纽约世博会。在以美国总统杜鲁门命名的棕榈树大道上，新艺术风格建筑林立，建筑表面均饰以描绘海地生活的彩色壁画。这些展馆会后作为政府办公楼被保留下来，成为太子港永久性建筑。

世博会最终迎来了25万游客，植物园、热带水族馆和棕榈树公园等受到游客欢迎。海地国家民俗艺术团在露天剧场进行了表演，海地文物也在这届世博会上展出，这些都是海地引以为傲的独特文化。

1949年太子港世博会园区手绘图
印刷品，1949年

Perspective Drawing of Expo Site
1949. Print.

旅游馆手绘图
印刷品,1949年

Sketch of Tourism Pavilion
1949. Print.

EXPO 1951 LILLE

里尔世博会

Theme: **Textile**
Location: **Lille, France**
Category: **Specialised Expo**
Dates: **1951.4.28-5.20**
Area (ha): **15**
Visitors: **1,500,000**
Participants: **24**

Textile Industry Gathering

[Lil]le, the center of the French textile industry, hosted a Specialised [Ex]po in 1951, which attracted more than 1.5 million visitors from all [ov]er the world, even though it was only open for three weeks. The [sit]e of the Expo was the Grand Palais de la Foire de Lille, which at the [ti]me had the largest pillar-free interior in Europe. It had been severely [da]maged during World War II, but was renovated in Lille for the Expo.

New Materials and Methods

[As] an international meeting place for the textile industry, this Expo [pr]ovided a platform for textile suppliers and designers to exchange [id]eas. The international participants presented production, expertise [an]d industrial achievements in textile machinery, dyes and finished [pr]oducts. Italy demonstrated the production of cotton and linen [fa]brics, as well as an artificial "thermo-fabrics". Japan showcased the [sim]ple and cost-effective mass production of garments from cotton [an]d rayon.

[Du]ring the Expo period, several theme days were set up, with separate [ev]ents dedicated to silk, rayon, nylon, wool and cotton. Debates, such [as] those organized by the General Assembly of the Wool Committee [or] the Cotton Union, were also held, creating opportunities for [ex]change between producers, designers and users. In addition to this, [th]e Expo demonstrated the multiple uses of fabrics in different fields. [So]me are well known, such as in the garment industry, while others [ar]e quite innovative, such as the application of textiles in sculptures or [pa]intings.

主题：纺织
举办地：法国里尔
类型：专业类世博会
日期：1951年4月28日至5月20日
占地（公顷）：15
参观者（人次）：1,500,000
参展方（个）：24

纺织业的聚会

里尔是法国的纺织业中心。1951年，里尔举办了一届专业类世博会，虽然只开放了三周，却吸引了世界各地150多万观众。世博会的会址选在里尔博览会大皇宫，这座建筑拥有当时欧洲最大的无柱内部空间。它在"二战"期间曾遭到严重破坏，但为了举办世博会，里尔对它进行了翻新改造。

新材料和新方法

作为国际纺织业的聚集地，世博会为纺织品供应商和设计师提供了交流的平台。各参展方展示了各自的纺织生产情况、纺织专业技术以及在纺织机械、染料和成品方面的工业成就。意大利展示了棉麻织物的生产，以及一种人造的调温面料。日本展示了如何简单又经济地用棉和人造丝大批量生产服装。

世博会期内设立了多个主题日，针对丝绸、人造丝、尼龙、羊毛和棉等不同主题分别开展活动。同时，世博会还举办各种辩论会，比如羊毛委员会大会和棉花联盟组织的辩论会，为生产商、设计师和用户创造交流的契机。除此之外，世博会还展示了织物在不同领域的多种用途，有一些是众所周知的，比如服装业，而另一些则颇具创新性，比如利用纺织品进行雕塑或绘画类的艺术创作。

观众观摩纺织品制作
印刷品，1951年

Visitors watching the production of textile.
1951. Print.

EXPO 1953 ROME

罗马世博会

Theme:
Agriculture
Location:
Rome, Italy
Category:
Specialised Expo
Dates: **1953.7.26-10.31**
Area (ha): **12**
Visitors: **1,700,000**

Modern Agriculture

Agriculture was one of the major economic and social problems faced by Italy during the post-war period as the country reformed the production structure. For this reason, in 1953 Rome hosted a specialised Expo on the theme of agriculture, to demonstrate the value of agriculture and to strengthen agricultural trade links through the presentation of modern and efficient agricultural practices.

The main building of this Expo covered 12 hectares and 190 hectares of outdoor exhibition space. The venue was divided into zones showcasing a range of agriculture-related elements, including agricultural irrigation systems, farm property and loans, cereal and maize production systems, agricultural machinery, and animal husbandry. The international section showcased different types of agricultural production from around the world. These vivid and realistic displays offered visitors a good opportunity to understand the modern agriculture. In addition to showcasing agricultural technology, various cultural events were organized throughout this Expo, including agricultural film festivals, art exhibitions, and national or international forums.

Legacy of the Expo

Expo 1953 Rome welcomed over 1.7 million people. Due to the great success of the Expo on the political, economic and cultural levels, Rome decided to adopt the model of this experience by organizing such agricultural expositions on a regular basis.

主题：**农业**
举办地：**意大利罗马**
类型：**专业类世博会**
日期：**1953 年 7 月 26 日至 10 月 31 日**
占地（公顷）：**12**
参观者（人次）：**1,700,000**

现代农业

进行战后生产结构改革时，农业是意大利面临的主要经济与社会问题之一。因此，罗马在 1953 年举办了一次以「农业」为主题的专业类世博会。这届世博会通过展示现代高效的农业生产实践，体现农业价值，加强农业贸易联系。

这届世博会的主建筑占地 12 公顷，除之外还有 190 公顷的户外展示空间。会场分为几个区域，展示一系列与农业有关的内容，包括农业灌溉系统、农场财产和贷款、谷物和玉米生产系统、农业机械以及畜牧业。国际展区展示了世界各地不同类型的农业生产。这些生动真实的展示让观众充分了解了何为现代农业。除了展示农业技术，世博会还组织了各种文化活动，包括农业电影节、艺术展以及国内或国际论坛。

世博遗产

1953 年罗马世博会的参观量达到了 170 万。由于世博会在政治、经济和文化层面都获得了极大成功，罗马决定延续这一经验模式，经常性地召开此类农业博览会。

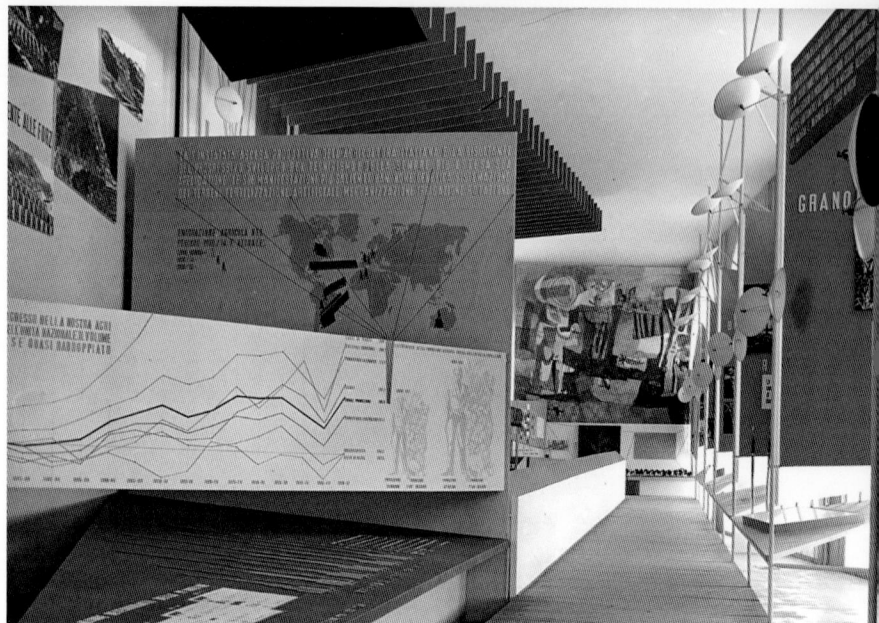

展览区域
照片,1953 年

Exhibition Area
1953. Photo.

EXPO 1953 JERUSALEM

耶路撒冷
世博会

Theme: **Conquest of the Desert**
Location: **Jerusalem**
Category: **Specialised Expo**
Dates: **1953.9.22-10.14**
Area (ha): **4.6**
Visitors: **600,000**
Participants: **13**

Conquest of the Desert

Under the name of Conquest of the Desert, Jerusalem hosted a specialised Expo in 1953, focusing on the development of desert areas and the settlement of populations. It explored how to conquer the desert for food and living space in the face of a growing population. In addition to scientific conferences on desert issues, the organizers added a cultural dimension to the Expo by arranging concerts and open-air performances in the evenings.

Apart from the participating countries, intergovernmental organizations such as UNESCO and the World Health Organization also took part in this Expo.

主题：**征服沙漠**
举办地：**耶路撒冷**
类型：**专业类世博会**
日期：**1953年9月22日至10月14日**
占地（公顷）：**4.6**
参观者（人次）：**600,000**
参展方（个）：**13**

征服沙漠

1953年，耶路撒冷举办了一届专业类世博会。这届世博会以沙漠地区的开发以及人口定居为议题，探讨了如何在人口日益增长的情况下，征服沙漠，赢得食物与住所。除了围绕沙漠问题举办各类科学会议，组织者在夜晚还安排了音乐会和露天戏剧表演，为这届世博会增加了文化色彩。联合国教科文组织、世界卫生组织等政府间组织也参加了此次世博会。

1953年耶路撒冷世博会场地:耶路撒冷会议中心
印刷品,1953年

Expo Avenue: Jerusalem Convention Center
1953. Print.

EXPO 1954 NAPLES

那不勒斯世博会

Theme:
Navigation
Location:
Naples, Italy
Category:
Specialised Expo
Dates: **1954.5.15-10.15**
Area (ha): **100**
Participants: **25**

Conquering the Seas

Expo 1954 Naples, also named as International Exhibition of Navigation, was held under the theme of Navigation, and focused on the topic of maritime industry in the age of globalization. The Expo dealt with various aspects of the maritime industry, such as global navigation technology, nautical instruments and equipment, sea transport, seafood, fishing and sea sports. As fishing was an important industry in southern Italy, the fishing section of the Expo attracted specialists and visitors, showcasing the latest fishing equipment and new systems for storing, distributing and displaying seafood. In addition to a wide range of models, a real ship and a lighthouse were on display at this Expo. The lighthouse was lit up at nighttime and put on a light show every evening.

Technology and Culture

Two important conferences were held during the Expo: the International Congress on Marine Technology and Navigation, which discussed how to improve navigation equipment at sea, with a focus on radar equipment, and the International Ethnography Conference, which explored the importance of the sea in the folk cultures of different countries.

Legacy of the Expo

The main building of this Expo, the Mostrad'Oltremare, is still in use today. The venue has an in-house fitness center and swimming pool, and often hosts Italian national and international sporting events.

主题：**航海**

举办地：**意大利那不勒斯**

类型：**专业类世博会**

日期：**1954年5月15日至10月15日**

占地（公顷）：**100**

参展方（个）：**25**

征服海洋

1954年那不勒斯世博会的主题是"航海"，旨在展示全球化时代下的航运业。世博会的展览内容涉及航运业的各个方面，比如全球导航技术、航海仪器与设备、海上运输、海产品、渔业以及海上运动等。由于渔业是意大利南部的重要产业，因此这届世博会上的渔业展区格外引人注目，展示了最新的捕鱼设备以及用于储存、分发和展示海产品的新系统，吸引了不少专业人士及普通观众。除了各式各样的模型，这届世博会上还展出了一艘真实的船和一座灯塔。灯塔每晚都会亮起，在园区内上演一场灯光秀。

技术与文化

世博会举行了两次重要会议：一次是国际海洋技术与导航大会，讨论如何改进海上导航设备，重点是雷达设备；另一次是国际人种学会议，探讨了海洋在不同国家民间文化中的重要性。

世博遗产

这届世博会的主建筑国际展览中心至今仍在使用。场馆内部设有健身中心和游泳池，经常举办意大利国内或国际体育赛事。

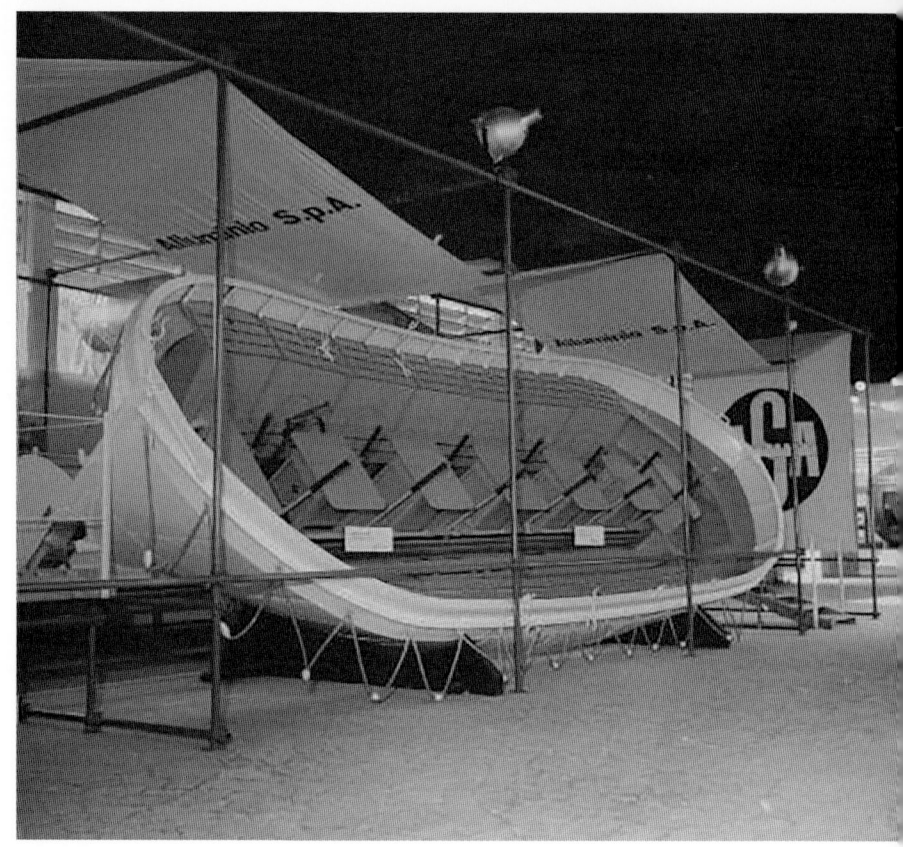

1954年那不勒斯世博会上展示的航海工具
照片，1954年

Navigation Equipment Display
1954. Photo.

EXPO 1955 TURIN

都林世博会

Theme:
Sport
Location:
Turin, Italy
Category:
Specialised Expo
Dates: **1955.5.25-6.19**
Visitors: **120,000**
Participants: **11**

Competition and Contest

Expo 1955 Turin was the third Specialized Expo that Italy hosted in a row, the first two being Expo 1953 Rome and Expo 1954 Naples. The theme of the Expo was sport, reflecting the increasingly important role that sport was playing in society and culture at the time. The Minister of State for Events, Tourism and Sport, Giovanni Ponti, addressed the opening ceremony of the Expo, stating: "If assertions and competitions should exist among Nations, they are in the fields of Art, Science and Sport." Eleven countries participated in the Expo, each with its own section, competed for medals in the areas of running, gymnastics, cycling, boxing, rowing and power boating.

Beyond Sports

The whole city of Turin was mobilized to participate in the organization of the Expo. Over the course of three weeks, the Expo attracted 120,000 visitors from Italy and other countries. Many visitors, as well as Turin residents, took part in the sports activities organized during the event. In addition to this, this Expo organized various events related to culture and sports, for instance, sports fashion shows at the Valentino Palace and movie festivals and projections of sports documentaries, attracting large numbers of visitors. After the event, people in Turin expected another Expo with the theme of sports in Turin.

主题：体育运动
举办地：意大利都灵
类型：专业类世博会
日期：1955 年 5 月 25 日至 6 月 19 日
参观者（人次）：120,000
参展方（个）：11

竞争与较量

1955 年都灵世博会是意大利连续第三年举办专业类世博会，前两次分别是 1953 年罗马世博会和 1954 年那不勒斯世博会。这届世博会以「体育运动」为主题，反映了当时体育运动在社会文化中发挥的越来越重要的作用。负责活动、旅游和体育事务的国务部长乔瓦尼·庞蒂在世博会开幕式上致辞，他说：「如果国家之间必须存在竞争和较量的话，那就应该在艺术、科学和体育领域内进行。」11 个国家参展了这届世博会，每个国家都设有自己的展区，并且在跑步、体操、自行车、拳击、赛艇和摩托艇等多个运动项目中角逐奖牌。

不只是体育

都灵全城的力量都被调动起来参与这届世博会的组织工作。在为期三周的时间里，世博会吸引了来自意大利以及其他国家的 12 万名游客。许多游客以及都灵本地居民都参加了会期内组织的体育活动。除此之外，世博会还举办了各种与体育有关的文化活动，例如在瓦伦蒂诺城堡举行体育时装表演、举办电影节放映体育纪录片等。这些活动都吸引了大批量的游客前来观看。人们热情高涨，急切呼吁在都灵再举办一次以体育为主题的世博会。

F.I.PA.B. SOFTBAL

意大利棒球垒球协会展区
照片，1955年

Exhibition Area of FIPAB
1955. Photo.

EXPO 1955 HELSINGBORG

赫尔辛堡世博会

Theme:
Modern Man in the Environment
Location:
Helsingborg, Sweden
Category:
Specialised Expo
Dates: **1955.6.10-8.28**
Participants: **10**

Great Show for Architects

This Specialised Expo held in Helsingborg, Sweden, in 1955, known as H55, was an exhibition of architecture, industrial design, and home furnishing. Under the theme of "The Modern Man in the Environment," it focused on modern design and architecture, emphasizing that even everyday objects, while enhancing their utility, should also realize the beauty of form as much as possible.

For many internationally renowned architects and designers, Expo1955 was a great show of experimentation. The French modernist architect Le Corbusier presented one of his most important works, the "Radiant City" in Marseille, as showcased at the Expo 1947 Paris. Finnish architect Alvar Aalto presented a minimalist apartment in Berlin. The Swedish Association of Architects presented models and pictures of urban development plans, as well as buildings of various structures and uses made of different building materials, for instance a collapsible house. Swedish furniture designer Björn Hultén presented his minimalist masterpiece—"H55 Lounge Chair".

The Most Successful Invention

A small but important invention at this Expo was the packing system design by Tetra Pak. In its triangular shape, this packing system was developed by the Swedish company Tetra Pak, was cheap and practice. Since its invention in the 1950s, it has been widely used in the milk product industry till now, this technology remains in extensive use.

主题：现代人类与环境
举办地：瑞典赫尔辛堡
类型：专业类世博会
日期：1955年6月10日至8月28日
参展方（个）：10

建筑师的乐园

1955年在瑞典赫尔辛堡举办的专业类世博会，被称为"H55"，是一次关于建筑、工业设计和家居的博览会。它以『现代人类与环境』为主题，重点展示现代设计与建筑，强调即便是日常用品，在提高实用性的同时也要尽可能实现形式之美。

对于众多国际知名建筑师和设计师来说，1955年的这届世博会是一个名副其实的实验乐园。法国现代主义建筑大师勒·柯布西耶展示了他最重要的作品之一——光辉城市（1947年巴黎世博会上他曾展示过另一件作品——马赛公寓）。芬兰著名建筑师阿尔瓦·阿尔托展示了他在柏林的一个设计项目——一套极简主义风格的公寓。瑞典建筑师协会展示了城市发展规划的模型和图片，以及采用不同建筑材料建造的各种结构和用途的建筑，其中还包含了一套可拆装的房屋。瑞典家具设计师比约恩·胡尔滕则展示了他的极简主义代表作——H55躺椅。

最成功的小发明

这届世博会上还展出了一项虽然小却十分重要的发明，那就是瑞典利乐公司用的三角锥形的利乐包装。利乐包装既便宜又实用，是一种保存牛奶等液体食品的创新技术，20世纪50年代发明后在整个乳制品行业推广。直至今天，这个70年前诞生的技术依然为我们日常所用。

1955 年赫尔辛堡世博会上展示的现代化厨房
照片,1955 年

1955年赫尔辛堡世博会上展示的客厅
照片，1955年

Home in Sweden: Living Room
1955. Photo.

EXPO 1956 BEIT DAGON

贝特达贡世博会

Theme:
Citrus
Location:
Beit Dagon, Israel
Category:
Specialised Expo
Dates: **1956.5.21-6.20**
Area (ha): **55**

Citrus Industry

In 1956, the specialized expo of Citriculture was organized in Beit Dagon. 250 to 300 delegates from more than 20 countries participated in the Expo. This Expo provided Israel with an opportunity to establish long-term trade cooperation with the international industry. Delegates from Mediterranean countries such as Spain, France, Morocco, Tunisia, as well as the USSR, Great Britain, New Zealand and Brazil participated in this Expo, covering both export and import industries of citrus.

The Expo was divided into three sections: the national production section, with exhibitors including the Israeli Ministry of Agriculture, the Citrus Marketing Board, and Agricultural Research Stations; the industrial section, featuring citrus production machinery and related materials; and the citrus export section. In addition, the Expo covered related industries, including essential oils, general citrus products and related equipment and machinery.

主题：**柑橘**

举办地：**以色列贝特达贡**

类型：**专业类世博会**

日期：**1956年5月21日至6月20日**

占地（公顷）：**55**

柑橘产业

1956年，贝特达贡举办了一届以柑橘栽培为主题的世博会。来自20多个国家的250至300名代表参加了这届世博会。这次世博会为以色列提供了与国际产业建立长期贸易合作的机会。柑橘产业出口国和进口国都派代表参加了此次世博会，包括西班牙、法国、摩洛哥、突尼斯等地中海国家以及苏联、英国、新西兰和巴西。

这届世博会分为三个部分：第一部分是国家生产展区，参展单位包括以色列农业部、柑橘营销委员会和农业研究站；第二部分是工业展区，展示柑橘生产器械和相关材料；第三部分是柑橘出口展区。另外，世博会还讨论了相关衍生行业的问题，比如精油、柑橘类产品以及相关设备和机械。

MEDITERRANEAN SEA

TEL AVIV

DAY OF ISSUE

1956年贝特达贡世博会纪念邮票，1956年

314 The Commemorative Stamp of Expo 1956 Beit Dagon
1956. Stamp.

EXPO 1957 BERLIN

柏林世博会

Theme: **Reconstruction of Hansa District**
Location: **Berlin, Germany**
Category: **Specialised Expo**
Dates: **1957.7.6-9.29**
Visitors: **1,000,000**
Participants: **13**

City in Ruins

In 1957, Berlin hosted the International Building Exhibition, a specialised Expo in Hansaviertel. With the theme of housing, the Expo site, where had been devastated during World War II, was in dire need of public funds to solve the housing problem. Berlin wanted to rebuild Hansaviertel with an Expo that would draw international attention to West Berlin and showcase a modern, democratic West Germany.

Architectural Design Competition

The Organizer of the Expo invited architects by calling for proposals of a residential building or a residential area in the region. By the opening of the Expo, more than 50 internationally renowned architects participated, including Walter Gropius, founder of the Bauhaus School, Finnish architect Alvar Alto, Danish architect Arne Jacobsen, Brazilian architect Oscar Niemeyer, French architect Le Corbusier, and many other important figures in architecture. However, Le Corbusier's controversial "Unitéd'Habitation" could not be realized in Hansaviertel. After several rounds of disputes with the municipal authorities, construction of the project finally began in Charlottenburg, another district of Berlin, six months before the opening of the Expo.

Living in the City of Tomorrow

The Organizer of the Expo aimed to build a "city of tomorrow", which was visited by a million people, many of whom applied to live in the buildings after visit. However, by the end of the Expo, only 601 of the 1,160 apartment units had been completed, and in the 1990s the buildings were preserved as a historic complex and became a part of Berlin's architectural heritage.

主题：重建汉萨维特尔
举办地：德国柏林
类型：专业类世博会
日期：1957年7月6日至9月29日
参观者（人次）：1,000,000
参展方（个）：13

废墟中的城市

1957年，柏林在汉萨维特尔地区举办了一届以住房为主题的专业类世博会。汉萨维特尔地区曾在"二战"炮火中遭到毁灭性打击，战后地方政府花费大量公共资金解决住房问题。柏林希望通过举办世博会重建汉萨维特尔，吸引国际社会对西柏林的关注，展示一个现代化的、民主的西德。

建筑设计竞赛

世博会的组织者邀请建筑师参与世博会，请每人设计一栋住宅楼或一片住宅区。截至世博会开幕时，有50多位国际知名建筑师参与其中，包括包豪斯学校的创办人瓦尔特·格罗皮乌斯、芬兰建筑大师阿尔瓦·阿尔托、丹麦建筑大师安恩·雅各布森、巴西建筑大师奥斯卡·尼迈耶、法国建筑大师勒·柯布西耶等。不过，勒·柯布西耶的设计"柏林公寓"引发了争议，无法在汉萨维特尔落地。与市政当局多轮争执后，"柏林公寓"最终在世博会开幕前六个月，在柏林的另一个区夏洛滕堡动工开建。

入住明日之城

世博会组织者的目标是建造一座"明日之城"，共计100万人次参观了这届世博会。许多柏林人参观后申请入住这些建筑。不过，世博会结束时，1,160套公寓单元中仅有601套完工。20世纪90年代，这些建筑作为历史建筑群受到保护，成为德国柏林的建筑遗产。

1957年柏林世博会园区内景
照片，1957年

Interior View of Expo 1957 Berlin
1957. Photo.

EXPO 1958 BRUSSELS

布鲁塞尔世博会

Theme:
**A World View:
A New Humanism**
Location:
Brussels, Belgium
Category:
World Expo
Dates: **1958.4.17-10.19**
Area (ha): **200**
Visitors: **41,454,412**
Participants: **39**

Symbol of the Time

As the first World Expo held in Europe after World War II, all participants showcased its own technological advances and progress in improving people's well-being. However, as King Baudouin I of Belgium said in his opening speech, "technology is not enough to make a civilization, it requires a parallel development of our moral conceptions". The Expo particularly emphasized international cooperation, with a number of international pavilions reflecting achievements in different fields. For example, the International Palace of Art was dedicated to the theme "50 Years of Modern Art", the Palace of Science showcased research on atoms and crystals, and pavilions such as the Palace of International Organizations and the Palace of World Cooperation explored and emphasized the four global challenges of population, food, energy, and transportation.

Bold Architecture

The Atomium, a landmark of this Expo, consists of nine spheres whose architectural form is an iron crystal structure enlarged 165 billion times. Additionally, French architect Le Corbusier was once again involved in Expos when he designed the Philips Pavilion for the Netherlands with Greek musician Iannis Xenakis. These architectural works abandoned the symmetrical structure of monumental buildings in favor of sloping or curved shapes, a design trend that came to be known as the "58 Style".

Movable Pavilions

After the Expo, the main venues, Centenary Palace complex and the Atomium were preserved in their original sites. However, some other pavilions were relocated after the event: the Austrian and Czechoslovakian Pavilions moved back to "home", the Côte d'Or chocolate pavilion is now a disco in Willebroek, the Wood Industry Pavilion is now a sports hall in Deurne, and the Canadian Pavilion is now a school in Genk.

主题：世界视野——新人文主义
举办地：比利时布鲁塞尔
类型：综合类世博会
日期：1958年4月17日至10月19日
占地（公顷）：200
参观者（人次）：41,454,412
参展方（个）：39

一个时代的象征

这是「二战」后欧洲举办的第一个综合类世博会，各参展方都展示了自身的技术进步以及在增进民生福祉方面取得的进展。然而，正如比利时国王博杜安一世在开幕致辞中所说：「技术不足以创造文明，我们的道德观念必须得到同步发展。」这届世博会尤为强调国际合作，设立多个国际馆体现不同领域的成就。例如，国际艺术宫的主题是「现代艺术50年」，科学宫展示了原子、晶体等方面的研究，国际组织宫和世界合作宫等场馆围绕人口、粮食、能源和交通四个全球性挑战进行探讨和展示。

大胆的建筑设计

原子球是这届世博会的标志性建筑，它由九个球体组成，其建筑外形是一个放大了1,650亿倍的铁晶体结构。另外，法国建筑大师勒·柯布西耶再次参与了世博会，他与希腊音乐家伊阿尼斯·泽纳基斯共同为荷兰设计了飞利浦馆。这些建筑作品都摒弃了纪念碑式建筑的对称性结构，转而采用斜面或曲线的造型，这种设计趋势后来被称为「58风格」。

会迁徙的场馆

布鲁塞尔展览中心和原子球作为这届世博会的主场馆保留在原址，但另一些场馆在会后迁往别处：奥地利馆和捷克斯洛伐克馆都「回国」了，克特多金象巧克力馆现在是维勒布鲁克市的一家迪斯科舞厅，木材工业馆现在是德尔纳市的一家体育馆，加拿大馆现在是亨克市的一所学校。

原子球是 1958 年布鲁塞尔世博会的地标性建筑，其建筑外形是一个放大了 1,650 亿倍的铁晶体结构印刷品，1958 年，原子球艺术设计博物馆馆藏

s the landmark of Expo 1958 Brussels, the Atomium takes the form of an iron
ystal structure magnified 165 billion times.
)58. Atomium + ADAM. SABAM. Print.

展区中央是 RAMAC 巨型计算机系统,它可以用十种语言回答游客在特定主题下提出的各种问题
印刷品,1958年,《这是美国:1958年布鲁塞尔世博会美国官方指南》,世博会博物馆馆藏

The central display was the giant "RAMAC" computer system which had been set up to answer questions of visitors on specific subjects in ten languages.
This is America, Official United States Guide Book Brussels World's Fair 1958.
1958. World Expo Museum Collection. Print.

工作人员正在向游客介绍原子能如何服务社区,这一展区重点展示了美国在和平利用原子能方面的发展历程 印刷品。1958 年,《这是美国:1958 年布鲁塞尔世博会美国官方指南》,世博会博物馆馆藏

taff explaining to visitors about how atomic energy could serve the community. This exhibit nowcased the development of the United States in the peaceful use of atomic energy. his is America, Official United States Guide Book Brussels World's Fair 1958. 958. World Expo Museum Collection. Print.

成年人不能进入儿童创意中心,只能在外面观察;而孩子们在里面游戏和创作,运用想象表达自我
印刷品。1958年,《这是美国:1958年布鲁塞尔世博会美国官方指南》,世博会博物馆馆藏

The kids-only Children's Creative Center, where adults could only observe from the outside. Inside, children could play and create, using their imagination to express themselves.
This is America, Official United States Guide Book Brussels World's Fair 1958.
1958. World Expo Museum Collection. Print.

EXPO 1961 TURIN

都林
世博会

Theme: **Man and his Work**
Location: **Turin, Italy**
Category: **Specialised Expo**
Dates: **1961.5.1-10.31**
Area (ha): **50**
Visitors: **5,000,000**
Participants: **19**

.chievements of the Century

ıe theme of Expo 1961 Turin was: Man and his Work—A Century of echnological and Social Developments: Achievements and Prospects. ırin invited each participants to showcase how they had developed different fields over the past century.

Iore Advanced Construction

or this Expo, Turin built the Palazzo del Lavoro, which was an xcellent example of the advanced level of labor and construction ork of the time. The floors, columns and facades of the Palazzo del avoro were made of marble, cement, steel and glass, while the panels eparating different sections were made of mirrored stainless steel.

Iore Sophisticated Technology

ineteen countries participated in the Expo. The six member states f the European Community jointly organized an exhibition on ıe theme of "Energy Sources", which demonstrated how new echnologies could be used to make better use of energy resource, s in the case of the first offshore tidal power station, which was still nder construction at the time. The United Kingdom's exhibition ocused on scientific progress, with a wide range of exhibits, from ansportation to nuclear energy. The United States, with its theme of Technological Progress in Industry", focused on achievements in the eld of communications. The highlight of the Expo was a model of the uman brain, which demonstrated how the brain processes images nd sounds.

Iore Diverse Images

isney's popular Fiat Circarama for 360° film were received by the isitors. With a capacity of 1,000 people at a time, the film was an nmersive experience of the Italian landscape. There were also two ide-screen theaters in the Palazzo del Lavoro equipped with a system ıat allowed simultaneous interpretation in four languages.

主题：**人与工作**
举办地：**意大利都灵**
类型：**专业类世博会**
日期：**1961年5月1日至10月31日**
占地（公顷）：**50**
参观者（人次）：**5,000,000**
参展方（个）：**19**

一百年的成就

1961年都灵世博会的主题是"人与工作——回顾一个世纪的技术进步与社会发展成就并展望未来"。都灵邀请每个参展方以此为题，展现各自一百年来在不同领域的发展。

更先进的建造

为了举办这届世博会，都灵专门建造了劳动宫，而劳动宫本身就极好地体现了当时劳动力与建筑工程的先进水平。劳动宫的地面、立柱和外墙由大理石、水泥、钢筋和玻璃构成，而分隔不同区域的隔板则采用了镜面不锈钢材料。

更尖端的技术

19个国家参加了这届世博会。欧洲共同体的六个成员国联合举办了以能源为主题的展览，展示如何用新技术更好地利用能源，当时还在建设中的第一个海上潮汐发电站就是其中一个案例。英国的展示重点是科学进步，展品范围广泛，从交通到核能涉及各个方面。美国以工业技术进步为主题，主要展示通信领域取得的成就。这届世博会上最亮眼的展品是人脑模型，它向观众演示了大脑是如何处理图像和声音的。

更多元的影像

迪士尼公司推出的菲亚特360度环幕电影广受欢迎，影院可同时容纳1,000人观看意大利风光片，令观众有如身临其境。另外，劳动宫内还设有两个宽银幕影院，配备了翻译系统，可以同声传译四种语言。

劳动宫外景
照片，1961年

Outside View of the Labor Palace
1961. Photo.

展馆内景
照片,1961年

334　Interior View of the Exhibition Hall
1961. Photo.

EXPO 1962 SEATTLE

西雅图世博会

Theme:
Man in the Space Age
Location:
Seattle, United States
Category:
World Expo
Dates: **1962.4.21-10.21**
Area (ha): **30**
Visitors: **9,000,000**
Participants: **49**

Conquering the Space

Under the theme of "Man in the Space Age", Expo 1962 Seattle was organized into five zones: the World of Science, the World of the 21st Century, the World of Commerce and Industry, the World of Art and the World of Entertainment. The Expo demonstrated how scientific research was affecting American life, with the core theme of space travel.

The Space Needle

The iconic architecture, the Space Needle, designed by American architect John Graham, symbolizes space travel. With a height of 185 meters, visitors can take a space-capsule shaped elevator to the revolving restaurant at the top. In addition to the Space Needle, there were other buildings at the Expo with highly innovative designs. American architect Paul Thiry designed a futuristic stadium for the Washington State Pavilion, now known as the Key Arena. Japanese-American architect Minoru Yamazaki, designer of the World Trade Center, designed the U.S. Science Museum, now the Pacific Science Center, a perfect blend of Japanese and Gothic architectural styles.

Seeing the Future

Many exhibits related to the future were displayed at the Expo, showing how people imagine living, working, playing, and traveling in the 21st century, such as a wall-size televisions, future homes and cars, electronic libraries, working models of hydroelectric dams, clocks running on gas, and fantasies of communicating with outer space. It is worth noting that IBM exhibited the first transistorized computer at the Expo.

主题：**太空时代的人类**
举办地：**美国西雅图**
类型：**综合类世博会**
日期：**1962年4月21日至10月21日**
占地（公顷）：**30**
参观者（人次）：**9,000,000**
参展方（个）：**49**

征服太空

1962年西雅图世博会的主题是"太空时代的人类"，共分为五个展区：科学的世界、21世纪的世界、工商业的世界、艺术的世界、娱乐的世界。这届世博会展现了科学研究如何影响美国人的生活，而其中最核心的话题无疑是太空旅行。

太空针

象征太空旅行的标志性建筑物就是美国建筑师约翰·格雷厄姆设计的太空针。太空针是一个高185米的尖塔，游客可以乘坐外形酷似太空舱的电梯到达顶部的旋转餐厅。除了太空针，世博会上还有一些建筑的设计也极具创新。美国建筑师保罗·蒂里为华盛顿州馆设计了一个具有未来主义风格的体育场，也就是现在的钥匙球馆。纽约世贸双子塔的设计师，日裔美国建筑师山崎实设计了美国科学馆，也就是现在的太平洋科学中心，完美融合了日式与哥特式两种建筑风格。

看见未来

这届世博会上展出了许多与未来有关的展品，展现了人们对于21世纪生活、工作、娱乐和旅行的想象，比如屏幕像墙一样宽的电视、未来的住宅和汽车、电子图书馆、水电大坝的工作模型、用煤气运行的时钟以及畅想与外太空通信等。值得一提的是，IBM公司在这届世博会上展出了第一台晶体管计算机。

1962 年西雅图世博会园区概念图
印刷品，约 1961 年，西雅图市府档案馆馆藏

Conceptual Drawing of Expo 1962 Seattle
1961. Courtesy Seattle Municipal Archives, Vertical File 435. Print.

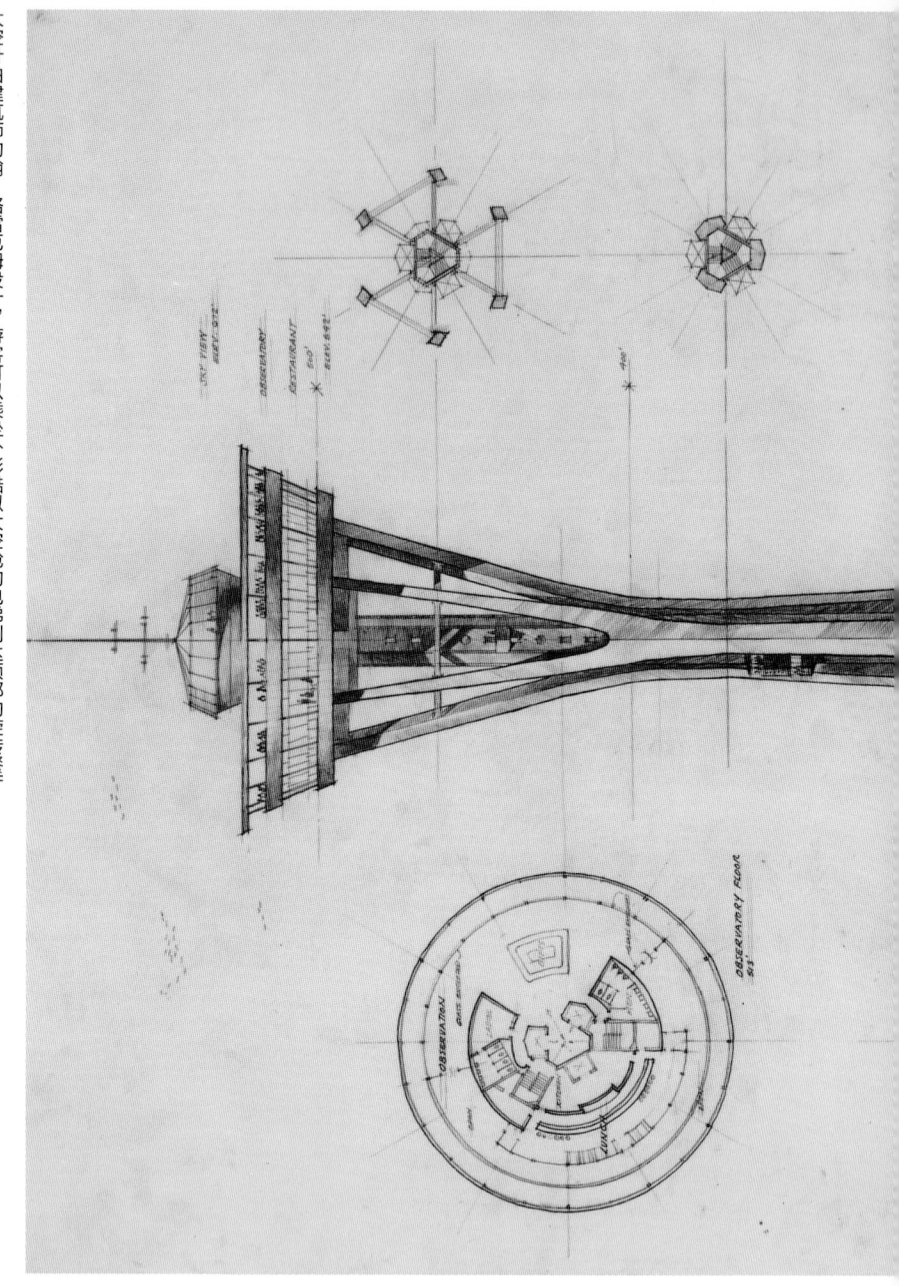

太空针由建筑师约翰·格雷厄姆设计，游客可以乘坐外形酷似太空舱的电梯到达顶部的旋转餐厅印刷品，1962年，华盛顿大学图书馆特别馆藏

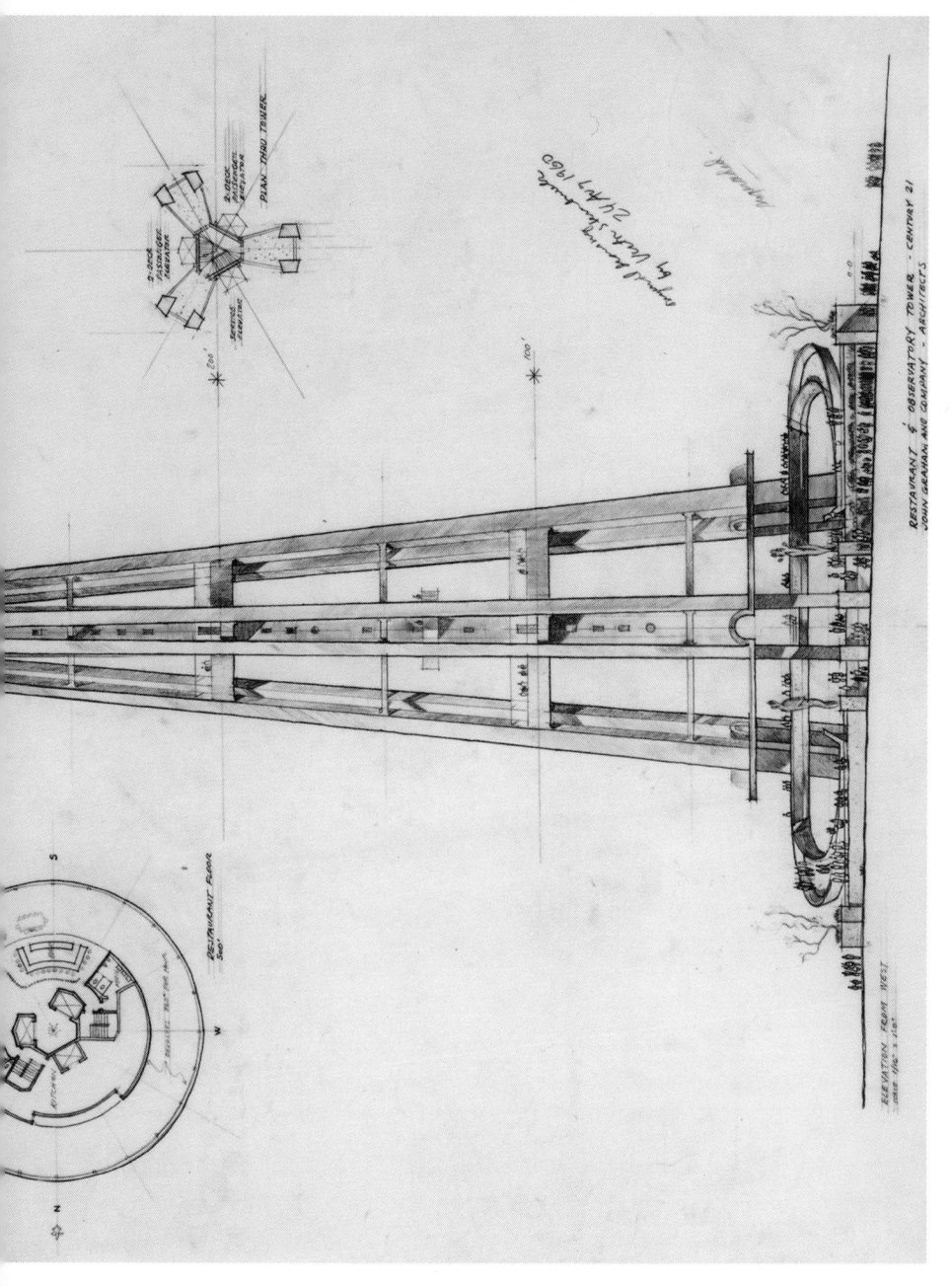

The Space Needle was designed by architect John Graham. Visitors could ride in an elevator shaped like a space capsule to reach the revolving restaurant at the top.
University of Washington Libraries, Special Collections UM14798. Print.

游客可以乘坐『宇宙飞船』模拟体验太空旅行,在此过程中感受逼真的火箭发射时的震感,并躲避流星雨的袭击印刷品,1962年5月,《生活》杂志,世博会博物馆馆藏

Visitors could experience a stimulated space travel in a "spaceship", feeling the vibrations a realistic rocket launch and dodging meteor showers.
Life. May 1962. World Expo Museum Collection. Print.

游客在美国国家航空航天局太空展区参观友谊 7 号航天器印刷品，1962 年 8 月，美国历史工业博物馆馆藏

owd viewing the Friendship 7 spacecraft at the NASA Space exhibit.
ugust 1962. MOHAI, 1987.59.131.35. Print.

1962年西雅图世博会上展出的通用汽车火鸟3号印刷品,1962年,西雅图市府档案馆馆藏

General Motors Firebird III at Expo 1962 Seattle
1962. Courtesy Seattle Municipal Archives, Item No.:78914. Print.

Theme: **Transport**
Location: **Munich, Germany**
Category: **Specialised Expo**
Dates: **1965.6.25-10.3**
Area (ha): **50**
Visitors: **2,500,000**
Participants: **31**

Modern Transportation

Expo 1965 Munich was the first Specialised Expo themed on transportation, showcasing a range of the latest transportation technologies, from space travel to high-speed rail. Surprisingly, when planning the Expo, the Organizer excluded the automotive industry, presenting car-related content only via a focus on road safety and urban mobility.

Inter-city Transport

The Expo highlighted the potential of public transportation to solve the problem of urban congestion, with themed areas devoted to road safety, urban mobility, public transportation, and the overall impact of transportation on people. The plans for the Munich subway and several models of subway trains were also displayed at the Expo, at that time the construction of the Munich subway network had only just begun. During the Expo, visitors could have the chance to take a test ride on the E03 high-speed trains between Munich and Augsburg. With a speed of 200 kilometers per hour, it was the fastest train in Germany at the time and covered the entire 62 kilometers in just 26 minutes.

Soaring into the Space

Just a few months before the opening of the Expo, the first unmanned rocket of the U.S landed on the moon. The Expo embodied the latest developments in aerospace engineering with a scale model of the Atlas, the first American manned spacecraft to orbit the Earth, and a rocket designed by Germany during World War I. Four years after the Expo, the U.S Apollo 11 made the first moon landing.

主题：交通
举办地：德国慕尼黑
类型：专业类世博会
日期：1965年6月25日至10月3日
占地（公顷）：50
参观者（人次）：2,500,000
参展方（个）：31

现代化的交通

1965年慕尼黑世博会是第一个以交通全系统为主题的专业类世博会，从太空旅行到高速铁路，展示了一系列最新的交通运输技术。不过出人意料的是，在规划这届世博会时，组织者排除了汽车行业，只在论及道路安全和城市交通时，才展示与汽车相关的内容。

在城市间驰骋

世博会着重强调了公共交通对于解决城市拥堵问题的潜力，专门设立主题展区展示道路安全、城市交通、公共交通，以及交通对人类的总体影响。世博会上还展出了慕尼黑地铁规划图和多个地铁列车模型，而当时慕尼黑地铁网络的建设才刚刚开始。世博会期间，游客还可以试乘慕尼黑至奥格斯堡的E03高速列车。列车时速200千米，是德国当时最快的列车，全程62千米只需26分钟即可到达。

在太空里翱翔

就在这届世博会开幕前几个月，美国第一枚无人驾驶火箭登上月球。这届世博会体现了航空航天工程的最新发展，展示了同比例大小的美国第一艘绕地球轨道飞行的载人航天器『阿特拉斯』的模型，以及德国在『一战』期间设计的火箭。这届世博会结束四年后，美国阿波罗11号实现登月。

国际宇航中心是 1965 年慕尼黑世博会的亮点,展示了航天工程领域的最新成果照片,1965 年

The International Centre of Astronautics was the highlight of the Expo 1965 Munich, showcasing the latest achievements in the field of aerospace engineering. 1965. Photo.

1965年慕尼黑世博会园区里的单轨火车
照片,1965年

Monorail in the Site of Expo 1965 Munich
1965. Photo.

EXPO 1967 MONTREAL

蒙特利尔世博会

Theme: **Man and his World**
Location: **Montreal, Canada**
Category: **World Expo**
Dates: **1967.4.28-10.29**
Area (ha): **400**
Visitors: **50,306,648**
Participants: **62**

Man and the World

Inspired by La Terre des Hommes, a collection of essays by French writer Antoine de Saint-Exupéry, author of The Little Prince, Expo 1967 Montreal chose its theme of "The Planet of Mankind". The Expo showcased scientific, technological and industrial advances, explored universal issues such as mankind's social responsibility and environmental awareness. The Organizer set up a number of thematic exhibitions based on the theme, such as Man and his Health, Man in the Community, Man and the Ocean, Man and the Space, Man the Creator, etc.

Progress of Humanity

The Expo showcased a series of significant exhibits from various countries. France displayed the results of Jacques Cousteau's underwater research discoveries, the Netherlands used a model to show the progress of the Zuiderzee project, and the Soviet Union displayed the space capsule in which Jurin Gagarin traveled, attracting 3 million visitors.

Habitat for Humanity

One of the Expo's landmarks was the Habitat 67, a residential complex of 158 standardized apartments, each of which was like a box made of reinforced concrete, providing a unique residential space for individuals in the midst of dense urban development. Another landmark was Buckminster Fuller's geodesic dome, a latticed spherical structure designed by Buckminster Fuller for the U.S. Pavilion. The Expo site was transformed into Parc Jean Drapeau, and the Fuller's dome became the Environmental Sciences Museum, and Habitat 67 became a true residential apartment.

主题：**人类与世界**
举办地：**加拿大蒙特利尔**
类型：**综合类世博会**
日期：**1967年4月28日至10月29日**
占地（公顷）：**400**
参观者（人次）：**50,306,648**
参展方（个）：**62**

人类与世界

1967年蒙特利尔世博会的主题是『人类与世界』，其灵感来源于法国作家、《小王子》的作者圣－埃克苏佩里的散文集《人类的大地》。这届世博会不仅展示了科学、技术和工业进步，还重点探讨了人类的社会责任和环保意识等普遍问题。组织者依据主题设置多个专题展，比如人类与健康、社会中的人、人类与海洋、人类与太空、人类创造者等等。

人类的进步

许多国家都有重要展品参展。法国展示了雅克·库斯托水下研究的发现成果，荷兰用模型展示了须德海围海造田工程的进展，苏联展示了宇航员加加林乘坐的太空舱，加加林是第一个进入太空的人，他乘坐的太空舱是这届世博会最受欢迎的展品之一，吸引了1,300万游客参观。

人类的栖居

栖居67是这届世博会的标志性建筑之一，它是一个由158套标准公寓组合而成的住宅建筑群，每套公寓都如同一个用钢筋混凝土打造的箱子，在密集的城市发展中为个体提供独特的住宅空间。另一个标志性建筑是巴克明斯特·富勒为美国馆设计的网格球形结构建筑——富勒球。会后，世博园区被改造为让·德拉佩奥公园，富勒球成为环境科学博物馆，栖居67成为真正的住宅公寓。

1967年蒙特利尔世博会园区鸟瞰图
印刷品，1967年，编号：P67-Y_2，蒙特利尔市档案馆馆藏

Bird's Eye View of Expo 1967 Montreal
1967. P67-Y_2. Archives de la Ville de Montréal. Print.

富勒球体现了建筑师巴克明斯特·富勒的设计理念:用最少的材料创造出最大的内部空间印刷品,1967年,摄影:日耳曼·博尚,魁北克国家图书馆与档案馆馆藏

The Buckminster Fuller's Geodesic Dome embodied the architect Buckminster Fuller's design philosophy of creating maximum interior space with minimum materials.
Photo by Germain Beauchamp. 1967. P809, S1, DBP061. Bibliothèque et Archives Nationales du Québec. Print.

栖居67的158套公寓像积木一样堆叠在一起,每套公寓都有独立的露台,以确保充足的采光与通风

印刷品,1967年,原魁北克电影局资料,魁北克国家图书馆与档案馆馆藏

he 158 apartments of Habitat 67 were stacked like building blocks. Each apartment had its
wn terrace, ensuring plenty of light and ventilation.
967. E6, S7, P6711600. Fonds Office du film du Québec. Bibliothèque et Archives Nationales du
)uébec. Print.

游客在迷宫馆的各个看台上观看加拿大国家电影局制作的多屏幕电影印刷品，1967年，国际展览局馆藏

Viewers were watching the multi-screen cinema produced by the National Film Board of Canada from a series of balconies in the Labyrinth Pavilion.
1967. BIE Archive. Print.

EXPO
1968
SAN ANTONIO
圣安东尼奥
世博会

Theme:
The Confluence of Civilizations in the Americas
Location:
San Antonio, United States
Category:
Specialised Expo
Dates: **1968.4.6-10.6**
Area (ha): **39**
Visitors: **6,384,482**
Participants: **23**

Gathering of the Western Hemisphere

As a bridge city between the United States and Latin America, the theme of Expo 1968 San Antonio was "The Confluence of Civilizations in the Americas", maximizing the participation of the countries of the Western Hemisphere. For this reason, Expo 1968 was also known as the HemisFair '68. In order to promote unity among the countries of the Americas and to make the best possible use of space, the Organizer allowed the five Central American countries and the eleven member countries of the Organization of American States to share the same venue.

New and Old buildings

The site of the park was originally a residential neighborhood, where was home to 22 historic buildings, some of which could be dated back to the 19th century with Spanish influence. The new venues, however, were built in contrast with explicit designs. The landmark is the 190-meter-high Tower of the Americas, which housed two revolving restaurant and an observation deck. The U.S. Pavilion screened a film on American cultural heritage, which was quite innovative at the time: at the beginning of the show, the audience was arranged in three separate theaters, each with a capacity of 400 people; then, as the show progressed, the walls and screens slowly rose to reveal a giant screen 43 meters wide and 12 meters high, as the largest screen in the world at the time.

Legacy of the Expo

After the Expo, the Expo site was transformed into the HemisFair Park, and many of the venues were preserved. The Henry B. Gonzales Convention Center is the most important legacy of the Expo, which allowed San Antonio to develop a successful convention industry and become a center for exchanges between the countries of the Americas.

主题：美洲文明的交汇
举办地：美国圣安东尼奥
类型：专业类世博会
日期：1968年4月6日至10月6日
占地（公顷）：39
参观者（人次）：6,384,482
参展方（个）：23

西半球的聚会

1968年圣安东尼奥世博会的主题是「美洲文明的交汇」。圣安东尼奥是连接美国和拉丁美洲的桥梁城市，世博会的组织者希望西半球国家都最大限度地参与进来。因而，这届世博会也被称为「68年半球博览会」。为了促进美洲各国的团结，也为了尽可能利用空间，世博会的组织者还让5个中美洲国家和美洲国家组织的12个成员国共用一个场馆。

新建筑和旧建筑

比较特别的是，园区所在地原本是一片住宅区，因而有22栋历史建筑保留在园区里，其中一些西班牙风格建筑的历史甚至可以追溯到19世纪。但是，新建的场馆大都采用了简洁的线条设计，两者形成鲜明对比。标志性建筑是190米高的美洲塔，塔内有旋转餐厅和观景台。美国馆放映了表现美国文化遗产的电影，其放映模式在当时颇具创新：演出开始时，观众被安排在三个独立的影院里，每个影院可容纳400人；之后伴随剧情的发展，墙面和屏幕缓缓升起，呈现出宽43米、高12米的巨型银幕，在当时堪称世界之最。

世博遗产

会后，世博园区被改造为半球博览会公园，许多场馆被保留下来。亨利·冈萨雷斯会议中心是世博会最重要的遗产，它让圣安东尼奥成功发展了会议产业，成为美洲各国之间交流的中心。

LYDA·LOTT CONSTRUCTORS

at HemisFair '68®, San Antonio, Texas . . .

1. TOWER OF THE AMERICAS
2. SAN ANTONIO CONVENTION COMPLEX
3. CHAMBER OF COMMERCE INFORMATION CENTER
4. SAN ANTONIO RIVER EXTENSION
5. FOREIGN EXHIBIT MODULES
6. LAKES AND WATERWAYS
7. MORMON CHURCH PAVILION
8. MINI-MONORAIL
• CITY PARKING GARAGE

A Joint Venture of General Contractors

DARRAGH-LYDA, INC.
AND
H. A. LOTT, INC.

DARRAGH-LYDA, INC.
SAN ANTONIO, TEXAS

H. A. LOTT, INC.
HOUSTON, TEXAS

Guide Map of Expo 1968 San Antonio
Hemisfair 1968 Official Souvenir Guidebook. 1968. World Expo Museum Collection. Print.

1968年圣安东尼奥世博会导览图印刷品，1968年，《1968年半球博览会官方纪念指南》，世博会博物馆馆藏

1968年圣安东尼奥世博会的地标性建筑之一——美洲塔印刷品，1968年，《1968年半球博览会官方纪念指南》，世博会博物馆馆藏

Tower of the Americas, one of the landmarks of Expo 1968 San Antonio. *Hemisfair 1968 Official Souvenir Guidebook*. 1968. World Expo Museum Collection. Print.

EXPO
1970
OSAKA

大阪
世博会

Theme: **Progress and Harmony for Mankind**
Location: **Osaka, Japan**
Category: **World Expo**
Dates: **1970.3.15-9.13**
Area (ha): **330**
Visitors: **64,218,770**
Participants: **77**

First Expo in Asia

In 1970, Osaka held the first World Expo in Asia. The theme of the Expo is "Progress and Harmony for Mankind", which was expressed through four sub-themes: Have a richer life and achieve better health; Utilize nature in more prosperous ways; Design a better everyday life; Mutually understand each other more deeply. The Organizer hoped to demonstrate the progress of the world's science and technology civilization, to promote world peace, to forge a consensus among mankind, and to work together with the international community to plan for a better future.

Ideal Future

The planning and architecture of the Expo site reflect the concept of futurism. Kenzo Tange and Uzo Nishiyama, the leading figures of Japan's Metabolist movement in the 1960s, planned the entire site, and Japanese art master Taro Okamoto designed the landmark building, Tower of the Sun. Renowned architects from home and abroad were practicing pioneering architectural concepts in this Expo. Corporate pavilions embodied the Japanese spirit of technology and innovation. The Fuji Pavilion, for instance, showed the first IMAX movie, whereas the Furukawa Pavilion had an appearance of a traditional pagoda, its interior showcasing state-of-the-art technology, such as voice-activated robots, cashless payment systems and an electronic "Computer Music Hall".

Realities in the Near Future

The highly experimental pavilions at the Expo inspired architects around the world. A few years later, inspired by the Metabolist architecture Takara Beautillion at the Osaka Expo, the world's first capsule hotel was created. Some of the technologies were also soon popularized around the world, such as the mobile phone and the "Washlet" toilets.

主题：**人类的进步与和谐**
举办地：**日本大阪**
类型：**综合类世博会**
日期：**1970 年 3 月 15 日至 9 月 13 日**
占地（公顷）：**330**
参观者（人次）：**64,218,770**
参展方（个）：**77**

亚洲第一次

1970 年大阪世博会是在亚洲举办的第一届世博会。这届世博会的主题是"人类的进步与和谐"，通过四个副主题得以体现："更富足和健康的生活""更多元地利用自然""更好地规划日常"和"更深入地相互理解"。世博会的组织者希望通过举办世博会，展示世界科技文明进步，促进世界和平，凝聚人类共识，与国际社会共同谋划美好的未来。

理想中的未来

世博园区的规划和建筑体现了未来主义的理念。日本 20 世纪 60 年代新陈代谢运动的领军人物丹下健三和西山夘三对整个园区进行了规划，日本艺术大师冈本太郎为园区设计了中心建筑太阳塔。许多日本国内或国际知名建筑师将世博会视为实践先锋建筑理念的试验场，日本企业馆则体现了当代日本的科技与创新精神。日本富士馆放映了第一部 IMAX 电影。古川馆的外形虽然是一座传统宝塔，但它内部展示的却是最先进的技术，比如声控机器人、无现金支付系统和电子音乐厅。

从未来到现实

世博会上极具实验风格的展馆启发着世界各地的建筑师。几年后，世界上第一家胶囊旅馆诞生，其灵感正是来源于大阪世博会上黑川纪章设计的新陈代谢派建筑宝美馆。世博会上展出的一些技术也很快在世界范围内得到普及，比如移动电话、卫洗丽智能马桶盖等。

1970年大阪世博会园区鸟瞰图
印刷品,1970年,世博会博物馆馆藏

黑川纪章为1970年大阪世博会设计了宝美馆,数年后,受宝美馆的启发,他设计出世界上第一家胶囊旅馆印刷品,1970年,世博会博物馆馆藏

At the Expo 1970 Osaka, Kisho Kurokawa designed the Takara Beautillion, which, a few years later, inspired him to design the world's first capsule hotel.
1970. World Expo Museum Collection. Print.

富士馆采用了先进的膜结构设计,1970年大阪世博会上多个同类建筑的出现,标志着膜结构时代的到来
印刷品,1970年,国际展览局馆藏

e Fuji Pavilion featured an advanced membrane structure design. Several similar uctures at the Expo 1970 Osaka signaled the era of membrane structures.
70. BIE Archive. Print.

天然气馆
印刷品，1970年，
国际展览局馆藏

378 The Gas Pavilion
1970. BIE Archive. Print.

游客在通信馆体验移动电话 1970年大阪世博会后,移动电话很快在世界范围内得到普及 印刷品,1970年,国际展览局馆藏

sitors trying cell phones at the Communications Pavilion.
ell phones quickly gained worldwide popularity after Expo 1970 Osaka.
970. BIE Archive. Print.

1970年大阪世博会上展出了人类采集的第一批月球岩石标本，月球岩石标本是当年最受欢迎的展品之一
印刷品，1970年，国际展览局馆藏

The first specimens of lunar rocks collected by man were exhibited at Expo 1970 Osaka. The lunar rocks were one of the most popular exhibits that year.
1970. BIE Archive. Print.

EXPO 1971 BUDAPEST

布达佩斯世博会

Theme: **The Hunt through the World**
Location: **Budapest, Hungary**
Category: **Specialised Expo**
Dates: **1971.8.27-9.30**
Area (ha): **35**
Visitors: **1,900,000**
Participants: **35**

Man and Nature

Expo 1971 Budapest was the first World Hunting Exhibition organized under the auspices of the Bureau International des Expositions, and the first Specialised Expo held in Eastern Europe. Hungary has a long tradition of hunting, and its national legend is also related to the hunting of stags. Budapest hoped to revive the hunting tradition by organizing this Expo, while it emphasized the relationship between man and nature, and paid attention to the protection and breeding of wild animals. With two slogans—"Nature conservation is a conservation of ourselves" and "Peace, Friendship, Nature, Health, Recreation and Sport", Budapest promoted sustainable hunting as a tool for wildlife conservation to the general public. The Wildlife Film Festival and the scientific symposiums were also organized during the Expo, leading to the signing of several international treaties, agreements and conventions on wildlife management and conservation.

New Standards

The Expo marked an important turning point for the recognition and evaluation of hunting trophies. In 1952, the International Council for Game and Wildlife Conservation (CIC) adopted a new set of internationally recognized guidelines for the measurement and evaluation of hunting trophies. The guidelines were first implemented at Expo 1971 Budapest, where hundreds of hunting trophies were evaluated by international scoring committees. To this day, the guidelines remain the recognized standard in the industry.

主题：世界狩猎
举办地：匈牙利布达佩斯
类型：专业类世博会
日期：1971 年 8 月 27 日至 9 月 30 日
占地（公顷）：35
参观者（人次）：1,900,000
参展方（个）：35

人与自然

1971 年布达佩斯世博会是国际展览局支持下举办的第一届世界狩猎博览会，也是第一届在东欧举办的专业类世博会。匈牙利有着悠久的狩猎传统，其民族传说也和狩猎雄鹿有关，因而，布达佩斯希望通过举办这届世博会，复兴狩猎的传统，但同时也强调人与自然的关系，关注野生动物的保护与饲养。布达佩斯提出两个口号——"保护自然就是保护我们自己"以及"和平、友谊、自然、健康、娱乐和体育"，把可持续狩猎作为一种保护野生动物的方式向大众推广。世博会还举办了野生动物电影节和科学研讨会，促成了多个与野生动物管理和保护有关的国际条约、协定和规范的签署。

新的标准

这届世博会对于狩猎战利品的认可与评估来说是一个重要的转折点。1952 年，国际狩猎和野生动物保护理事会颁布了一套新的国际公认的准则，用于衡量和评估狩猎战利品。这套准则在 1971 年布达佩斯世博会上第一次得到实施，相关国际评估分委员会对数百件狩猎战利品进行了评比。直至今天，这套准则依然是行业内公认的标准。

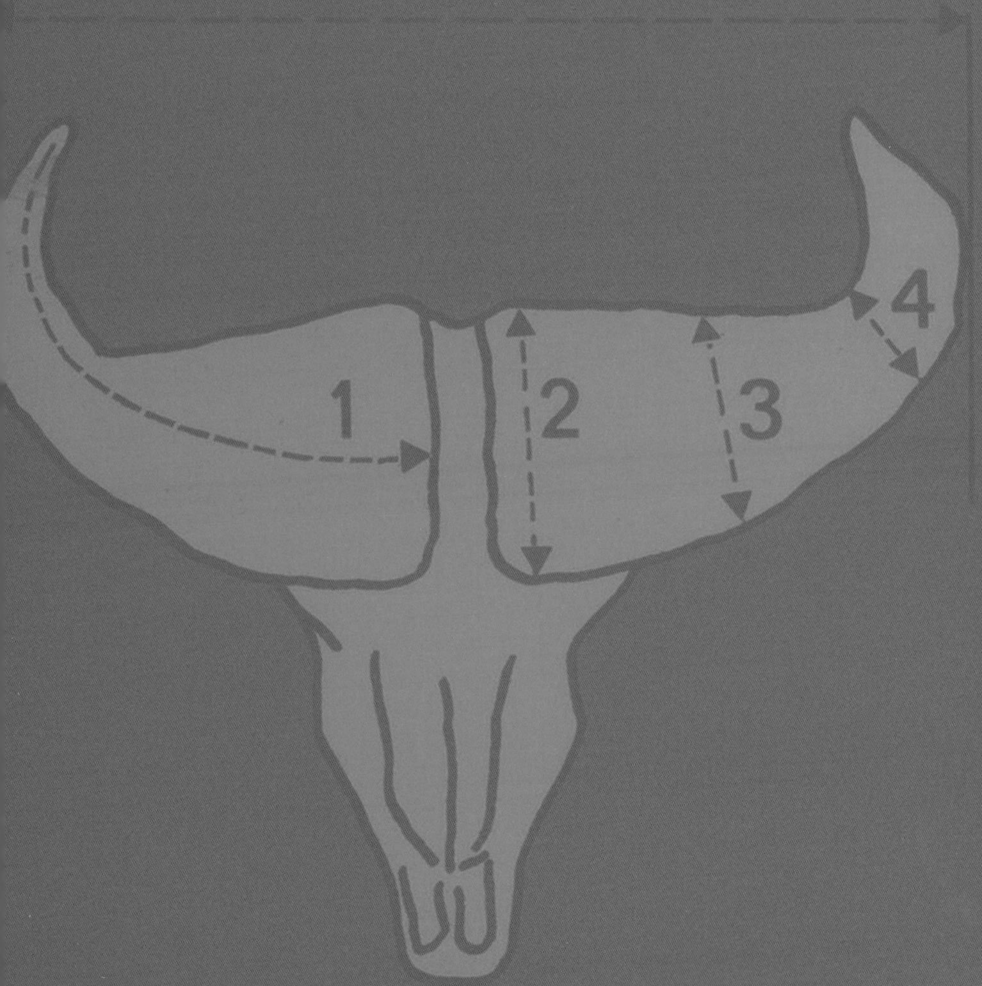

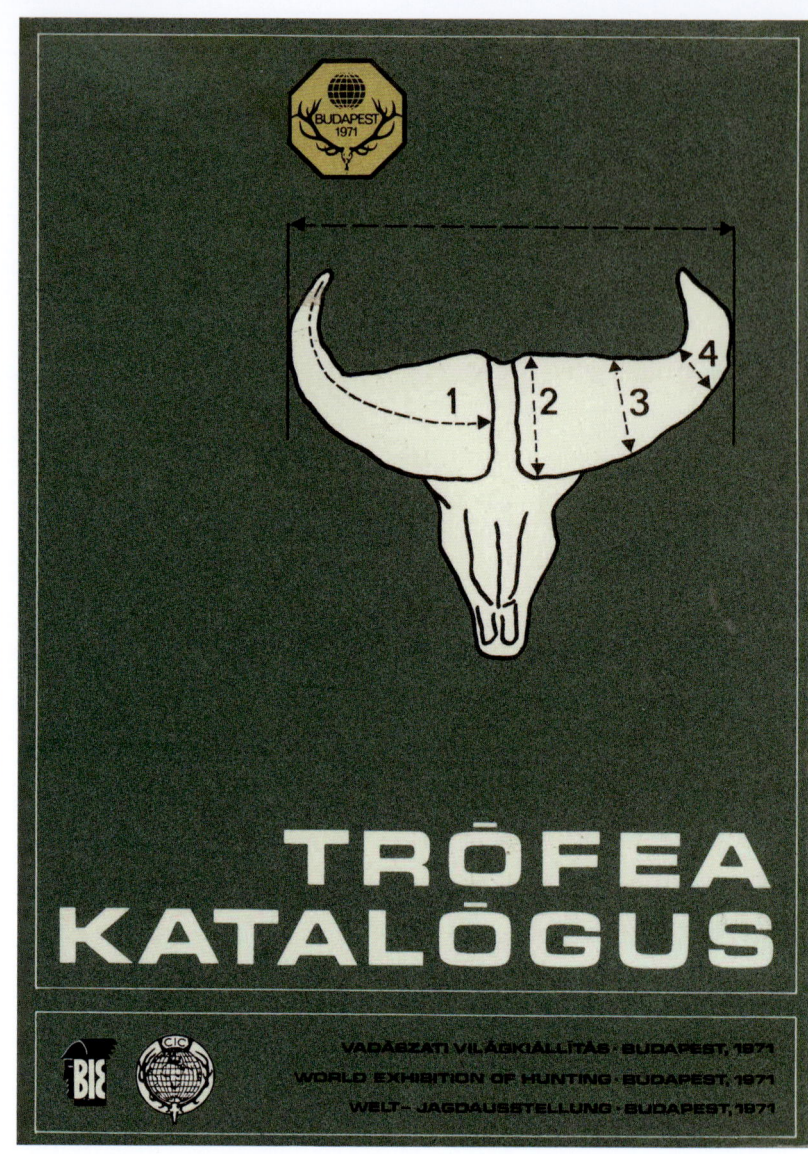

相关国际评分委员会对数百件狩猎战利品采用新准则进行了评比,这套准则从那时起一直沿用至今。1971年,《狩猎战利品目录》,世博会博物馆馆藏

Hundreds of hunting trophies were judged by the relevant international scoring committee using the new guidelines, which have been in use ever since.
TrōfeaKatalōgus. 1971. World Expo Museum Collection. Print.

EXPO 1974 SPOKANE

斯波坎
世博会

Theme: **Celebrating Tomorrow's Fresh New Environment**
Location: **Spokane, United States**
Category: **Specialised Expo**
Dates: **1974.5.4-11.2**
Area (ha): **40**
Visitors: **5,600,000**
Participants: **10**

Progress without Pollution

In 1974, a Specialised Expo was held in Spokane, Washington, USA, the first to focus on the theme of environment. The slogan of the Expo was "Progress without Pollution". Spokane's economy was dependent on extractive industries, and the local Spokane River was significantly impacted by the regional industry. By hosting the Expo, Spokane hoped to revitalize the decaying downtown area and keep pace with the economic and cultural development of the United States.

Cleaning Up the City and the River

The site of the Expo was originally a Great Northern Railroad Depot, an area long been criticized. By hosting the Expo, Spokane transformed the area and undertook a massive environmental cleanup in and around the city. On the opening day of the Expo, organizers released 1,974 trout in the Spokane River, demonstrating that Spokane's environment has improved significantly. The U.S. Pavilion was the highlight of the Expo, showcasing U.S. programs to address environmental issues and showing one of the first IMAX films, "Man Belongs to the Earth".

New Thoughts of Sustainability

At a time when environmental protection was not yet mainstream, the Expo Spokane was the first to raise concerns about sustainable development and the Earth's environment, and served as a platform for discussion of environmental issues among participating countries. This Expo also witnessed the first United Nations World Environment Day. The U.N. recognized and applauded Spokane's role in protecting the environment, and Spokane took advantage of the Expo to clean up decaying industrial buildings and revitalize its downtown. As a result, the city of Spokane has benefited from increased recognition and it saw continued economic growth.

主题：歌颂明日的崭新环境
举办地：美国斯波坎
类型：专业类世博会
日期：1974年5月4日至11月2日
占地（公顷）：40
参观者（人次）：5,600,000
参展方（个）：10

无污染的进步

1974年，在美国华盛顿州斯波坎市举行了一届专业类世博会，这是第一个以环境为主题的世博会。这届世博会的口号是『无污染的进步』。斯波坎的经济依赖于采掘业，当地的斯波坎河对区域经济具有重要影响和作用。斯波坎希望通过举办世博会，振兴颓败的市中心区域，追赶美国经济与文化发展的脚步。

清理城市与河流

世博会的所在地原本是大北方铁路车站，这一地区长期以来饱受诟病。斯波坎通过举办世博会，改造了这一地区，并对城市及其周边开展大规模环境清理。世博会开幕当天，组织者在斯波坎河放生了1,974条鳟鱼，表明斯波坎的环境治理已经得到显著改善。美国馆是这届世博会的亮点，展示了美国解决环境问题的相关计划，并放映了电影《人类属于大地》，这是世界上最早的IMAX电影之一。

领先时代的思考

在环境保护尚未成为主流认知的年代，斯波坎世博会率先提出了对可持续发展以及地球环境的关注，成为聚集各方讨论环境问题的平台。同年，在首个联合国世界环境日上，联合国认可和称赞了斯波坎世博会在环境保护方面发挥的作用，而斯波坎也借由世博会清理了破败的工业建筑，使市中心重新焕发生机。斯波坎的知名度由此不断提高，迎来经济持续增长。

1974年斯波坎世博会园区鸟瞰图
印刷品，1974年，世博会博物馆馆藏

Aerial View of Expo 1974 Spokane
1974. World Expo Museum Collection. Print.

开幕当天,1974年斯波坎世博会组织者在斯波坎河放生了1,974条鳟鱼,表明斯波坎的环境治理已经得到显著改善印刷品,1974年,《官方纪念指南》,世博会博物馆馆藏

On the opening day of the Expo, the Organisers released 1,974 trout into the Spokane River, symbolising the significant improvement in Spokane's environmental management.
Official Souvenir Program. 1974. World Expo Museum Collection. Print.

美国馆在其显著位置展示了西雅图酋长的一句名言:"大地不属于人类,而人类是属于大地的印刷品",1974年,《发言人评论报》图片档案

A quote from Chief Seattle, "The earth does not belong to man, man belongs to the earth", was displayed prominently at the U.S. Pavilion. 1974. *The Spokesman-Review.* Photo Archive. Print.

苏联馆前总是排着很长的等候参观的队伍
印刷品，1974年，《发言人评论报》图片档案

394 There was always a long line for the Show at the Soviet Pavilion.
1974. *The Spokesman-Review* Photo Archive. Print.

EXPO 1975 OKINAWA

冲绳
世博会

Theme: **The Sea We would like to See**
Location: **Okinawa, Japan**
Category: **Specialised Expo**
Dates: **1975.7.20-1976.1.18**
Area (ha): **100**
Visitors: **3,485,750**
Participants: **35**

Man and the Sea

After the great success of Expo 1970 Osaka, Japan came up with the plan to hold another Expo on the island of Okinawa. The theme of this Expo is "The sea we would like to see". The site was divided into four thematic zones: The People and History cluster showcased shipping and cultural and trade exchanges in the Pacific region; The Science and Technology cluster emphasized international cooperation and research in marine and water conservation; The Fish cluster showcased aquatic species and maritime trade; and The Ship cluster featured oceanic adventures and the Expo Port pavilion.

Instead of allowing participants to build their own pavilions, this Expo encouraged participates to rent prefabricated rectangular or hexagonal space modules, each measuring approximately 250 square meters. The USSR Pavilion was memorable, which featured the world's first large-scale map of the oceans. Another impressive pavilion was the United States Pavilion, which demonstrated ocean thermal power plants and advances in the study of ocean-atmosphere interactions.

The Future is at Sea

The landmark of the Expo 1975 Okinawa was Aquapolis, a floating city 32 meters above the sea. Designed by Japanese Metabolist architect Kiyonori Kikutake, Aquapolis was a prototype for a future ocean society. After the Expo, Aquapolis was preserved and attracted visitors for decades until 1993, when it was closed. The Expo site was transformed into the Okinawa Commemorative National Government Park, also known as Ocean Expo Memorial Park. The park contains a museum, botanical garden, and aquarium, including the Okinawa Churaumi Aquarium, which was one of the largest aquariums in the world.

主题：**我们希望看到的海洋**
举办地：**日本冲绳**
类型：**专业类世博会**
日期：**1975 年 7 月 20 日至 1976 年 1 月 18 日**
占地（公顷）：**100**
参观者（人次）：**3,485,750**
参展方（个）：**35**

人类与海洋

在 1970 年大阪世博会取得巨大成功后，日本计划在冲绳岛再次举办世博会。这届世博会的主题是"我们希望看到的海洋"。整个园区分为四个主题区：人类与海洋的历史展区展示了太平洋地区的航运和文化贸易交流；海洋科技展区强调在海洋和水资源保护方面开展国际合作与研究；渔业展区展示水生物种以及海上贸易；航运展区以海洋探险为主题，还特别设置了一个世博港。

这届世博会没有像往届那样让参展方自行建造展馆，而是鼓励各参展方租用预制的长方形或六角形空间模块，每个模块的面积约为 250 平方米。令人印象深刻的国家馆包括苏联馆和美国馆。苏联馆展示了世界上第一张大比例尺海洋地图，美国馆演示了海洋热能发电厂以及海气相互作用的研究进展。

未来在海上

1975 年冲绳世博会的地标性建筑是海上都市，它高出海面 32 米，是一座漂浮在海上的城市。海上都市由日本新陈代谢派建筑师菊竹清训设计，是未来海洋社会的雏形。世博会结束后，海上都市得以保留，数十年来一直吸引着游客，直到 1993 年才关闭。世博园区被改造为国营冲绳纪念公园，又称海洋博公园。公园内有博物馆、植物园和水族馆，其中冲绳美丽海水族馆是世界上最大的水族馆之一。

1975年冲绳世博会园区鸟瞰图
印刷品,1976年,《冲绳国际海洋博览会官方记录》,世博会博物馆馆藏

erial View of Expo 1975 Okinawa
fficial Record of International Ocean Exposition, Okinawa 1975.
976. World Expo Museum Collection. Print.

Aquapolis was a prototype for a future ocean society, and an exploration of how human beings could live and work on ocean.
Official Record of International Ocean Exposition, Okinawa 1975. 1976. World Expo Museum Collection. Print.

海上都市构建了一种未来海洋社会的雏形,试图探索人类如何在海洋环境中生活和工作印刷品,1976年,《冲绳国际海洋博览会官方记录》,世博会博物馆馆藏

1975年冲绳世博会上展示了构想中的未来海底城市，交通工具、生产设备都运用仿生学原理被设计成海洋生物的形态印刷品；1975年，《海洋博览会的纪念相册》，世博会博物馆馆藏

At the Expo, a future undersea city was envisioned, where transportation and production facilities were designed to resemble sea creatures based on bionic principles.
The Souvenir Album of Expo '75. 1975. World Expo Museum Collection. Print.

EXPO 1981 PLOVDIV

普罗夫迪夫
世博会

Theme:
Earth - Planet of Life
Location:
Plovdiv, Bulgaria
Category:
Specialised Expo
Dates: **1981.6.14-7.12**
Area (ha): **51**
Participants: **70**

Modern Hunting

In 1981, the city of Plovdiv in Bulgaria hosted a Specialised Expo on the theme of hunting. Focusing on the historical relationship between humans and wildlife, and the range of environmental issues associated with it. It was the one of the first Expos to focus on ecological issues. Many hunting trophies were exhibited at the Expo, and the evaluation of hunting trophies was not simply a matter of categorizing them using a scoring system, but more importantly of providing information on the number of species, environmental changes, genetics, and breeding. Various events were also organized during the Expo, such as equestrian, fishing, shooting, hunting dog trial and falconry shows, as well as a film festival on the theme of nature.

Hunting and the Environment

A scientific symposium was an important part of Expo 1981 Plovdiv. Representatives from international scientific institutions spent the five-day session discussing issues such as the conservation and rational use of natural resources. The symposium emphasized the theme of the Expo, that mankind is responsible for life on earth and has an obligation to preserve biodiversity. The symposium, entitled "Game and Environment", was divided into two parts: "Agriculture, Forest and Game" and "Safety and Production of Game Animals". Discussions focused on the effective management of wildlife breeding, the domestication of new breeds and the breeding of new hybrids that are resistant to harmful environmental impacts. In addition, several round tables related to veterinary and food medicine were organized during the Expo.

主题：**地球——生命的星球**

举办地：**保加利亚普罗夫迪夫**

类型：**专业类世博会**

日期：**1981年6月14日至7月12日**

占地（公顷）：**51**

参展方（个）：**70**

现代狩猎

1981年，保加利亚普罗夫迪夫市举办了一届以狩猎为主题的专业类世博会。这届世博会重点探讨了人类与野生动物之间的历史关系，以及与之相关的一系列环境问题，是较早关注生态问题的世博会之一。世博会上展示了许多狩猎战利品，对狩猎战利品的评估不是简单地用计分系统做分类，而是提供物种数量、环境变化、遗传和繁殖情况等信息。世博会还组织了各种活动，比如马术、钓鱼、射击、猎犬比赛和猎鹰表演，以及以自然为主题的电影节。

狩猎与环境

科学研讨会是1981年普罗夫迪夫世博会的重要组成部分。来自国际科学机构的代表们在五天的会期里就自然资源的保护和合理利用等问题开展讨论。研讨会强调了世博会的主题，认为人类应对地球上的生命负责，有义务保护生物的多样性。研讨会的议题是狩猎动物与环境，分为两个部分：「农业、森林与狩猎」和「狩猎动物的安全与生产」。研讨会重点讨论了有效管理野生动物饲养、驯化新品种以及培育能够抵御有害环境影响的杂交新品种。除此之外，这届世博会还组织了几次与兽医和食品医学有关的圆桌会议。

1981年普罗夫迪夫世博会纪念章印刷品，1981年，《狩猎战利品目录》，世博会博物馆馆藏

mmemorative Stamps of Expo 1981 Plovdiv
talogue of Hunting Trophies. 1981. World Expo Museum Collection. Print.

1981年普罗夫迪夫世博会纪念章
印刷品,1981年,《狩猎战利品目录》,世博会博物馆馆藏

Commemorative Stamps of Expo 1981 Plovdiv
Catalogue of Hunting Trophies. 1981. World Expo Museum Collection. Print.

EXPO 1982 KNOXVILLE

诺克斯维尔世博会

Theme: **Energy turns the World**
Location: **Knoxville, United States**
Category: **Specialised Expo**
Dates: **1982.5.1-10.31**
Area (ha): **29**
Visitors: **11,127,780**
Participants: **16**

Energy Turns the World

In 1982, Knoxville, Tennessee, USA, hosted a Specialised Expo under the theme "Energy Turns the World". Knoxville chose the energy theme, as the city was a major energy center in the United States, home to the Tennessee Valley Authority and Oakridge National Laboratory, one of the world's leading nuclear research site. The Expo site was adjacent to the Museum of Science and Energy and the popular Smoky Mountain National Park.

The Sunsphere

The sun is a source of energy that nourishes life on Earth. The landmark of this Expo was the Sunsphere, 81 meters high and a five-story tower structure. Visitors can take an elevator to the top where they could enjoy the views of the Expo area from an observation deck or dine in a restaurant.

Sixteen international participants constructed their national pavilions at the Expo. The U.S. Pavilion was partially powered by solar panels on the roof. Through interactive touchscreens and visual technologies such as IMAX, the U.S. Pavilion showed visitors the history of energy production and utilization in the United States. As an energy-producing country, Saudi Arabia displayed giant solar collectors at the Expo. On the other hand, the Italy Pavilion displayed a model of an energy generator.

Expo Legacy

After the Expo, the site was transformed into a park, retaining several cultural and recreational facilities. The former Japanese Pavilion is now the Knoxville Museum of Art, and the Tennessee Amphitheater hosts a variety of concerts, while the Sunsphere, a symbol of Knoxville, was reopened to visitors in 2007.

主题：能源推动世界
举办地：美国诺克斯维尔
类型：专业类世博会
日期：1982年5月1日至10月31日
占地（公顷）：29
参观者（人次）：11,127,780
参展方（个）：16

能源推动世界

1982年，美国田纳西州诺克斯维尔市举办了一届专业类世博会，主题是『能源推动世界』。之所以以能源为主题，是因为诺克斯维尔是美国重要的能源中心，田纳西河流域管理局和世界领先的核研究基地美国橡树岭国家实验室都设在这里。世博园区的选址毗邻科学与能源博物馆，以及游客众多的大雾山国家公园。

太阳球

太阳是能量的源泉，滋养着地球上的生命。这届世博会的地标性建筑就是太阳球。太阳球高达81米，内有五层结构，游客可以乘坐电梯到达顶部，在观景台上俯瞰世博园区或在餐厅用餐。

16个国际参展方在世博会上设立了展馆。美国馆的部分供电来源于屋顶的太阳能板。通过互动触摸屏和IMAX等视觉技术，美国馆向游客展示了美国能源生产与利用的历史。作为能源生产国，沙特阿拉伯在世博会上展示了巨型的太阳能集热器。意大利馆则展示了能源发电机模型。

世博遗产

世博会结束后，园区被改造为公园，保留了多个文化娱乐设施。原先的日本馆现在是诺克斯维尔艺术博物馆，田纳西露天剧场则成为各类音乐会的举办场所。2007年，太阳球作为诺克斯维尔的象征再次向游客开放。

1982年诺克斯维尔世博会上展出的节能屋明信片，1982年，世博会博物馆馆藏

Energy Saving House at Expo 1982 Knoxville
1982. World Expo Museum Collection. Postcard.

The comic series *Adventures of Shoney's Big Boy* launched an Expo special edition with a story of the Big Boy who visited the Expo with a robot and caught thieves. *Adventures of Shoney's Big Boy.* 1982. World Expo Museum Collection. Print.

Theme:
The World of Rivers - Fresh Water as a Source of Life
Location:
New Orleans, United States
Category:
Specialised Expo
Dates: **1984.5.12-11.11**
Area (ha): **34**
Visitors: **7,335,000**
Participants: **15**

The First Official Mascot

The theme of Expo 1984 New Orleans was "A World of Rivers: Fresh Water as a Source of Life". In keeping with the theme, the Expo site was chosen along the banks of the Mississippi River. The mascot for this year's Expo was a white pelican wearing blue tuxedo, called Seymore D. Fair. It was the first official mascot in the history of the Expo.

Urban Renewal and Upgrading

New Orleans hoped to host the Expo to renovate and update the city's facilities, redevelop the Warehouse District, and position itself as an attractive tourist destination and high-level convention center. To this end, New Orleans built a new monorail system to transport large numbers of tourists, effectively avoiding traffic congestion in the Warehouse District and downtown area. Many of the streets and buildings in the Warehouse District were renewed and the appearance of the city was greatly improved. After the event, these buildings were utilized for commercial or residential purposes and continue to serve the city. The Expo's series of improvements greatly contributed to the development of the New Orleans Warehouse District, and to this day, the area remains popular for its restaurants and art galleries.

The Ernest N. Morial Convention Center is the greatest legacy of this Expo. It served as the Louisiana Pavilion during the Expo and reopened as a convention center in 1985, now being the sixth largest convention center in the United States. Another noteworthy Expo legacy is the shopping center built on the waterfront, then home to the International Pavilion, whose presence has integrated both banks of the Mississippi River into the New Orleans urban life cycle.

主题：**河流的世界——淡水是生命之源**
举办地：**美国新奥尔良**
类型：**专业类世博会**
日期：**1984 年 5 月 12 日至 11 月 11 日**
占地（公顷）：**34**
参观者（人次）：**7,335,000**
参展方（个）：**15**

第一个吉祥物

1984 年新奥尔良世博会的主题是『河流的世界——淡水是生命之源』。为契合主题，世博园区选址在密西西比河畔。这届世博会的吉祥物是一只身穿蓝色礼服的白色鹈鹕，名叫塞默尔。塞默尔是世博历史上第一个官方吉祥物。

城市更新与升级

新奥尔良希望通过举办世博会，改造更新城市设施，重新开发仓库区，把新奥尔良打造成有吸引力的旅游胜地和高级会议中心。为此，新奥尔良新建了单轨铁路系统，用来运送大量游客，有效避免了仓库区和市中心区的交通拥堵。仓库区的许多街道和建筑也焕然一新，城市面貌得到极大改善。会期结束后，这些建筑被用作商业或住宅用途，继续服务于这座城市。世博会的一系列改造工程极大促进了新奥尔良仓库区的发展，直至今日，这一地区的餐馆和艺术画廊仍很受欢迎。

新奥尔良莫里尔会议中心是这届世博会最大的遗产。世博会期间，它曾是路易斯安那州馆。1985 年，这里作为会议中心再度开放，目前已成为美国第六大会议中心。另一个值得一提的世博遗产是在滨水区建造的购物中心，它当时是国际场馆的所在地，它的存在让密西西比河两岸都融入了新奥尔良的城市生活圈。

1984年新奥尔良世博会园区示意图
印刷品，1984年，《1984年新奥尔良世博会官方指南》，世博会博物馆馆藏

Sketch of the Site of Expo 1984 New Orleans
1984 World's Fair in New Orleans: the Official Guidebook, 1984.
World Expo Museum Collection. Print.

Monorail and Enterprise Space Shuttle at the Expo 1984 New Orleans.
Enterprise Space Shuttle was the world's first space shuttle.
1984. World Expo Museum Collection. Print.

1984年新奥尔良世博会上的单轨火车和企业号航天飞机,企业号航天飞机是世界上第一架航天飞机印刷品,1984年,世博会博物馆馆藏

游客可乘坐空中缆车MART穿越密西比河，俯瞰1984年新奥尔良世博会园区及城市全景，MART还设有老年及残障人士专用车印刷品，1984年，《1984年新奥尔良世博会官方指南》，世博会博物馆馆藏

Visitors could cross the Mississippi River on the aerial gondola, MART, which also featured senior and handicapped-accessible vehicles, while admiring the panoramic views of the Expo and the city.
1984 World's Fair in New Orleans: the Official Guidebook, 1984.
World Expo Museum Collection. Print.

Theme: **Dwellings and Surroundings - Science and Technology for Man at Home**
Location: **Tsukuba, Japan**
Category: **Specialised Expo**
Dates: **1985.3.17-9.16**
Area (ha): **100**
Visitors: **20,334,727**
Participants: **48**

Expo in the City of Science

Expo 1985 Tsukuba was one of the most visited Specialised Expos to date, with a total of 20.3 million visitors. Tsukuba is known as a science city, and the Organiser wanted to demonstrate the relationship between human beings and science and technology, so that the public could enhance their knowledge and understanding of science and technology through visit and experience.

Technology Shaping the Future

The Expo's Theme Pavilion was divided into two sub-themes: "My Land", which focused on the diversity of nature, Japan's local natural resources, and the technology needed to utilize them; and "My Life", which demonstrated that human beings belong to nature, explained the role of human beings in nature, and envisioned the future. The Japanese corporate pavilions were also very popular with visitors, especially the Mitsubishi Future Pavilion, which featured a monorail system that later appeared at the Expo 1988 Brisbane, Australia, transporting visitors to and from the Expo. In addition, the U.S. Pavilion focused on Artificial Intelligence, with "Robots that think" demonstrating how a robot can recover a Rubik's Cube or solve complex math problems.

Learning through Play

The Expo also featured a Children's Plaza, which was designed to encouraged children to learn about science and technology while playing. Fun Tube was one of the popular facilities, consist of a large, winding pipe in which children can experience wind, rain, fog, echoes, reflections and other feelings. The Mechanical Zoo was also popular among children and contained a variety of machines that mimic terrestrial and aquatic animals.

主题：**居住与环境——人类家居科技**

举办地：**日本筑波**

类型：**专业类世博会**

日期：**1985年3月17日至9月16日**

占地（公顷）：**100**

参观者（人次）：**20,334,727**

参展方（个）：**48**

科学城里的世博会

日本筑波以科学城闻名。1985年，筑波举办了专业类世博会，组织者希望展示人类与科技的关系，让公众通过参与和体验增进对科技的认知和了解。当年共有2030万游客参观了这届世博会。

科技塑造未来

世博会的主题馆分为两大副主题：『我的土地』，主要展示自然多样性、日本当地的自然资源，以及利用自然资源所需的技术；『我的生活』，表明人类属于自然，明确人类在自然中扮演的角色，并畅想未来的生活。日本各个企业馆很受观众欢迎，特别是三菱未来馆的单轨列车系统，之后又出现在1988年澳大利亚布里斯班世博会的现场，运送往来游客，继续服务世博会。另外，美国馆重点展示了人工智能，馆内有一个『会思考的机器人』，向观众演示机器人如何复原魔方或解决复杂的数学问题。

在玩乐中学习

世博会还设有儿童广场，趣味管道。它由一个蜿蜒曲折的大型管道组成，儿童可以在其中体验风、雨、雾、回声、反光等各种感受。机械动物园也很受孩子们欢迎，里面有各种各样模仿陆生和水生动物的机器。

1985年筑波世博会上的HSST-03磁悬浮列车（HSST 意为高速地面运输）印刷品，1985年，世博会博物馆馆藏

The HSST-03 Maglev Train (HSST: High Speed Surface Transport) at Expo 1985 Tsukuba 1985. World Expo Museum Collection. Print.

The Solar Ray Concentration Transmission System, displayed at the Expo, could capture solar energ and transmit it to a designated area, inspiring the future energy utilisation designs.
1985. World Expo Museum Collection. Print.

1985年筑波世博会上展出的太阳能聚光传输系统,可采集太阳能并传输至指定区域,对未来能源利用具有启示作用印刷品,1985年,世博会博物馆馆藏

富士机器人剧场展出的机器人马可印刷品，1985年，世博会博物馆馆藏

Marco Robot at Fuyo Robot Theatre
1985. World Expo Museum Collection. Print.

EXPO 1985
PLOVDIV
普罗夫迪夫
世博会

Theme: **Inventions**
Location: **Plovdiv, Bulgaria**
Category: **Specialised Expo**
Dates: **1985.11.4-11.30**
Area (ha): **5.8**
Visitors: **1,000,000**
Participants: **54**

Special Arrangement

In 1984, Bulgaria expressed to the BIE its wish to organise a Specialised Expo in Plovdiv on the occasion of the International Year of Youth in 1985. At that time, the BIE had already approved the applications for Expo 1985 Tsukuba and Expo 1986 Vancouver, so Bulgaria's application was against the regulatory framework of that time, which required a minimum of two years between Expos and a four-year waiting period after the first one as Plovdiv had already hosted an Expo in 1981. However, taking into account the shorter duration and the beneficial theme of the Expo, and the support of the World Intellectual Property Organization (WIPO), the 95th General Assembly of the BIE voted to accept the recognition of Expo 1985 Plovdiv.

Gathering of Young Inventors

Under the theme "Achievements of Young Inventors", Expo 1985 Plovdiv encouraged participants to present the results of their scientific research and to take part in conferences and symposiums Some 10,550 inventions by young inventors were exhibited. The relevant international jury awarded 198 gold medals and 4 special prizes, while 35 prizes were awarded by relevant Bulgarian organizations. Jointly organised with the WIPO, a seminar entitled "Inventions for Development" was held during the Expo.

In addition, the Expo led to the establishment of the Federation of Inventors' Associations of Africa, which was founded on November 1985, by 16 African countries that met in Plovdiv to discuss the formation of a provisional committee to draw up the regulations.

主题：**青年发明家的成就**
举办地：**保加利亚普罗夫迪夫**
类型：**专业类世博会**
日期：**1985年11月4日至11月30日**
占地（公顷）：**5.8**
参观者（人次）：**1,000,000**
参展方（个）：**54**

一次破格申请

1984年，保加利亚向国际展览局表示，希望在1985年国际青年年之际在普罗夫迪夫举办一届专业类世博会。当时，国际展览局已经通过了1985年筑波世博会和1986年温哥华世博会的申请，因此保加利亚的再度申请违反了当时国际展览局制定的规则，即两届世博会之间至少间隔两年，以及首次举办世博会后需等待四年方可再度申请，而普罗夫迪夫在1981年刚刚举办过一届世博会。然而，考虑到这届世博会的会期较短、主题有益，以及得到联合国机构世界知识产权组织的支持，国际展览局第95次大会表决认可举办这届世博会。

青年发明家的聚会

1985年普罗夫迪夫世博会以『青年发明家的成就』为主题，鼓励与会者介绍各自的科研成果，参加各种会议和专题讨论会。世博会展出了大约10,550件青年发明家的发明。相关国际评委会颁发了198枚金奖和4个特别奖。保加利亚相关组织也颁发了35个奖项。世界知识产权组织在会期内举办了题为『发明促进发展』的研讨会。

另外，这届世博会还促成了非洲发明家协会联合会的成立。16个非洲国家在普罗夫迪夫世博会上举行会议，讨论成立一个临时委员会来制定章程，并最终在1985年11月8日成立了非洲发明家协会联合会。

EXPO 1986 VANCOUVER
温哥华
世博会

Theme:
Transportation and Communication: World in Motion - World in Touch
Location:
Vancouver, Canada
Category:
Specialised Expo
Dates: **1986.5.2-10.13**
Area (ha): **70**
Visitors: **22,111,578**
Participants: **55**

World in Motion

With transportation as its theme, Expo 1986 Vancouver showcased various modes of transportation: a 5.4-kilometer monorail connected the site, the SkyTrain system that allowed visitors to travel between the main site and the Canada Pavilion by the harbour, and two gondola skyrides provided visitors with an unobstructed view of the site, and all of transportation facilities were free of charge. International participants showcased their latest advances in transportation, such as the Japanese Pavilion, which presented a prototype of a maglev train, and the German Pavilion, which showed buses powered by a hybrid electric and gasoline engine.

Flying into the Space

This was the first Expo in which aviation power such as the Soviet Union, the United States, and China participated together, and space travel was the focus of their exhibits. The Soviet Pavilion displayed a 8-meter-tall replica of the Soviet space station, which visitors could enter to see the laboratories inside. The U.S. Pavilion displayed models of spacecraft, including the Space Shuttle Columbia, and facilities and equipment. The Chinese Pavilion presented models of communication satellites and space rockets.

Continued Benefit for Vancouver

The theme of the Expo had a profound effect on Vancouver. The SkyTrain and the Alex Fraser Bridge, a cable-stayed bridge over the Fraser River, were both built for the Expo. The SkyTrain has now grown to be the longest driverless rapid transit system in the world, and the Fraser Bridge was the longest bridge of its kind at the time of its opening. The Canada Pavilion was transformed into Vancouver's new marina after the Expo, and its iconic white sails remain in place and becoming one of Vancouver's landmarks.

主题：**交通与通信**
　　　　——运转中的世界，联系中的世界
举办地：**加拿大温哥华**
类型：**专业类世博会**
日期：**1986年5月2日至10月13日**
占地（公顷）：**70**
参观者（人次）：**22,111,578**
参展方（个）：**55**

运转中的世界

1986年温哥华世博会以交通为主题，各式各样的交通工具因而成为世博园区里的亮点。5.4千米长的单轨铁路将世博园区各个地点串联起来，架空列车让游客轻松往返主会场和港口边的加拿大馆，两条空中缆车线则方便游客俯瞰园区美景，而且园区里的这些交通工具都是免费的。国际参展方展示了各自在交通方面的最新进展，比如日本馆展示了磁悬浮列车的原型，德国馆展出了油电混合动力驱动的公共汽车。

飞向太空

这届世博会是苏联、美国、中国首次共同参与的世博会，太空旅行成为它们展示的重点。苏联馆展示了高33米的苏联空间站复制品，游客可以进入这个空间站参观里面的实验室。美国馆展示了包括哥伦比亚号航天飞机在内的航天器模型和设施设备。中国馆则展示了通信卫星和太空火箭的模型。

运转中的温哥华

这届以交通为主题的世博会对温哥华影响至深。拉桥阿力克斯·菲沙桥都是为这届世博会而新建的。架空列车和横跨在菲沙河上的斜拉无人驾驶快速交通系统，而菲沙桥在开通时也是同类桥梁中最长的。加拿大馆会后被改造成为温哥华的新码头，其标志性的白帆依然保留，成为温哥华的地标之一。

Aerial View of Expo 1986 Vancouver
Canadian Geographic. 1986. World Expo Museum Collection. Print.

1986年温哥华世博会鸟瞰图
印刷品，1986年，《加拿大地理》杂志，世博会博物馆馆藏

Space Station Model behind the USSR Pavilion
1986. World Expo Museum Collection. Print.

苏联馆展示了礼炮号空间站复制品印刷品，1986年，世博会博物馆藏

《阿奇的世界》系列漫画推出世博会特辑，本页描绘的正是主人公阿奇和朋友们途径苏联馆，看到礼炮号空间站复制品印刷，1986年，《阿奇的世界》，世博会博物馆馆藏

The comic series *The World of Archie* launched an Expo special edition, featuring a story that Archie and his friends visiting a model of the space station in the Soviet Union Pavilion.
The World of Archie. 1986. World Expo Museum Collection. Print.

EXPO 1988 BRISBANE

布里斯班世博会

Theme: **Leisure in the Age of Technology**
Location: **Brisbane, Australia**
Category: **Specialised Expo**
Dates: **1988.4.30-10.30**
Area (ha): **40**
Visitors: **18,560,447**
Participants: **36**

Leisure as A Form of Culture

The theme of Expo 1988 Brisbane was "Leisure in the Age of Technology", which demonstrated the common pursuit of leisure by people from different culture backgrounds and the important link between leisure and culture. Each participating country presented its own distinctive leisure style: the Swiss Pavilion featured a 40-meter-long ski slope, the German Pavilion had a beer garden, and the U.S. Pavilion featured sports, inviting a number of top athletes to perform in its outdoor stadium. To facilitate outdoor activities and performances, the Expo site was planned with many tent-shaped shade facilities and lush vegetation to shield visitors from the blazing Queensland sun.

From Tsukuba to Brisbane

Visitors could tour the park by monorail, which traveled directly through the Queensland Pavilion. This monorail system was the same one that operated in the Mitsubishi Future Pavilion at the Expo 1985 Tsukuba, and it came to Brisbane three years later. The Queensland Pavilion recreated the Australian outback and showed legendary stories about the Aboriginal people.

Legacy of the Expo

The Expo site was converted from a decaying industrial area near the harbor, and after the Expo, it was transformed into South Bank Parklands. The Expo's original theme park, World Expo Park, was converted into the Brisbane Convention and Exhibition Center.

主题：科技时代的休闲方式
举办地：澳大利亚布里斯班
类型：专业类世博会
日期：1988年4月30日至10月30日
占地（公顷）：40
参观者（人次）：18,560,447
参展方（个）：36

休闲也是文化

1988年布里斯班世博会的主题是『科技时代的休闲方式』，展现不同文化背景的人对休闲的共同追求，体现追求休闲与发展文化之间的重要联系。各参展方围绕主题展现各自极具特色的休闲方式：瑞士馆内建造了坡道长达40米的滑雪场；德国馆内设有一个啤酒花园；美国馆以体育为特色，邀请众多顶级运动员在其建造的户外运动场表演。为了便于进行户外活动和表演，世博园区在规划时设计了许多帐篷形状的遮阳设施和郁郁葱葱的植被，为游客遮挡昆士兰的烈日。

从筑波到布里斯班

游客可以乘坐单轨列车游览园区，列车直接从昆士兰馆的建筑体中穿堂而过。这套单轨列车系统正是1985年在筑波世博会三菱未来馆内运行的系统，三年后它又来到了布里斯班。昆士兰馆再现了澳大利亚内陆地区的风貌，讲述着有关原住民的传奇故事。

世博遗产

世博园区是由港口附近一个破旧的工业区改建而成的，世博会结束后，它又被改造成南岸公园。世博会原来的主题公园世博园，现在则被改建为布里斯班会展中心。

Aerial View of Expo 1988 Brisbane
World Expo 88. 1988. World Expo Museum Collection. Print.

1988年布里斯班世博会鸟瞰图
印刷品,1988年,《88年世博会》,世博会博物馆馆藏

单轨列车从昆士兰馆穿行而过,这套单轨列车系统正是1985年在筑波世博会三菱未来馆内运行的系统印刷品,1988年,摄影:约翰·布莱克,《88年世博会》,世博会博物馆馆藏

The monorail running through the Queensland Pavilion. This monorail system was the same system that operated in the Mitsubishi Future Pavilion at Expo 1985 Tsukuba.
Photo by John Black. *World Expo 88.* 1988. World Expo Museum Collection. Print.

三米高的机器人「蓝」是澳大利亚馆特殊的主持人，负责引导游客参观印刷品，1988年，摄影：吉尔·德宁，《88年世博会》，世博会博物馆馆藏

Blue, the 3-metre-high robot, who was the special host to guide visitors through the Australian Pavilion.
Photo by Jill Dening. *World Expo 88*. 1988. World Expo Museum Collection. Print.

在维多利亚馆展出的部分高科技展品印刷品,1988年,摄影:吉尔・德宁,《88年世博会》,世博会博物馆馆藏

Part of the High-tech Display inside the Victorian Pavilion
Photo by Jill Dening. *World Expo 88*. 1988. World Expo Museum Collection. Print.

EXPO 1991 PLOVDIV

普罗夫迪夫
世博会

Theme:
The Activity of Young People in the Service of a World of Peace
Location:
Plovdiv, Bulgaria
Category:
Specialised Expo
Dates: **1991.6.7-7.7**
Participants: **9**

Inviting Young People

After 1985, Plovdiv, Bulgaria, in cooperation with the World Intellectual Property Organization (WIPO), again organized a specialised Expo in 1991. As before, the Expo continued to emphasize the creativity of young people and sought to demonstrate the positive role they play in promoting world peace. To encourage young inventors from all over the world to participate in the Expo, a the crew of the second joint Soviet-Bulgarian space flight in 1988 extended an invitation to young people to participate in Expo 1991 Plovdiv.

Inventions and Iinnovations

More than 3,000 inventions and innovations were showcased at the Expo, which were classified into 14 categories by theme. To encourage youth, no inventor participating in the Expo was older than 45. About 10% of all inventions on display were invented by school students under the age of 18, 22% by young people between the ages of 18 and 25, and 59% by inventors between the ages of 25 and 35. The relevant international jury awarded 187 gold medals and 40 special prizes for the most innovative inventions among them.

The Government of Bulgaria and the World Intellectual Property Organization organized an international seminar entitled "Young Inventors and Innovators in the Context of Economic and Technological Development". Representatives from 25 countries participated in the three-day seminar. A total of 140 reports and lectures were published and 180 scientific and cultural events, including 45 conferences, were organized throughout the Expo period. Plovdiv created platforms and opportunities for scientists, entrepreneurs, inventors and technologists from all over the world to exchange ideas.

主题：**青年服务世界和平**

举办地：**保加利亚普罗夫迪夫**

类型：**专业类世博会**

日期：**1991 年 6 月 7 日至 7 月 7 日**

参展方（个）：**9**

邀请年轻人

继 1985 年之后，保加利亚普罗夫迪夫联合世界知识产权组织在 1991 年再次举办了专业类世博会。与之前一样，这届世博会依然强调了青年的创造力，力图表现青年对推动世界和平所发挥的积极作用。为鼓励世界各地的青年发明家参加世博会，早在 1988 年，苏联－保加利亚第二次联合太空飞行的机组人员就向年轻人发出邀请，请他们参加 1991 年普罗夫迪夫世博会。

发明与创新

世博会上展出了 3,000 多项发明和创新，这些发明和创新按主题分为 14 类。参加世博会的发明家年龄都不超过 45 岁。在展出的所有发明中，约有 10% 是由 18 岁以下的在校学生发明的，有 22% 是由 18 岁至 25 岁的年轻人发明的，有 59% 是由 25 岁至 35 岁的发明家发明的。相关国际评委会为其中最具创新性的发明项目颁发了 187 个金奖和 40 个特别奖。

保加利亚政府和世界知识产权组织举办了国际研讨会，题为『经济技术发展背景下的青年发明家和创新者』。来自 25 个国家的代表参加了这次为期三天的研讨会。整个世博会期间，相关报告和演讲共计发表 140 篇，各种科学文化活动共计组织 180 场，其中包括 45 场会议。普罗夫迪夫为世界各地的科学家、企业家、发明家和技术人员创造了交流的平台和机会。

EXPO 1992 SEVILLE

塞维利亚世博会

Theme: **The Age of Discovery**
Location: **Seville, Spain**
Category: **World Expo**
Dates: **1992.4.20-10.12**
Area (ha): **215**
Visitors: **41,814,571**
Participants: **108**

The Road of Discovery

In 1992, Seville, in the south of Spain, hosted the World Expo under the theme "The Age of Discovery" to commemorate the 500th anniversary of Columbus' discovery of the Americas. The site of the Expo was chosen on the island of Cartuja, where Columbus was said to have lived before setting sail. The main road of the Expo was called the "The Road of the Discoveries", along which 10 thematic pavilions were located, where visitors can take a journey through time and witness the evolution of science, technology and culture over the past 500 years.

The Expo's mascot was Curro, a nickname for Francisco in Andalusia. It was designed by Heinz Edelman, the designer who created the animated short film "Yellow Submarine" for the Beatles. At the time, 23 designs from 15 countries participation for the competition of mascot for Expo 1992 Seville.

Festive Revelry

The Expo site was filled with a joyous and festive atmosphere, and the Expo organized a wide variety of cultural events to welcome visitors around the clock. Every night, the fireworks and light show on the Lake of Spain launched the beginning the "Expo Night", with opera, symphony, theater, jazz, flamenco, and salsa performances until 4:00 a.m. the next morning.

Urban Renewal

In order to organize a high quality Expo, Seville underwent an extensive urban renewal process, which included the construction of a new airport terminal, train station, highway, a new high speed train line to shorten the drive from Madrid to Seville, and the construction of four bridges to facilitate transportation between the Expo site and the city. After the Expo, the island of Cartuja, where the Expo was located, was transformed into "Cartuja 93", the new center of technological and economic development in Seville.

主题：**发现的时代**

举办地：**西班牙塞维利亚**

类型：**综合类世博会**

日期：**1992年4月20日至10月12日**

占地（公顷）：**215**

参观者（人次）：**41,814,571**

参展方（个）：**108**

发现之路

1992年，西班牙的南部城市塞维利亚举办世博会，主题是『发现的时代』，以此纪念哥伦布发现美洲新大陆500周年。世博园区选址在卡图哈岛，据说哥伦布在启航之前曾居住在此。世博园区的主干道名为『发现之路』，沿途分布十个主题馆，游客在此踏上时间之旅，见证500年来科学、技术与文化的演变进程。这届世博会的吉祥物是科罗，这个名字是西班牙男性常用名弗朗西斯科的昵称。它的设计者是曾经为披头士乐队创作过动画短片《黄色潜水艇》的设计师海茵茨·爱德尔曼。当时，有来自15个国家的23份设计方案共同参与了比选。

节日狂欢

世博会现场洋溢着欢乐的节日氛围。世博会组织了丰富多彩的文化活动，不分昼夜地迎接着游客。每晚，西班牙湖上的焰火与灯光表演拉开『世博之夜』的帷幕，歌剧、交响乐、戏剧、爵士舞、弗拉门戈舞、萨尔萨舞表演轮番上演，直到次日凌晨4点。

城市更新

为举办一届高质量的世博会，塞维利亚进行了大规模的城市更新，包括修建新的航站楼、火车站、高速公路，开辟新的高铁线路缩短马德里到塞维利亚的车程，以及架设四座桥梁方便世博园区与市内的交通。世博会结束后，世博园区所在地卡图哈岛即转变为『卡图哈93』，成为塞维利亚新的技术和经济发展中心。

1992年塞维利亚世博会园区鸟瞰图
照片，1992年，塞维利亚公共资产管理公司档案

Aerial View of Expo 1992 Seville
1992. 055 Vistas Aéreas 1992-05. EPGASA. Photo.

461

西班牙湖建设之前的样貌，西班牙湖沿岸是1992年塞维利亚世博会主要的娱乐演出地点 印刷品，1988年，《1992年塞维利亚世博会项目与工程》，世博会博物馆馆藏

Most of the entertainment and performance took place along the Lake of Spain. This photo shows the site before construction.
Expo '92 Sevilla Proyectos y Obras. 1988. World Expo Museum Collection. Print.

西班牙湖的设计图
印刷品，1988年，《1992年塞维利亚世博会项目与工程》，世博会博物馆馆藏

Design scheme of the Lake of Spain
Expo '92 Sevilla Proyectos y Obras. 1988. World Expo Museum Collection. Print.

1992年塞维利亚世博会上展出了阿里亚娜4型火箭，阿里亚娜系列火箭由欧洲航天局研制，承担大量商业卫星发射业务。照片，1992年，摄影：安娜·伊莱亚斯，塞维利亚公共资产管理公司档案

Ariane 4 at the Expo 1992 Seville. The Ariane Series, designed by the European Space Agency, specialised in the launch of commercial satellites.
Photo by Anna Elias. 1992. 0061 Pabellón del Futuro. EPGASA. Photo.

EXPO
1992
GENOA

热那亚
世博会

Theme:
Christopher Columbus: The Ship and the Sea
Location:
Genoa, Italy
Category:
Specialised Expo
Dates: **1992.5.15-8.15**
Area (ha): **6**
Visitors: **817,045**
Participants: **52**

A Celebrity from Genoa

Two Expo were held in 1992, a Specialised Expo in Genoa and a World Expo in Seville. Both Expos were organized in the same year to commemorate the 500th anniversary of Columbus' discovery of the Americas. Genoa is the hometown of Columbus, while Seville is where he used to live.

Many exhibits related to Columbus' discovery of the Americas were displayed at the Expo Genoa. The Bahamas was the first place Columbus landed after arriving in the Americas, and the Bahamas Pavilion exhibited scenic photographs of the first island Columbus landed on, as well as artifacts from the local natives. Sailing was also an important theme at this Expo. The Japan Pavilion showcased a walking robot dressed in samurai clothing, highlighting the importance of nautical theme to Japan.

City of Genoa

Renzo Piano, the famous Italian designer and a native of Genoa, was responsible for planning the entire Expo site. He proposed a plan for the construction of the site that can be seen as an urban renewal program, including the construction of two permanent buildings, a large mixed-use facility center and the largest aquarium in Italy with 12,000 marine species. Genoa is an important industrial port city in Italy, and this plan connected the run-down port to the city center, spurring the development of the entire area. The highlight of the Expo was the Grande Bigo, a panoramic lift, which remains as a landmark attraction of Genoa today. Inspired by cargo cranes, the lift consists of eight large masts that allow visitors to rise to a height of 40 meters and enjoy the panoramic view of the port and the old town.

主题：**克里斯托弗·哥伦布——船与海**
举办地：**意大利热那亚**
类型：**专业类世博会**
日期：**1992 年 5 月 15 日至 8 月 15 日**
占地（公顷）：**6**
参观者（人次）：**817,045**
参展方（个）：**52**

热那亚人

1992 年举办了两届世博会，分别是热那亚专业类世博会和塞维利亚综合类世博会。同一年举办的这两届世博会都是为了纪念哥伦布发现美洲新大陆 500 周年。热那亚是哥伦布的故乡，而塞维利亚则是他曾经生活过的地方。

热那亚世博会上展示了许多与哥伦布发现新大陆有关的展品。巴哈马是哥伦布到达美洲后首先登陆的地方，巴哈马馆展示了哥伦布登陆的第一个岛屿的风景照片，以及当地土著的文物。航海同样是这届世博会上重要的主题。日本馆展出了一个身着武士服、会说话的机器人，向游客介绍航海对于日本的重要性。

热那亚城

意大利著名设计师伦佐·皮亚诺，也是热那亚人，他负责规划整个世博园区。皮亚诺提出的园区建设方案，也可以看作是一个城市改造计划。这个计划包括建造两座永久性建筑，即一座大型综合设施中心和一座拥有 1.2 万种海洋生物的意大利最大的水族馆。热那亚是意大利重要的工业港口城市，这个方案把原本破败的港口连通至市中心，带动了整个区域的发展。世博会上的亮点是戈全景升降机，如今它也是整个热那亚的地标性景点。它的设计灵感来源于货轮起重机。升降机由八根大桅杆组成，游客可以升到 40 米的高度俯瞰港口和老城区。

EXPO
1993
DAEJEON
大田
世博会

Theme:
The Challenge of a New Road of Development
Location:
Daejeon, Republic of Korea
Category:
Specialised Expo
Dates: **1993.8.7-11.7**
Area (ha): **90.1**
Visitors: **14,005,808**
Participants: **141**

Development and Environment

Korea built its first national pavilion at Expo 1893 Chicago. As a centennial commemoration, Korea hosted a Specialised Expo in Daejeon in 1993. The theme of the Expo was "The Challenge of a New Road of Development" with two sub-themes: "Traditional and Modern Science and Technology for the Developing World" and "Effective Use of Resources and Recycling", reflecting the growing concern of society awareness about the environmental issues associated with economic development at that time.

Han'bit-Ap

Han'bit-Ap, or the Tower of Great Light, is a tower with a height of 93 meters located in the center of the Expo site and is still open today. Inspired by light, science and the universe, the tower showcased the connection between the past, present and future. The base of the tower was made of 1993 granite blocks to pay tribute to Cheomseongdae, Korea's ancient astronomical observatory; the middle of the tower represented the present, depicting the progress of science in Korea at that time; and the top of the tower symbolized the future, embodying Korea's determination to progress.

Environmentally Friendly

International participants showcased its progress in utilizing clean and renewable energy sources, as well as innovations in the field of transportation and mobility around. The France Pavilion highlighted its achievements in transportation and urban planning, such as a model of the TGV high-speed train, a prototype of an electric car, and innovative solutions for handling industrial and domestic waste. The Canada Pavilion displayed a car simulator that allowed visitors to drive around the streets of Quebec, Canada. The Russia Pavilion presented an equivalent-sized model of the Mir space station, as well as new materials and technologies that can reduce environmental pollution.

主题：**新发展道路的挑战**
举办地：**韩国大田**
类型：**专业类世博会**
日期：**1993年8月7日至11月7日**
占地（公顷）：**90.1**
参观者（人次）：**14,005,808**
参展方（个）：**141**

发展与环境

在1893年芝加哥世博会上，韩国第一次设立国家馆。1993年，作为百年纪念，韩国在大田举办了一届专业类世博会。当时正值韩国经济快速发展之际，世博会的主题是"新发展道路的挑战"，另有两个副主题："发展中国家的传统与现代科技"以及"资源的有效循环利用"，反映出当时社会已经越来越关注经济发展对环境的影响。

韩光塔

韩光塔，高93米，位于世博园区中心位置，至今仍在开放。它以光、科学和宇宙为设计灵感，展现出过去、现在、未来三者之间的联系。塔的底部由1,993块花岗岩砌成，用以表达对韩国古代天文观测台瞻星台的致敬；塔的中部代表现在，描绘了韩国当时的科学发展进程；塔的顶部象征未来，体现韩国进步的决心。

环境友好

各参展方围绕主题展示各自在利用清洁与可再生能源方面的进展，以及交通出行领域的创新成果。法国馆强调了其在交通与城市规划方面的成就，比如TGV高速列车模型、电动汽车的原型车以及处理工业和生活垃圾的创新解决方案。加拿大馆展出了一台汽车模拟器，游客可以模拟驾驶在加拿大魁北克的街道上。俄罗斯馆展出了和平号空间站同等大小的模型，以及可以减少环境污染的新材料和新技术。

1993年大田世博会地标性建筑——韩光塔,塔的底部、中部、顶部以不同形式分别象征过去、现在与未来印刷品,1994年,《大田世博会官方报告》,世博会博物馆馆藏

Han'bit-Ap, the landmark of Expo Daejeon, signified the past, present and future in the upper, middle and lower parts respectively.
The Taejon International Exposition Official Report. 1994. World Expo Museum Collection. Print.

The Korean Maglev Train at Expo 1993 Daejeon
1993. BIE Archive. Print.

1993年大田世博会上运行的磁悬浮列车
印刷品，1993年，国际展览局馆藏

梦精灵机器人是1993年大田世博会的吉祥物,通过接收飞碟内部的机器指令完成所有动作,充电一次可运行6小时。印刷品,1994年,《大田世博会官方报告》,世博会博物馆馆藏

Kumdori robot is the mascot of Expo 1993 Daejeon. All the movements of Kumdori were conducted by machines stored inside the UFO and 1 time recharge could last for 6 hours.
The Taejon International Exposition Official Report. 1994. World Expo Museum Collection. Print.

EXPO 1998 LISBON

里斯本世博会

Theme:
**The Oceans:
a Heritage for
the Future**
Location:
Lisbon, Portugal
Category:
Specialised Expo
Dates: **1998.5.22-9.30**
Area (ha): **50**
Visitors: **10,128,204**
Participants: **160**

Legacy for the Future Humanity

In view of the increasing pressure on marine life and growing awareness of the health of the oceans, the United Nations General Assembly proclaimed 1998 as the International Year of the Ocean, and Portugal organized Expo 1998 Lisbon under the theme "The Oceans: A Heritage for the Future", reaffirming its willingness to take positive action to protect the oceans and their limited resources. The Expo provided tens of millions of visitors with a broad education in marine science and fostered an active international dialog on ocean governance.

An Expo Dedicated to the Future

From its preparation stage, the Expo had been recognized as a strategically important project for the region and was a central part of the transformation plan for the eastern part of Lisbon, originally a heavily polluted industrial area. The Expo had transformed the area into a mixed-use residential, commercial and cultural district with plentiful green spaces and access to public transportation, establishing a multi-modal transport hub that connected the site to the metro, rail and bus networks throughout Lisbon and beyond. After the Expo, the site became a modern urban neighborhood built from the associated venues and facilities. The success of Lisbon in integrating the organizing the Expo with the future development of the city and the needs of the local people was an example of urban renewal in Portugal.

主题：**海洋——未来的遗产**
举办地：**葡萄牙里斯本**
类型：**专业类世博会**
日期：**1998 年 5 月 22 日至 9 月 30 日**
占地（公顷）：**50**
参观者（人次）：**10,128,204**
参展方（个）：**160**

人类未来的遗产

在新时代背景下，海洋生物的生存压力与日俱增，但人们对海洋健康的认知也在不断提高。1998 年，联合国大会宣布当年为国际海洋年，葡萄牙在里斯本举办以「海洋——未来的遗产」为主题的世博会，重申愿意采取积极行动，保护海洋及其有限的资源。这届世博会为上千万游客提供广泛的海洋科学教育，促进国际社会在海洋管理方面展开积极对话。

为未来而建的世博会

这届世博会从筹备之初起，就被当地视为一个重要的战略项目，是里斯本东部地区改造计划的核心部分。里斯本东部地区原本是一个受污染严重的工业区，当地通过筹办世博会将这一区域改造成绿地面积庞大、公共交通便利、集住宅、商业和文化等多种功能于一体的综合街区。围绕园区的交通基础设施得到改善，形成多式联运的枢纽，将园区与整个里斯本甚至更广泛地区的地铁、铁路和公共汽车网络连接起来。世博会结束后，世博园区成为一个现代化的城市街区，原本为世博会而建的相关场馆和设施成为这个街区的主要部分。里斯本将世博会的组织工作与城市未来发展以及当地居民的需求紧密联系为一体，成功为葡萄牙城市更新改造树立了榜样。

1998年里斯本世博会园区全景
印刷品，1998年，里斯本市府档案馆馆藏

Aerial View of Expo 1998 Lisbon
1998. Arquivo Municipal de Lisboa. Print.

Ocean Exploration Exhibits at Expo 1998 Lisbon
1998. BIE Archive. Print.

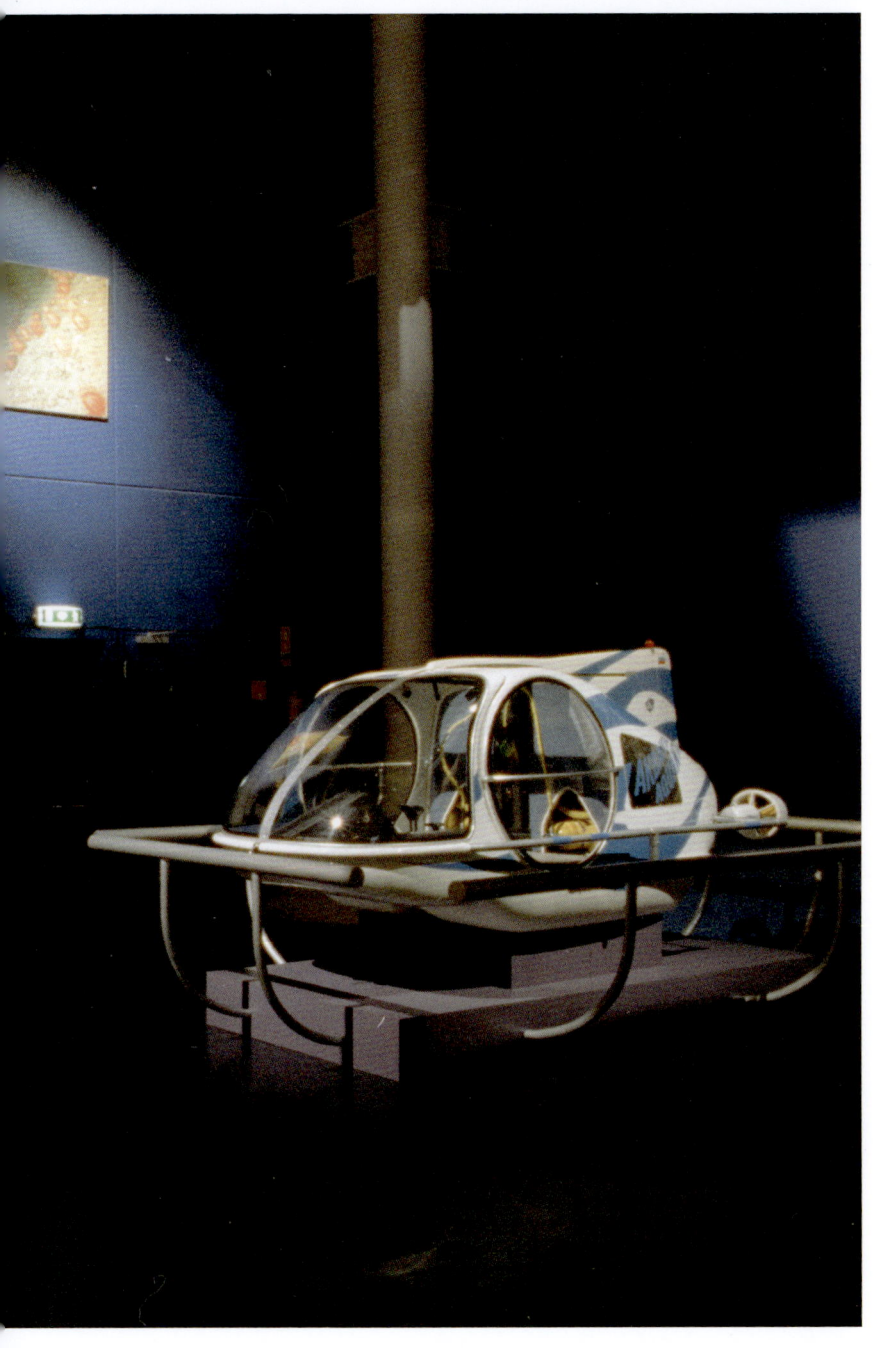

1998年里斯本世博会上的海洋探索展项
印刷品，1998年，国际展览局馆藏

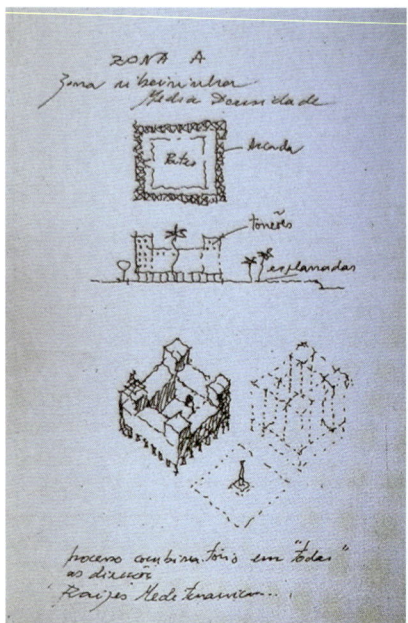
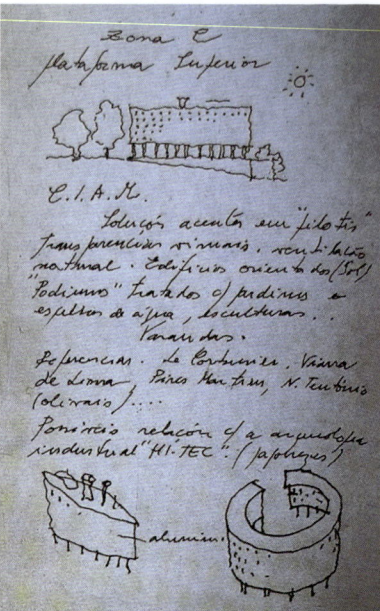

Detailed Plan of the Expo Site (partial)
Lisbon World Expo 98. Projects. 1996. World Expo Museum Collection. Print.

EXPO 2000 HANNOVER

汉诺威
世博会

Theme: **Humankind - Nature - Technology**
Location: **Hannover, Germany**
Category: **World Expo**
Dates: **2000.6.1-10.31**
Area (ha): **160**
Visitors: **18,100,000**
Participants: **174**

Sustainable Development

Expo 2000 Hannover, under the theme "Humankind - Nature - Technology", embodied the aims and principles of Agenda 21, which was agreed upon at the 1992 Earth Summit. The Expo fully implemented a resolution adopted by the General Assembly of the BIE in 1994 on sustainable development of Expos. This resolution required the Organizer of the Expo to plan for the re-use of the Expo site and facilities at the beginning of the preparations for the event. This Expo used the existing Hannover Messe as the main exhibition hall, while the rest of the site was developed as part of the Kronsberg Eco-district. The residential area became a model eco-city for its by passive buildings and low-energy buildings.

Hannover Principals

The development of the site adhered to the Hannover Principals. With sustainability as the guideline, many pavilions were constructed using bold and advanced technologies. The Swiss Pavilion was made up of more than 40,000 logs without the use of any adhesive materials. The Japan Pavilion was constructed by recycled paper from Germany as the building material and paper tube technology. The Netherlands Pavilion accommodated a tulip fields, a forest, sand dunes, wind turbines and other elements in a limited space, forming an environmentally friendly system that was self-sufficient in electricity and had a closed-loop water system.

Projects around the World

Expo 2000 Hannover launched a call for "Projects around the World", which solicited examples of sustainable development practices from all over the world, and the selected cases were exhibited in the "Global House". The Global House was the predecessor of the Best Practices Area, which has been a mandatory part of all World Expos since Expo 2010 Shanghai.

主题：**人类、自然、科技**
举办地：**德国汉诺威**
类型：**综合类世博会**
日期：**2000年6月1日至10月31日**
占地（公顷）：**160**
参观者（人次）：**18,100,000**
参展方（个）：**174**

可持续发展

2000年汉诺威世博会以『人类、自然、科技』为主题，体现了1992年联合国环境与发展大会上达成的《21世纪议程》的宗旨和原则。同时，这届世博会还彻底贯彻了1994年国际展览局大会通过的关于可持续发展世博会的一项决议。这项决议要求世博会的组织者在筹办之初即做好会后重新利用场馆与设施的计划。汉诺威世博会以现有的汉诺威展览中心为主要展馆，其余场地则开发成为康斯柏格生态住宅区的一部分。该住宅区以被动式低能耗建筑为特色，是有名的生态示范城区。

汉诺威原则

园区开发严格遵守汉诺威原则。以可持续发展为指导方针，许多展馆的建造采用了大胆而先进的技术。瑞士馆由4万多块原木构成，没有使用任何粘胶材料。日本馆以德国产的再生纸为建筑材料，运用纸管技术建造而成。荷兰馆在有限的空间里容纳了郁金香花田、森林、沙丘、风电机组等多种元素，形成一套电力自给、水路闭环的环保系统。

世界项目

汉诺威世博会发起一项名为『世界项目』的征集，向世界各地征集可持续发展的实践案例，入选案例在『全球之家』展出。『全球之家』是最佳实践区的前身，之后从2010年上海世博会开始，最佳实践区成为每届世博会必须展示的内容。

2000年汉诺威世博会园区局部鸟瞰图
印刷品，2000年，《世博建筑文献：为2000年汉诺威世博会所做的贡献》，世博会博物馆馆藏

Partial View of Existing Fair Site
EXPO Architecture Documents: Contributions for the World Exposition EXPO 2000 in Hanover.
2000. World Expo Museum Collection. Print.

The Switzerland Pavilion
2000. BIE Archive. Print.

瑞士馆
印刷品，2000 年，国际展览局馆藏

日本馆内景
印刷品，2000年，国际展览局馆藏

Interior of the Japan Pavilion
2000. BIE Archive. Print.

荷兰馆
印刷品，2000年，国际展览局馆藏

德国安全工作系统展览入选了2000年汉诺威世博会的「世界项目」，传达了「技术应该适应人的需求，而非让人去适应技术」的理念印刷品，2000年，《全球互联：为了可持续的未来，〈21世纪议程〉在行动》，世博会博物馆馆藏

Listed in the "Projects Around the World" of the Expo 2000 Hannover, The German Safe Work System Exhibition conveyed the concept that "not mankind has to adapt to technology, but technology has to adapt to mankind."
Global Network for a Sustainable Future Agenda 21 in Action. 2000. World Expo Museum Collection. Print.

EXPO 2005 AICHI

爱知
世博会

Theme:
Nature's Wisdom
Location:
Aichi, Japan
Category:
World Expo
Dates: **2005.3.25-9.25**
Area (ha): **173**
Visitors: **22,049,544**
Participants: **121**

No Environment Burdens

The theme of this Expo, "Nature's Wisdom", echoed and reflected the resolution adopted by the General Assembly of the BIE in 1994, which codified that the theme of the Expo held in the 21st century must reflect environmental protection. At the same time, based on the 1997 Kyoto Protocol (the United Nations Framework Convention on Climate Change), the Organizer of the Expo Aichi conducted a comprehensive environmental evaluation of the site and sought to minimize the impact of construction on the surrounding environment. In order to reduce the environmental load on the ground, the Organizer also constructed a 2.6-kilometer-long circular promenade, the "Global Loop", which was 14 meters above the ground.

The 3R Principle

Strictly following the 3R principle of "Reduce, Reuse, Recycle", the Expo adopted a range of new technologies conducive to sustainable development in its construction and management. From giant laser projection screens to automated solar production systems, the Expo showcased a variety of innovations designed to improve quality of life while protecting the environment. In addition, the Organizer have set up a comprehensive recycling system in the site to separate waste and increase recycling efficiency, and had introduced a virtual currency system called "Eco-Money" to encourage people to use fewer plastic bags and more public transportation to build an environmental friendly society.

Making Way for the Eagle

The site of the Expo was originally set to be located within Kaisha Forest in Seto municipality, but realizing that the construction would have an impact on the survival of the local wildlife, the eagles, the Organizer reduced the size of the Seto site and used it only as a secondary venue. Nagakute was chosen as the main site. After the Expo, the Seto site was transformed into the Aichi Kaisho Forest Center, which continued to protect the Kaisho Forest, while the Nagakute site was transformed into the Moricoro Park, where the animation theme park Ghibli Park was open on this site in 2022.

主题：**自然的睿智**
举办地：**日本爱知**
类型：**综合类世博会**
日期：**2005 年 3 月 25 日至 9 月 25 日**
占地（公顷）：**173**
参观者（人次）：**22,049,544**
参展方（个）：**121**

不给环境添负担

2005 年爱知世博会的主题是『自然的睿智』，呼应并体现了 1994 年国际展览局大会通过的一项决议，决议规定 21 世纪举办的世博会其主题必须反映环境保护。同时，以 1997 年《联合国气候变化框架公约》京都议定书为基础，爱知世博会的组织者对场地环境进行全面评估，力求将建设对周围环境的影响降至最低。为了减少对地面的环境负荷，组织者还在园区修建了离地 14 米高、长 2.6 千米的空中回廊——『全球环路』。

3R 原则

世博会严格遵循『减少（Reduce）、再利用（Reuse）、再循环（Recycle）』的 3R 原则，采用有利于可持续发展的新技术进行建设和管理。从巨型激光投影屏幕到自动太阳能生产系统，世博会上展示的各种创新技术都旨在提高生活质量以及保护环境。此外，组织者在园区内还建立了全面的回收系统，将垃圾进行分类，以提高回收效率；推出虚拟货币系统——『环保市』，鼓励人们少用塑料袋、多乘坐公共交通，建设环境友好型的社会。

为苍鹰让路

世博会原本选址在濑户的海上之森，但意识到建设会对当地野生动物苍鹰的生存造成影响，组织者缩小濑户会场的面积，只将其作为副会场，另选长久手作为主会场。会后，濑户会场被改造为爱知海上之森中心，继续保护海上之森；长久手会场则被改造为爱·地球博纪念公园，2022 年"动画主题公园吉卜力公园也在此开园。

2005年爱知世博会长久手会场局部鸟瞰图
照片，2005年

Partial View of the Nagakute Site
2005. Photo.

Following the Expo, most of the Nagakute site was transformed into a wide parkland known as Moricoro Park (named after the Expo mascots, Morizo and Kikkoro). 2005. Photo.

2005年爱知世博会结束后,长久手会场被改造为爱·地球博纪念公园

照片,2005年

长久手日本馆的建筑体具有双层结构，这种结构如同蚕茧一般，既保护了内部生命体，又与周遭环境保持联系

印刷品，2005年，《日本馆》，世博会博物馆馆藏

506　The dual-layered structure of Japan Pavilion Nagakute evokes the image of a cocoon, which shelters life forms within while also being linked to its surrounding environment.
Japan Pavilions. 2005. World Expo Museum Collection. Print.

单座未来概念车 i-Unit 和载人步行机器人 i-Foot 上演了多场机器人表演秀
丰田汽车公司版权所有

-Unit, a single-seat concept car, and i-Foot, a passenger robot,
taged a number of robot shows.
© Toyota Motor Corporation

i-Unit 目前在世博会博物馆展出，由丰田汽车公司捐赠。i-Unit 可依据车速改变形态，博物馆展出的是其低速行驶时的形态照片，2018年，世博会博物馆馆藏

The i-Unit is currently on display at the World Expo Museum, donated by Toyota Motor Corporation. The i-Unit can change shape depending on its speed, and the one on display is shown in its low speed configuration. 2018. World Expo Museum Collection. Photo.

EXPO 2008 ZARAGOZA

萨拉戈萨
世博会

Theme:
Water and Sustainable Development
Location:
Zaragoza, Spain
Category:
Specialised Expo
Dates: **2008.6.14-9.14**
Area (ha): **25**
Visitors: **5,650,943**
Participants: **108**

Water Resource Management

Expo 2008 Zaragoza, under the theme "Water and Sustainable Development", emphasized the urgency of water management and called on the international community to face the challenges and propose solutions for the future. Located on the banks of the Ebro River, the Expo's master plan was based on the principle of sustainable development, with zones named after geographic features such as islands, rainforests, oasis, temperate forests, snow and ice, mountains, river and flat planes, grasslands and deserts. The Expo site featured several thematic plazas, each with a number of water-themed art installations, reflecting various topics such as thirst, clean energy, river basin governance, urban water and more.

The Zaragoza Charter

The Water Tribune, as a special establishment of the Expo Zaragoza, was designed to bring together the world's wisdom on water management issues. It provided a space for discussion and exchange between researchers, technical engineers, governments and businesses, encouraging ideas and visions. As a concrete outcome, *The Zaragoza Charter*, provided clear recommendations for the sustainable management of water resources and guided the forward direction for the world.

Water for Life

After the Expo, Zaragoza became the first Spanish City to host headquarters of a United Nations Agency: the United Nations International Decade for Action: Water for Life 2005-2015. The Expo also improved the city's transportation infrastructure, with the construction of new roads and bridges, and a bicycle rental program was established since the Expo and which remains in place today.

主题：**水与可持续发展**
举办地：**西班牙萨拉戈萨**
类型：**专业类世博会**
日期：**2008年6月14日至9月14日**
占地（公顷）：**25**
参观者（人次）：**5,650,943**
参展方（个）：**108**

水资源管理

萨拉戈萨世博会以『水与可持续发展』为主题，强调了水资源管理问题的紧迫性，号召国际社会共同面对挑战，提出未来应对之策。世博会的总体规划遵循可持续发展的原则，选址在埃布罗河畔，以地理特征命名各个区域，比如岛屿、雨林、绿洲、温带森林、冰雪、山脉、河流平原、草原，以及沙漠。世博园区设有不同主题的广场，每个广场都设置了许多与水主题相关的艺术装置，反映干涸、清洁能源、河流治理、城市水资源等各类话题。

《萨拉戈萨宣言》

萨拉戈萨世博会专门设立水论坛，为水资源管理问题凝聚世界智慧。它为科研者、技术工程师、政府以及企业方提供讨论和交流的空间，鼓励各方提出主张和愿景，并最终发布了《萨拉戈萨宣言》。该宣言为水资源的可持续管理提出明确建议，为全世界指明了方向。

生命之水

世博会结束后，联合国将『国际"生命之水"十年行动2005—2015』的总部设在萨拉戈萨，使萨拉戈萨成为西班牙第一个设有联合国机构总部的城市。萨拉戈萨世博会同时也改善了城市的交通基础设施，新的道路和桥梁因此而建设，自行车租赁方案也从世博会开始一直在这座城市里施行。

2008年萨拉戈萨世博会园区手绘图
印刷品，约2008年，《2008年萨拉戈萨世博会总目录》，世博会博物馆馆藏

The Drawings of Expo 2008 Zaragoza
General Catalogue: Exposición Internacional Zaragoza 2008.
2008. World Expo Museum Collection. Print.

2008年萨拉戈萨世博会以水为主题，选址在埃布罗河畔，图为艺术家乔玛·帕兰萨为世博会设计的作品《埃布罗之魂》

印刷品，2008年，《2008年萨拉戈萨世博会总目录》，世博会博物馆馆藏

Themed on water, the Expo 2008 Zaragoza chose its site along the River Ebro. This photo is a print of Alma del Ebro, an artwork created by Jaume Plensa specifically for the Expo.
General Catalogue: Exposición Internacional Zaragoza 2008. 2008. World Expo Museum Collection. Print.

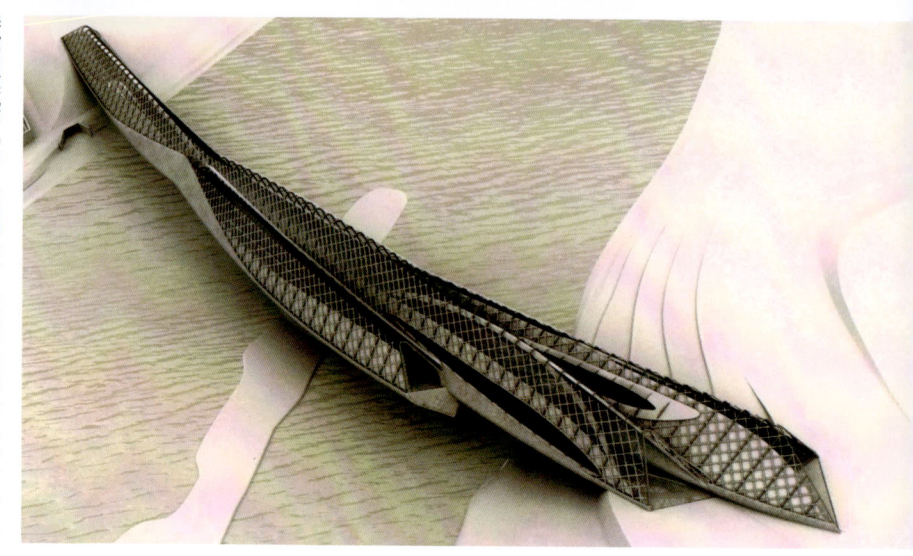

桥馆由建筑师扎哈·哈迪德设计,她将桥馆定义为"一个从河流和岸边自然生长出来的物体"。印刷品,约2008年,《2008年萨拉戈萨世博会总目录》,世博会博物馆馆藏

The Bridge Pavilion is Designed by architect Zaha Hadid. The design team defines it as "an object born from the natural conditions of the river and its bank".
General Catalogue: Exposición Internacional Zaragoza 2008. 2008. World Expo Museum Collection. Print.

EXPO 2010 SHANGHAI

上海
世博会

Theme: **Better City, Better Life**
Location: **Shanghai, China**
Category: **World Expo**
Dates: **2010.5.1-10.31**
Area (ha): **523**
Visitors: **73,085,000**
Participants: **246**

A Record-breaking Expo

Expo 2010 Shanghai was the most visited Expo in history, boasting a total of 73 million visitors, with the highest attendance of 1.03 million visitors in a single day. The area of the Expo site and the number of international participants also reached a record high at that time.

Better City, Better Life

Entering the 21st century, the urban population has increased dramatically, causing a series of social challenges such as population mobility, social stability and sustainable development. Shanghai adopted "Better City, Better Life" as the theme of the Expo, advocating the international community to face urban problems together and showcase their own solutions to urban challenges. The highlight of the Expo was the Urban Best Practices Area, which showcased nearly 80 case studies to inspire the future development of cities around the world.

Long Lasting Impact of Expo

The massive renovation projects along the Huangpu River in the center of Shanghai for the Expo were a perfect illustration of the theme of the Expo. Large areas of old factories were transformed into the Expo site, a new area fully integrated into modern city life. Steel mills and power plants were transformed into sculpture gardens and museums, and the Expo site and pavilions were developed into parks and cultural venues after the Expo. In 2017, the World Expo Museum, the official museum of the BIE, was inaugurated on the former site of the Expo.

Shanghai Declaration and World Cities Day

On the closing ceremony of Expo 2010 Shanghai, the *Shanghai Declaration* was issued, which proposed that the closing day of the Expo, October 31, to be designated as the World Cities Day. Three years later, the United Nations General Assembly adopted the World Cities Day, which will be celebrated annually. Another significant legacy of the Expo is the *Shanghai Manual*, jointly compiled by the UN-Habitat, the BIE, and the Shanghai Municipality.

主题：城市，让生活更美好

举办地：中国上海

类型：综合类世博会

日期：2010年5月1日至10月31日

占地（公顷）：523

参观者（人次）：73,085,000

参展方（个）：246

创纪录的世博会

2010年上海世博会是有史以来参观人数最多的一届世博会，参观了这届世博会，单日最高客流量达到103万人次。这届世博会的园区面积、国际参展方数量也都达到历史新高。

城市，让生活更美好

进入21世纪，城市人口急剧上升，引发人口流动、社会安定、可持续发展等一系列社会问题。上海以『城市，让生活更美好』作为世博会的主题，倡导国际社会共同面对城市问题并提出解决方案。这届世博会的亮点是城市最佳实践区，展示了近80个城市案例，为世界各地城市未来的发展带来启发。

世博效应持续发力

为举办世博会，上海对市中心的黄浦江两岸开展大规模重建，其本身就是对世博会主题最好的注解。大片的旧厂区被改造为世博园区，成为一个完全融入现代城市生活的新区域。钢铁厂、发电厂转变为雕塑园、博物馆、世博园区及场馆也会在会后重新开发为公园和文化场所。国际展览局官方博物馆——世博会博物馆也在园区旧址上新建，于2017年正式开放。

《上海宣言》和世界城市日

上海世博会在闭幕时发表《上海宣言》，并建议将闭幕这一天10月31日设为世界城市日。三年后，联合国大会通过决议，每年庆祝世界城市日。另外，由联合国人居署、国际展览局和上海政府共同主编的《上海手册》也是一项重要的世博遗产。

2010年上海世博会浦东片区鸟瞰图
照片，2010年，摄影：项欣荣，世博会博物馆馆藏

Aerial View of the Pudong site of Expo 2010 Shanghai
Photo by XIANG Xinrong. 2010. World Expo Museum Collection. Photo.

中国馆
照片,2010年,摄影:项欣荣,世博会博物馆馆藏

China Pavilion
Photo by XIANG Xinrong. 2010. World Expo Museum Collection. Photo.

城市最佳实践区展示的城市案例为城市未来发展带来新启示，图为宁波滕头案例馆照片，2010年，世博会博物馆馆藏

Case studies showcased in the Urban Best Practices Area inspired the future development of cities around the world. This photo shows the Ningbo Case Pavilion.
2010. World Expo Museum Collection. Photo.

World Expo Museum
Photo by YUAN Ji. 2020. World Expo Museum Collection. Photo.

世博会博物馆照片,2020年,摄影:袁稷,世博会博物馆馆藏

2010年上海世博会园区在会后得到充分规划与利用，逐步发展成为政务办公、会展商务、文化博览与绿色生态相融合的综合性场域照片，2024年，摄影：IP SHANGHAI 徐介明

According to the holistic post-Expo plan, the site has been gradually developed into a hub of government departments, business, convention and exhibition industries, cultural and ecological centers.
Photo by IP SHANGHAI XU Jieming. 2024.Photo.

EXPO 2012 YEOSU
丽水世博会

Theme:
The Living Ocean and Coast
Location:
Yeosu, Republic of Korea
Category:
Specialised Expo
Dates: **2012.5.12-8.12**
Area (ha): **25**
Visitors: **8,203,956**
Participants: **103**

Shared Destiny for Human and Ocean

Located on the southern coast of Korea, Yeosu has been a historical hub of marine transportation since ancient times, linking China, Japan and Korea. Yeosu located in the richest regions in East Asia in terms of marine life species. With the theme of ocean and coast, the Expo considered that ocean and coasts are the source of human life and the regulator of the earth's ecosystem, attaching great importance to human life and development. However, continued exploitation of coastal areas, overuse of marine resources and pollution were threatening the balance of these two fragile ecosystems. The Expo advocated focusing on the sustainable development of the oceans, as human survival is closely linked to the health of the oceans and coasts.

An Expo Site by the Sea

The Expo site was located in the harbor on the southeast coast of Yeosu. Without damaging the surrounding environment, the Expo constructed an environmentally friendly international leisure harbor, an international tourist resort and a coastal residential area, meeting the operational needs during the Expo, as well the efficient utilization after the Expo.

Yeosu Declaration

As a practice, a declaration was also issued during this Expo. The *Yeosu Declaration* provided a new perspective for the world to realize green growth (meaning a low-carbon, sustainable economic development model) by paying attention to the marine environment. Expo 2012 Yeosu called on governments and civil society to work in solidarity and cooperation towards the common goals for the oceans.

主题：生机勃勃的海洋与海岸
举办地：韩国丽水
类型：专业类世博会
日期：2012年5月12日至8月12日
占地（公顷）：25
参观者（人次）：8,203,956
参展方（个）：103

人类与海洋命运与共

丽水坐落于韩国南部海岸，可连通中、日、韩三国，自古以来就是海洋运输的枢纽，其所处的东亚地区是海洋生物物种最为丰富的区域之一。丽水世博会以『生机勃勃的海洋与海岸』为主题，认为它们是人类生命之源，也是地球生态系统的调节器，对于人类生存与发展关系重大。然而，沿海地区的持续发展、海洋资源的过度利用和污染，正在威胁这两个脆弱的生态系统的平衡。丽水倡导关注海洋的可持续发展，因为人类的生存与海洋、海岸的健康紧密相连。

依海而建的园区

世博园区位于丽水东南部海岸的港口。在不破坏周围环境的前提下，丽水世博会建造了环保型国际休闲港、国际旅游度假区和滨海住宅区。这片区域不仅能满足世博会期间的运营需求，还能在世博会结束后被高效利用。

《丽水宣言》

和之前一样，这届世博会也发表了宣言。《丽水宣言》为世界提供了一个新的视角，即关注海洋环境，实现绿色增长（指一种低碳、可持续的经济发展模式）。丽水世博会呼吁各国政府和民间社会团结合作，为共同的海洋目标不懈努力。

2012年丽水世博会园区鸟瞰图
照片,2012年,摄影:项欣荣,世博会博物馆馆藏

Bird's Eye View of Expo 2012 Yeosu
Photo by XIANG Xinrong. 2012. World Expo Museum Collection. Photo.

主题馆内上演了一场秀,讲述濒临灭绝的儒艮与少年的友情,借此引发人们思考如何保护海洋印刷品,2013年,《世博遗产的传承、研究和利用——世博会博物馆丽水世博会研讨会暨考察文集》,世博会博物馆馆藏

A show in the Theme Pavilion told the story of the friendship between an endangered dugong and a teenager, which provoked people to think about how to protect the oceans.
Investing in the Future, the Legacy of Expos: Collected Papers of Forum & Survey on Expo 2012 Yeosu Korea by World Expo Museum. 2013. World Expo Museum Collection. Print.

天塔是 2012 年丽水世博会园区里最高的建筑,由废弃的水泥筒仓改造而成,其外部安装了管风琴,声音可传至 6,000 米远

印刷品,2013 年,《海洋的故事——韩国 2012 年丽水世博会》,世博会博物馆馆藏

The Sky Tower, the tallest building of the Expo site, was converted from an abandoned cement silo. With an organ installed on its exterior, the building could make sound up to six kilometers away.
The Story of Ocean and Coast: Expo 2012 Yeosu Korea. 2013. World Expo Museum Collection. Print.

2012年丽水世博会地标性建筑——Big-O印刷品，2013年，《海洋的故事——韩国2012年丽水世博会》，世博会博物馆馆藏

Big-O, the Centerpiece of Expo 2012 Yeosu
The Story of Ocean and Coast: Expo 2012 Yeosu Korea.
2013. World Expo Museum Collection. Print.

EXPO 2015 MILAN

米兰
世博会

Theme: **Feeding the Planet, Energy for Life**
Location: **Milan, Italy**
Category: **World Expo**
Dates: **2015.5.1-10.31**
Area (ha): **110**
Visitors: **21,500,000**
Participants: **139**

Food for Thought

Centered on food, Expo 2015 Milan addressed the global issues and challenges, such as food production, dietary health, population growth, waste prevention and efficient use of natural resources, and called for the countries all over the world to unite in the fight against the food crisis.

Inspired by the ancient Roman camp, the Expo site featured 2 vertical axes: the 1.5-km east-west Decumano (World Avenue) and the 350-meter north-south Cardo (Street of Italy). Several of the Expo's thematic pavilions provided a full interpretation of the theme: Pavilion Zero told the history of mankind's relationship with food, the Future Food Pavilion featured an interactive supermarket and an innovative kitchen, the Parco Biodiversita housed gardens and greenhouses, and the Children's Park allowed younger visitors to learn about food through games.

In addition, some of the international participants participate the Expo via "Clusters". These clusters were categorized on the basis of agricultural specialty or climatic type, i.e. Rice, Cocoa and Chocolate, Coffee, Fruit and Legumes, Spices, and Cereals and Tubers, Arid Zones, Bio-Mediterraneum, and Islands, Sea and Food, reflecting the thematic character of this Expo.

The *Milan Charter*

The Expo published the *Milan Charter*, setting principles and objectives related to nutrition, sustainable development and the right to food. Additionally, the mayors of more than 100 cities around the world co-signed the Milan Urban Food Policy Pact. The Pact, supported by the Food and Agriculture Organization of the United Nations, called on cities to develop sustainable and healthy food systems while promoting biodiversity and reducing waste.

主题：滋养地球，生命能源
举办地：意大利米兰
类型：综合类世博会
日期：2015年5月1日至10月31日
占地（公顷）：110
参观者（人次）：21,500,000
参展方（个）：139

聚焦粮食

米兰世博会以食物为主题，直面粮食生产、饮食健康、人口增长、避免浪费和有效利用自然资源等全球问题与时代挑战，呼吁世界各国团结起来共同应对食物危机。

世博园区的设计灵感来源于古罗马兵营，设有两条垂直的中轴线：东西向1.5千米长的德库马努斯中轴线（世界大道）和南北向350米长的卡多中轴线（意大利大道）。世博会的几大主题馆对主题展开充分演绎：零号馆讲述人类与食物的关系史，未来食物馆内设有互动超市和创新厨房，生物多样性公园内有花园和温室，儿童乐园让孩子们通过游戏学习有关食物的知识。

另外，部分国际参展方以集群的方式参展。这些集群基于农业特点或气候类型分类，分别是：稻米集群、可可和巧克力集群、咖啡集群、水果和豆类集群、香料集群、谷物和薯类集群、干旱集群、海岛海洋和食物集群、生态地中海集群。这种特殊的集群方式体现了这届世博会的主题特色。

《米兰宣言》

这届世博会发表了《米兰宣言》，宣言设定了与营养、可持续发展、食物权有关的原则和目标。此外，全球100多个城市的市长联合签署了《米兰城市粮食政策公约》。该公约得到联合国粮食及农业组织的支持，呼吁各城市在促进生物多样性和减少浪费的同时，发展可持续和健康的粮食系统。

Panoramic View of Expo 2015 Milano
Expo Milano 2015 the Making of.
2015. World Expo Museum Collection. Print.

2015年米兰世博会园区全景印刷品，2015年，《建造2015年米兰世博会》，世博会博物馆馆藏

Pavilion Zero was the first themed pavilion upon entering the Expo site, and its theme was closely related to the Zero Hunger Challenge advocated by the United Nations.
Expo Milano 2015 Official Report. 2018. World Expo Museum Collection. Print.

零号馆是游客进入2015年米兰世博会园区后参观的第一个主题馆，它的展示主题与联合国倡导的『零饥饿挑战』密切相关印刷品，2018年，《2015年米兰世博会官方报告》，世博会博物馆藏

2015年米兰世博会呼吁参与者"设计和建造临时性的、可持续的建筑,关注材料生命周期及其对环境的影响"。印刷品,2018年,《2015年米兰世博会官方报告》,世博会博物馆藏

Expo 2015 called participants to "design and create temporary, sustainable buildings, focusing on environmental impact and life cycle of the materials and the components". *Expo Milano 2015 Official Report.* 2018. World Expo Museum Collection. Print.

EXPO 2017 ASTANA

阿斯塔纳世博会

Theme: **Future Energy**
Location: **Astana, Kazakhstan**
Category: **Specialised Expo**
Dates: **2017.6.10-9.10**
Area (ha): **25**
Visitors: **3,977,545**
Participants: **137**

Future Energy

With the theme of "Future Energy", Expo 2017 Astana demonstrated Kazakhstan's intention to contribute to the global dialogue on energy security, to actively develop and utilize alternative sources of energy, and to transition to a green economy.

The Kazakhstan Pavilion, Nur-Alem, the centerpiece of the Expo, is the world's largest spherical structure with a diameter of 80 meters. Its architectural surface is covered with 3,535 pieces of double-glazed glass and is powered by renewable energy through silent wind turbines and photovoltaic technology. It was the most visited pavilion during the Expo and housed the Museum of Future Energy, introducing six types of energy generation: space, solar, wind, organic, kinetic and water. The top floor was the "City of the Future" gallery, which depicted how new technologies and smart grids would shape the future of Astana.

In addition, the Energy Best Practices area at the Expo showcased more than 20 sustainable energy management solutions from around the world, such as an off-grid power generation system using solar energy to supply oxygen to treat pneumonia, and a sidewalk that generates electricity from the kinetic energy of pedestrians walking.

The *Manifest of Values and Principles*

Expo 2017 Astana hosted 3,500 events over the three-month period, and the most important series of those events was the Future Energy Forum. The Forum gathered together scientists, energy experts and political representatives from all over the world for in-depth discussions on the sustainable production, storage, distribution and consumption of energy. The Forum provided the basis for the compilation of the *Manifest of Values and Principles* for Expo 2017 Astana, which provided guidance and recommendations for the promotion of energy-efficient lifestyles and the widespread use of renewable energy sources.

主题：未来能源
举办地：哈萨克斯坦阿斯塔纳
类型：专业类世博会
日期：2017年6月10日至9月10日
占地（公顷）：25
参观者（人次）：3,977,545
参展方（个）：137

未来能源

阿斯塔纳世博会的主题是"未来能源"，表明哈萨克斯坦有意促成能源安全全球对话，积极开发和利用替代能源，向绿色经济转型的意愿。

努尔－阿列姆哈萨克斯坦国家馆是这届世博会的中心建筑，它是世博会期间参观人数最多的展馆，馆内设有未来能源博物馆，详细介绍宇宙能源、太阳能源、风能源、生物能源、动力能源和水能源等六种能源生产方式。努尔－阿列姆馆的顶层是"未来城市"展厅，描绘新技术和智能电网将如何塑造阿斯塔纳的未来。

另外，世博会上的能源最佳实践区展示了来自世界各地的20多个可持续能源管理方案，比如利用太阳能供氧治疗肺炎的离网发电系统、利用行人步行的动能发电人行道等。

《价值观与原则宣言》

阿斯塔纳世博会在三个月会期内共举办了3,500场活动，其中最重要的系列活动就是未来能源论坛。论坛汇聚了全球科学家、能源专家和政界代表，围绕能源的可持续生产、储存、分配和消费展开深入讨论。论坛为《2017年阿斯塔纳世博会的价值观与原则宣言》的编纂提供了基础，该宣言为提倡节能生活方式和广泛使用可再生能源提供指导和建议。

2017年阿斯塔纳世博会园区效果图
印刷品，2018年，《未来能源——2017年阿斯塔纳世博会》，世博会博物馆馆藏

Rendering of the Site of Expo 2017 Astana
Future Energy: Kazakhstan Astana Expo 2017. 2018. World Expo Museum Collection. Print.

553

Nur-Alem Kazakhstani Pavilion
Photo by DAI Xiaoli. 2017. World Expo Museum Collection. Photo.

努尔-阿列姆哈萨克斯坦国家馆照片,2017年,摄影:戴晓珂,世博会博物馆馆藏

努尔－阿列姆哈萨克斯坦国家馆的宇宙能源展区展示了登月飞船的等比例模型印刷品，2018年，《未来能源——2017年阿斯塔纳世博会》，世博会博物馆馆藏

The Kazakhstan Pavilion, Nur-Alem, featured a scale model of the spacecraft that landed on the moon in the section of space energy.
Future Energy: Kazakhstan Astana Expo 2017. 2018. World Expo Museum Collection. Print.

EXPO 2020 DUBAI

迪拜世博会

Theme: **Connecting Minds, Creating the Future**
Location: **Dubai, United Arab Emirates**
Category: **World Expo**
Dates: **2021.10.1-2022.3.31**
Area (ha): **438**
Visitors: **24,102,967**
Participants: **200**

Future for All

Expo 2020 Dubai was the first Expo in the Middle East, Africa and South Asia (MEASA) region. With the theme "Connecting Minds, Creating the Future", Dubai invited the nations of the world to join in the creation of a new world for the future, to face the new challenges and to seek the future solution. The main theme encompassed three sub-themes: "Opportunity", "Mobility" and "Sustainability".

Connecting the World

The center of the Expo site is Al Wasl Plaza, whose dome structure is the world's largest immersive 360-degree projection surface. Al Wasl is the historic name of Dubai, which means "connection". The plaza connected three zones of the Expo: Opportunity Zone, Mobility Zone and Sustainability Zone.

The each thematic zones anchored by its own thematic pavilion. Mission Possible - Opportunity Pavilion inspired optimism that everyone can make a difference in the future and demonstrated the positive changes that can result from cooperation; Alif - Mobility Pavilion (Arif is the pronunciation of the first letter of the Arabic alphabet) allowed visitors to "meet" with historical explorers to discover the world of continuous progress; and the Terra - Sustainability Pavilion told the story of mankind and nature, presented the impact of mankind on the environment, and guided visitors to protect nature.

Expo 2020 Dubai was a grand and diverse event, providing visitors with visual beauty and intellectual inspiration. Using sustainable building materials and cutting-edge technologies to create architectural masterpieces, the site was designed to be ready for after-use. The Expo site is now being gradually transformed into Expo City Dubai, a model district for future cities that will serve as a global reference.

主题：沟通思想，创造未来
举办地：阿联酋迪拜
类型：综合类世博会
日期：2021年10月1日至2022年3月31日
占地（公顷）：438
参观者（人次）：24,102,967
参展方（个）：200

所有人的未来

迪拜世博会是第一次在中东、非洲和南亚地区举办的世博会。这届世博会的主题是『沟通思想，创造未来』，迪拜邀请世界各国加入创造未来新世界的行列中，共同面对新的挑战，寻求未来发展之路。主标题下设有三个副标题，分别是：『机遇』『流动性』和『可持续发展』。

连接世界

世博园区的中心是阿尔瓦斯尔广场，其穹顶结构是世界上最大的沉浸式360度投影面。阿尔瓦斯尔是迪拜历史上的曾用名，意为『连接』。阿尔瓦斯尔广场在园区里也发挥了连接的作用，与其相连的是三片『花瓣』，即机遇区、流动性区和可持续发展区三个主题区。

主题区设有特定的主题馆：『可行的使命——机遇馆』，激发人人都能在未来有所作为的乐观精神，展现合作产生的积极变化；『阿里夫——流动性馆』（阿里夫是阿拉伯字母表第一个字母的发音），让游客与历史上的探索者『见面』，探索持续进步的世界；『地球——可持续发展馆』，讲述人类与自然的故事，阐明人类对环境的影响，引导游客保护自然。

迪拜世博会规模盛大，极具多样性，为游客带来视觉上的美感与思想上的启迪。园区运用可持续建筑材料和尖端技术创造了多个建筑杰作，并在建设之初就为后续开发做好准备，目前正逐步转型为迪拜世博城，将成为值得全球借鉴的未来城市示范区。

2020年迪拜世博会园区夜景
2020年迪拜世博会官方版权所有

Aerial View at Night of Expo 2020 Dubai
© Expo 2020 Dubai

"地球——可持续发展馆"夜景
2020年迪拜世博会官方版权所有

Aerial View at Night of Terra - The Sustainability Pavilion
© Expo 2020 Dubai

The exhibits in the Mission Possible –Opportunity Pavilion were centered on the UN Sustainable Development Goals (SDGs).
© Expo 2020 Dubai

站在『阿里夫——流动性馆』门前的吉祥物——机器人Opti，利用人工智能等多项技术为游客提供参观指引服务

2020年迪拜世博会官方版权所有

In front of the Alif - Mobility Pavilion was its mascot, Opti, which could provide visitor's guidance service based on AI and other technologies.
© Expo 2020 Dubai

EXPO 2025 OSAKA KANSAI

大阪
世博会

Theme:
Designing Future Society for Our Lives
Location:
Osaka Kansai, Japan
Category:
World Expo
Dates: **2025.4.13-10.13**
Area (ha): **155**

Designing Future Society for Our Lives

The theme, "Designing Future Society for Our Lives", makes individuals think how they want to live and how they can maximise their potential. This theme also aims to drive co-creation by the international community in designing a sustainable society that supports individuals' ideas of how they want to live. In other words, the Expo will ask a straightforward question for the first time: "What is the happy way of life?" The Expo is taking place at a time when new social challenges, including expanding economic gaps and heightened conflicts, are emerging, while science technologies are evolving, including AI and biotechnology, that will present changes to humankinds, for example, extended life spans.

Saving Lives, Empowering Lives, and Connecting Lives are the three subthemes of the Expo. Japanese culture has long been based on the belief that any material, from all living creatures to even a pebble along the road, has an inherent life. With this in mind, the Expo welcomes the consideration of 'life' not just for human beings but also in a broader sense of diverse creations and nature that surround humans.

The concept of Expo 2025 Osaka Kansai is "People's Living Lab." This concept represents the Expo's approach toward putting its theme into practice and serves as a guideline for the practical implementation of projects. The most distinctive characteristic of the Expo will be the endeavour to give a realistic picture of a future society not just through thought, but also through action. This endeavour is being launched before the Expo, by inviting diverse participants to come together with various initiatives to tackle challenges with solutions that will help achieve the SDGs, either on or off the Expo site.

Information provided by the Expo Organiser

主题：**设计未来社会，让生命绽放光彩**

举办地：**日本大阪关西**

类型：**综合类世博会**

日期：**2025 年 4 月 13 日至 10 月 13 日**

占地（公顷）：**155**

设计未来社会，让生命绽放光彩

2025 年大阪世博会以『设计未来社会，让生命绽放光彩』为主题，促发人们思考如何生活以及最大限度地发挥个人潜能，推动国际社会共同创造一个支持个体意愿的可持续发展的社会。换言之，世博会将首次提出一个明确的问题：『什么是幸福的生活方式？』大阪世博会举办之时，一方面诸如贫富差距增大、社会冲突加剧等新时代下的挑战不断涌现，而另一方面，人工智能、生物技术等科技迅速发展，将给人类带来寿命延长等变化。

『拯救生命』『赋能生命』『链接生命』是这届世博会的三个副主题。日本文化一直认为任何物质，大到所有的生物，小到路边的一粒石子，都具有其内在的生命力。因此，世博会鼓励思考『生命』，不仅思考人类的生命，还在更广泛的意义上思考人类周围的各种创造物和大自然的『生命』。

2025 年大阪世博会的理念是『人们的生活实验室』。这一理念既是世博会将主题付诸实践的方法，也为项目的实际实施提供了指导。这届世博会将不仅通过思想，还要通过行动，努力描绘未来社会的现实图景。在开幕之前，世博会组织者就发起各种倡议，汇聚不同方面的参与者，面对挑战并提出方案，共同推动联合国可持续发展目标的实现。

注：以上信息来源于世博会主办方。

2025年大阪世博会园区设计效果图
2025年大阪世博会官方版权所有

Design Rendering of Expo 2025 Osaka
© Expo 2025 Osaka Kansai

EXPO 2027 BELGRADE
贝尔格莱德世博会

Theme:
Play for Humanity - Sport and Music for All
Location:
Belgrade, Serbia
Category:
Specialised Expo
Dates: **2027.5.15-8.15**
Area (ha): **25**

Play for Humanity – Sport and Music for All

Expo 2027 Belgrade is an opportunity for the world to see the real potential of the region. It will showcase that Serbia is not only keeping up with the latest global trends in infrastructure, tourism, science, technology, artificial intelligence etc., but also that it has the capacity to be the leader in such domains. In these globally challenging times, Serbia's hope is that Expo 2027 Belgrade will commence a bright new chapter of history marked by harmony, friendship, and celebration.

The theme, "Play for humanity: Sport and Music for All", was designed with the purpose of exploring the ways in which humanity can use the power of play for building resilience of individuals and communities in a world full of insecurities. Play is perceived as a superpower of the future, enabling humans to create, innovate and grow. The proposed theme has been further developed into sub-themes to allow international participants to present themselves in the best possible way with ideas and solutions that give answers to the defined problem statement: How to prepare the human body, mind, and logic for a technology-led world full of insecurities and make humans more resilient for the coming decades? The theme will allow Expo 2027 Belgrade to be the largest celebration of global recovery shaped by the power of play and embellished with music and sport.

Information provided by the Expo Organiser

主题：**玩动世界——体育音乐，你我共享**
举办地：**塞尔维亚贝尔格莱德**
类型：**专业类世博会**
日期：**2027 年 5 月 15 日至 8 月 15 日**
占地（公顷）：**25**

玩动世界——体育音乐，你我共享

2027 年贝尔格莱德世博会将成为塞尔维亚向世界展现其潜能的机会，证明其不仅在城市建设、旅游、科学、技术、人工智能等领域达到国际先进水平，还有能力成为这些领域的领军者。在这个充满挑战的时代，塞尔维亚相信 2027 年贝尔格莱德世博会将开启以和谐、友谊和庆祝为主题的历史新篇章。

2027 年贝尔格莱德世博会的主题是『玩动世界——体育音乐，你我共享』，旨在探索人类如何利用游乐的力量，在这个充满不安全感的世界中增强个人与社会的复原力。游乐被视为未来的超能力，可以帮助人类创造、创新和成长。这届世博会将围绕游乐这一主题，发展出多个副主题，让各个参展方能够以最适合的方式展现各自一个共同问题的回答，那就是：『如何让我们的身体、思想和逻辑做好准备，应对这个以技术为主导的、不安定的世界，并且让我们在未来几十年更具复原力？』在这一主题下，通过体育和音乐充分发挥游乐的力量，2027 年贝尔格莱德世博会将成为全球复苏最大的庆典。

注：以上信息来源于世博会主办方。

2027年贝尔格莱德世博会园区设计效果图
2027年贝尔格莱德世博会官方版权所有

Design Rendering of Expo 2027 Belgrade
© Expo 2027 Belgrade

EXPO 2030 RIYADH

利雅得
世博会

Theme:
Foresight for Tomorrow
Location:
Riyadh, Saudi Arabia
Category:
World Expo
Dates:
2030.10.1-2031.3.31

Foresight for Tomorrow

World Expos weave together a rich history of global innovation and progress. At Expo 2030 Riyadh, nations from around the world will build on this important legacy, together. Expo 2030 Riyadh will be a global platform for collective action through which all countries can work together to solve common challenges, and advance shared prosperity and progress.

The theme for Expo 2030 Riyadh, "Foresight for Tomorrow", encapsulates the Kingdom of Saudi Arabia's commitment to create Expo 2030 as a global platform that accelerates progress towards achieving the Sustainable Development Goals (SDGs). Riyadh will work with the global community under three inclusive sub-themes, to harness science and innovation in service of a better future, for all humanity and our planet:

Transformational Technology - Exploring how the power of innovation can be harnessed to drive positive change. From developing smart cities to promoting responsible digital innovations and accelerating scientific breakthroughs, Transformational Technology will be leveraged to showcase how technology can reshape our world for the better.

Sustainable Solutions - Highlighting innovative approaches to climate adaptation, clean energy, and ecosystem regeneration. Sustainable Solutions is about finding the delicate balance between progress and environmental stewardship to safeguard our planet for future generations.

Prosperous People - Emphasising that true progress is inclusive. Prosperous People will explore how to improve global health, provide resources for all, and ensure abundant opportunities. Prosperous People is about creating a world where prosperity is a shared reality, not a privilege for the few.

Information provided by the Expo Organiser

主题：**预见未来**

举办地：**沙特阿拉伯利雅得**

类型：**综合类世博会**

日期：**2030 年 10 月 1 日至 2031 年 3 月 31 日**

预见未来

世博会见证了全球创新与进步的伟大历程。2030 年利雅得世博会将成为汇聚行动与力量的平台，世界各国将在世博会重要遗产的基础上携手前进，合作应对共同挑战，促进全球繁荣发展。

2030 年利雅得世博会的主题是『预见未来』，体现了沙特阿拉伯希望通过举办世博会加快全球实现联合国可持续发展目标的意愿。利雅得拟定了三个副主题，鼓励国际社会开展合作，运用科学与创新的力量为全人类和我们生存的地球创造更美好的未来：

『变革性的技术』——探索如何利用创新的力量推动积极的变革。从发展智慧城市到促进数字创新和加速科学突破，『变革性的技术』将展示技术如何重塑我们的世界，使之变得更加美好。

『可持续的解决方案』——主要展示与气候适应、清洁能源和生态系统恢复有关的创新方案。『可持续的解决方案』就是要在发展与环境之间找到微妙的平衡，为子孙后代保护我们的地球。

『繁荣的人类』——强调真正的发展是具有包容性的。『繁荣的人类』将探讨如何改善全球健康，为所有人供给资源，并提供充足的机会。『繁荣的人类』所创造的繁荣属于所有人，而非少数人的特权。

注：以上信息来源于世博会主办方。

2030利雅得世博会园区设计效果图
2030利雅得世博会官方版权所有

Design Rendering of Expo 2030 Riyadh
© Expo 2030 Riyadh

图书在版编目（CIP）数据

从过去向未来：引领时代进步的世博会 / 世博会博物馆编.
-- 上海：上海人民美术出版社, 2025.4.
ISBN 978-7-5586-3123-8
Ⅰ.G245-64
中国国家版本馆 CIP 数据核字第 2025M3R292 号

从过去向未来：引领时代进步的世博会

| 编　　　者：世博会博物馆
| 主　　　编：刘文涛
| 统　　　筹：王　姝　洪丽娜
| 出 品 人：侯培东
| 总 策 划：邱孟瑜
| 书籍设计：董　伟
| 排　　　版：懂书文化
| 责任编辑：沈丹青
| 技术编辑：齐秀宁
| 摄　　　影：徐介明
| 文字整理：周翠梅　顾　艳
| 出版发行：上海人民美术出版社
| （上海市闵行区号景路 159 弄 A 座 7F 邮编：201101）
| 印　　　刷：上海雅昌艺术印刷有限公司
| 开　　　本：889×1194　1/32　19.5 印张
| 版　　　次：2025 年 4 月第 1 版
| 印　　　次：2025 年 4 月第 1 次
| 书　　　号：ISBN 978-7-5586-3123-8
| 定　　　价：398.00 元

本书图片来源涵盖世博会博物馆馆藏资源、面向全球的世博文献征集成果以及公开渠道素材。图片已尽可能获取授权并标明出处，若发现未授权使用，请即刻联系。

Infographic of Expos 世博信息表

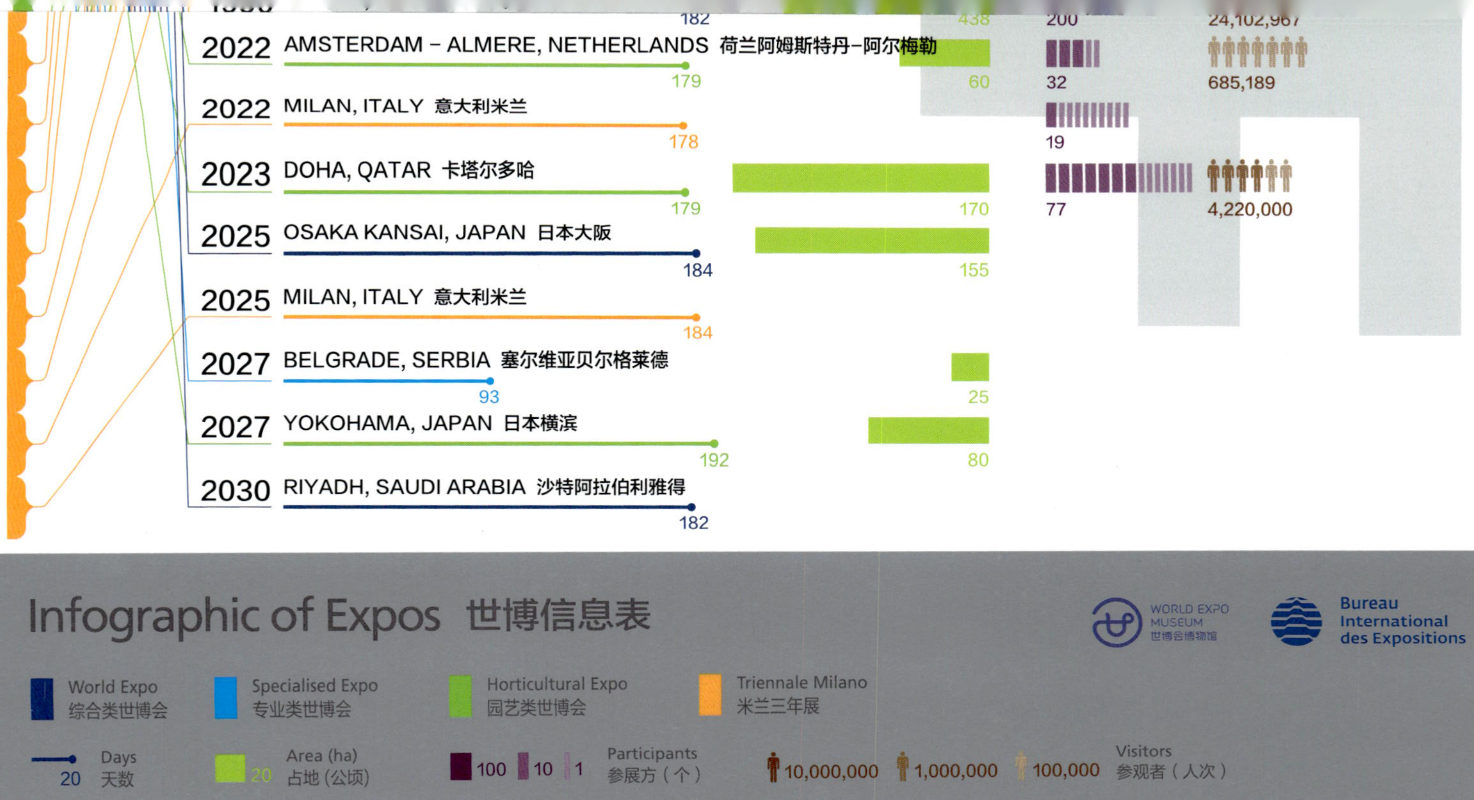

World Expo 综合类世博会	Specialised Expo 专业类世博会	Horticultural Expo 园艺类世博会
	Triennale Milano 米兰三年展	

- 2030 RIYADH, SAUDI ARABIA 沙特阿拉伯利雅得
- 2027 YOKOHAMA, JAPAN 日本横滨
- 2027 BELGRADE, SERBIA 塞尔维亚贝尔格莱德
- 2025 MILAN, ITALY 意大利米兰
- 2025 OSAKA KANSAI, JAPAN 日本大阪
- 2023 DOHA, QATAR 卡塔尔多哈
- 2022 MILAN, ITALY 意大利米兰
- 2022 AMSTERDAM – ALMERE, NETHERLANDS 荷兰阿姆斯特丹-阿尔梅勒

Days 天数 20
Area (ha) 占地（公顷） 100 / 10 / 1
Participants 参展方（个） 10,000,000 / 1,000,000 / 100,000
Visitors 参观者（人次）

182, 179, 178, 179, 184, 93, 192, 182

60, 155, 170, 184, 25, 80

438, 200, 32, 19, 77

24,102,961, 685,189, 4,220,000

WORLD EXPO MUSEUM 世博会博物馆
Bureau International des Expositions

1027 PARIS, FRANCE 法国巴黎

155

11

680,000